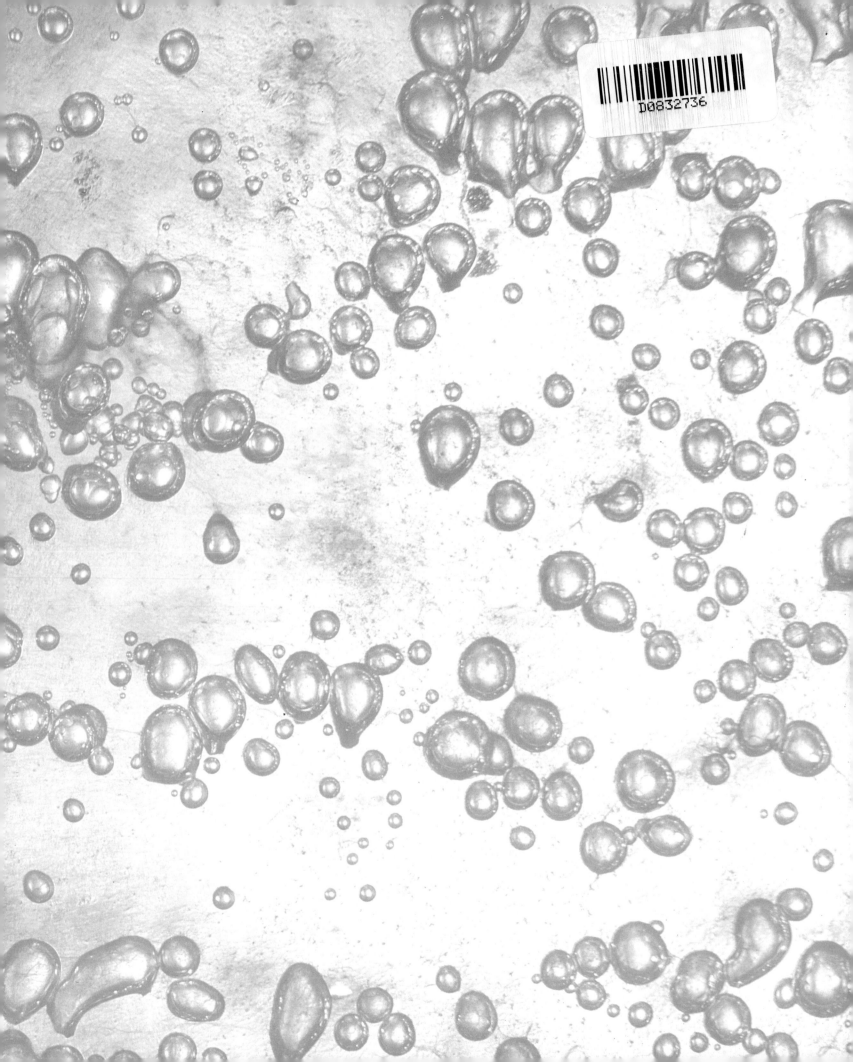

THE
COMPLETE
AQUARIUM

THE COMPLETE AQUARIUM

PETER W. SCOTT

PHOTOGRAPHY BY
JANE BURTON
and Kim Taylor

DORLING KINDERSLEY
London • New York • Stuttgart

A DORLING KINDERSLEY BOOK

For Alastair, Emma and, always, Zena

Senior Editor
Krystyna Mayer

Art Editor
Ursula Dawson

Editors
Tom Fraser
Jonathan Hilton
Roger Tritton

Managing Art Editor
Derek Coombes

First published in Great Britain in 1991 by
Dorling Kindersley Limited,
9 Henrietta Street,
London WC2E 8PS

Copyright © 1991
Dorling Kindersley Limited, London
Text copyright © 1991 Peter W. Scott

A CIP catalogue record for this book is available
from the British Library

ISBN 0-86318-603-3

Reproduced by Colourscan, Singapore
Printed and bound in Italy by Graphicom, Trento

CONTENTS

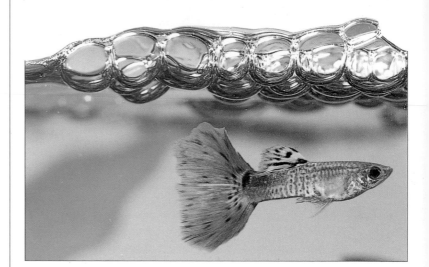

THE NATURAL ENVIRONMENT

THE FISH

THE FRESHWATER AQUARIUM

THE BRACKISH-WATER AQUARIUM

THE MARINE AQUARIUM

TANK AND WATER MANAGEMENT

FEEDING, BREEDING, AND HEALTHCARE

INTRODUCTION

Seventh-century terracotta vessel decorated with birds and fishes

Cotton manuscript dating from the reign of the Roman emperor Tiberius

Fishes have a truly ancient lineage, one stretching back more than 400 million years. By way of comparison, whales, masters of the great oceans as they seem to us, have existed for just 55 million years; and mankind, the merest flicker of geological time – a few hundred thousand years. Yet, for all the long history of fishes, we know surprisingly little about them. Their domain, the aquatic regions of the world comprising some 70 per cent of the Earth's surface, became available to serious scientific study only about 50 years ago. The breakthrough came with the invention of Scuba-diving equipment, which gave ichthyologists an opportunity to observe, relatively unhindered, the natural behaviour of many species of fish.

From archaeological evidence, we know that fishes have been important as a food source since prehistoric times to coastal tribes and people living near rivers and lakes. Shallow-swimming fishes were taken with rudimentary spears or clubs; deeper-swimming ones perhaps with nets. But it was not until ancient Egyptian times that we know that fishes were kept and bred not only as a ready supply of food but, more importantly from the aquarist's point of view, because of their ornamental attributes.

As a food source the Egyptians favoured the rearing of tilapia species, while for their beauty they kept mormyrids, which were revered as sacred animals. There is also tenuous evidence indicating that goldfish, selectively bred

Illustration from 1879 showing the interior of Brighton Aquarium

Fossilized fish (*Knightia* spp.), discovered in the Green River, Wyoming, U.S.A.

Boat-fishing in late-nineteenth-century China

Nineteenth-century Japanese scroll painting entitled "Sadatora carp with bog bean"

carp, date back to the Tang dynasty of China (AD 618 to 907), but stronger evidence certainly exists for their presence in China during the Sung dynasty (AD 970 to 1278).

The introduction of goldfish into Europe was somewhat delayed, however, and they did not reach England until the end of the seventeenth century, probably around 1691. But over the next hundred years they did become widespread in ornamental ponds and lakes. They seem to have reached across the Atlantic to the United States sometime before 1859, at which date Arthur M. Edwards wrote in his book, *Life Beneath the Waters, or the Aquarium in America*, that goldfish could be taken from the Schuykill River.

Back in Europe in the mid-nineteenth century, fishkeeping was becoming a serious affair. In 1853 the London Zoological Society established a public aquarium with the assistance of Philip Gosse, who had spent some time developing his concept of the "balanced aquarium", one in which there were aquatic plants and fishes. Other aquaria were opened in Paris in 1859 and in Hamburg in 1864. Soon after this date, German hobbyists began breeding ornamental fishes and commenced an export trade to the United States that continues to this very day.

Gosse's concept of the balanced aquarium has been crucial in the development of fishkeeping as we presently know it. Many early aquaria were temperate tanks that housed fishes caught locally

Cosby gourami
Trichogaster trichopterus sumatranus

Ancient Iraqi depiction of a fisherman

Spalding's diving bell,
illustrated in 1821

in rivers or found in rock pools. They were thus tanks loosely related to a single habit, or biotope tanks – ones based on a single habitat. With the advent of air travel, exotic fishes from all over the world became available and with them came the concept of community aquaria. In these, mixed populations from widely differing habitats were introduced together; the only thing these fishes had in common, apart from tolerating the same general water conditions, was an easy-going and indulgent nature.

Central to *The Complete Aquarium* is Philip Gosse's concept of balance: balance in recreating the types of conditions that a fish would have encountered in the wild; the types of plant in which it would have sheltered; and the water colour and chemistry in which it would have evolved. Although it is true that most fishes now available are captive-bred and that many species are relatively tolerant of water conditions, this does not mean that they will not do even better if you make some effort to duplicate the kind of water conditions in which their ancestors evolved.

To help you in this, the book begins with a consideration of many of the natural aquatic environments. These range from forest pools and open oceans to deep, tropical lakes and wide, shallow rivers. This is followed by an outline of the physiology of fishes – literally how fishes work, and how their bodies have developed to enable them to take full

Scuba-diving among
yellowtail snappers (*Octyrus
chrysurus*)

Elaborate indoor aquarium,
highly fashionable in the
nineteenth century

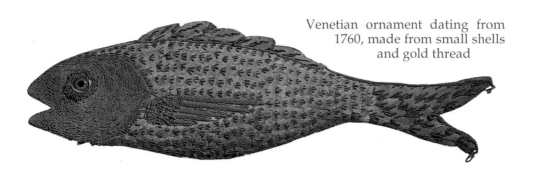

Venetian ornament dating from 1760, made from small shells and gold thread

advantage of the medium in which they live, which supports them, brings them food, and supplies them with life-sustaining oxygen. Next, via the establishment of a freshwater community aquarium, the general principles of setting up a tank are explained, before looking in detail at a range of habitats, and how to go about recreating them as closely as possible. A similar approach is used with the setting up of a marine community tank to illustrate broader principles of establishing such systems. In all, 16 different tank environments are covered in step-by-step detail.

Throughout, liberal cross-referencing allows much of the technical aspects of fishkeeping to be separated into the remaining chapters. The sections on tank and water management, filtration, heating, and lighting provide the background to the hardware, while those dealing with plants, troubleshooting, feeding, breeding, and healthcare give the essential information on the living ingredients.

It is possible in these relatively few pages to reflect only a flavour of the diversity of life in the world's lakes, rivers, pools, streams, swamps, estuaries, and seas, but hopefully you can build on the approach here when creating your own aquarium. To help you in the task of researching and recreating new habitats, a bibliography is provided that will lead you into more specialized texts, and assist you in your search for your own complete aquarium.

Mid-nineteenth-century design for a window aquarium

Typically ornate aquarium, dating from 1859

Silver sand

THE
NATURAL
ENVIRONMENT

To encourage you to enjoy your fishes to the fullest, and to
understand their needs in terms of water type and tank
layout, this chapter provides an important insight into
the varied natural environments from which many
popular aquarium fishes originate. Suitable aquarium
fishes from tropical and temperate regions live in marine
and freshwater habitats ranging from rapidly flowing
streams and rivers, through sluggish pools and lakes, to
the great continent-spanning oceans. Between these

Richly coloured bogwood

Distinctively striped rocks

extremes of fresh and salt water, brackish waters, such as swamps and estuaries, are the natural environments of yet other species of fish suitable for aquaria. Within this chapter you will find descriptions and photographs of the major aquatic environments of the world, along with notes on their geography and climate, and on whether the waters are fast- or slow-moving, clear or murky, acid or alkaline. The marine section describes how fishes and other animals, such as corals, have adapted to this unique habitat.

Congo anubias
Anubias congensis

Pebbles with prominent
natural features

WATER

When the Earth began to form, from dust and gases, the constituents that were to make up water were tied up in a range of chemical compounds. Very early in the Earth's history – too early for geological record – water collected to form the first sea, the Tethys Sea (*see* p. 26). As rain began to fall, fresh water collected on the land too, creating rivers, streams, and lakes.

Today two-thirds of the Earth's surface is covered in water, and almost all of this (97.7 per cent) is in the sea. The remaining water is locked in icecaps and glaciers, suspended in the atmosphere, or contained in rivers, streams, and lakes. The amount in rivers, streams, and lakes is, compared to the volume of water in the sea, a tiny trickle: less than 0.01 per cent of the Earth's water.

The prime difference between fresh and sea water is their salt content. Different levels of salt present different problems for fishes' kidneys and most fishes are restricted to either a freshwater or marine habitat. Few have adapted themselves to live in both environments. Notable fishes like the salmon breed and spend their early life in fresh water before migrating out to sea where they can eat the plankton and reach maturity before returning. A number of hardy species that normally live in fresh water, such as several of the tilapia, can tolerate very high levels of salt too.

SEA WATER

The sheer vastness of the sea makes it a very stable environment. The sea is composed of about 96.4 per cent pure water, and 3.6 per cent dissolved minerals. Of these minerals, three-quarters is common salt (sodium chloride).

THE WATER CYCLE

Rain, falling on the hills, disappears into porous rock, or runs over impervious rock. Underground or on the surface, the water is concentrated into streams, which combine as rivers.

The rivers flow into the seas, where they replace the waters lost by evaporation into clouds. As the clouds drift over land, they cool, allowing condensation of water into rain.

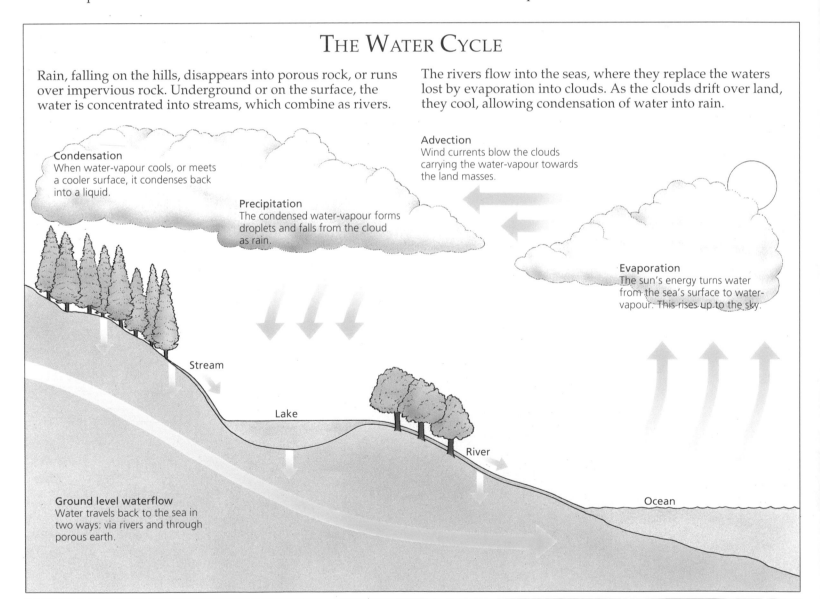

Condensation
When water-vapour cools, or meets a cooler surface, it condenses back into a liquid.

Precipitation
The condensed water-vapour forms droplets and falls from the cloud as rain.

Advection
Wind currents blow the clouds carrying the water-vapour towards the land masses.

Evaporation
The sun's energy turns water from the sea's surface to water-vapour. This rises up to the sky.

Stream

Lake

River

Ocean

Ground level waterflow
Water travels back to the sea in two ways: via rivers and through porous earth.

MINERALS IN SEA WATER

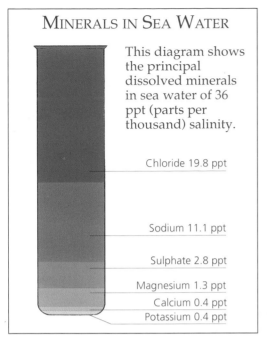

This diagram shows the principal dissolved minerals in sea water of 36 ppt (parts per thousand) salinity.

Chloride 19.8 ppt

Sodium 11.1 ppt

Sulphate 2.8 ppt

Magnesium 1.3 ppt

Calcium 0.4 ppt

Potassium 0.4 ppt

GLACIAL WATERS MEETING THE SEA *On a calm day, the surface discontinuity caused by low-salinity waters from a glacier flowing out to the open sea is clearly visible.*

The mineral content of sea water is due to the rain dissolving minerals from the land over millions of years, or simply washing land away into the sea. The world's highest "mountain" is, in fact, underwater, off the mouth of the Amazon River, where sediments have been deposited to a height of some 11,000 m (37,000 ft).

The concentration of minerals in the early Tethys Sea (*see* p. 26), was nine ppt (parts per thousand). Today the seas of the world are saltier, and have a concentration of minerals of around 36 ppt. This figure does vary slightly in different parts of the world. Heavy evaporation in the subtropical regions, particularly the Sargasso Sea and the Caribbean, results in high water salinity of up to 37 ppt, while the level reaches 40 to 41 ppt in the Red Sea. High rain levels in some areas, such as the Amazon basin, cause flood water to flow out to sea, where the salinity level is reduced. To some extent these local differences are counterbalanced by the mixing of waters caused by ocean currents and winds.

Although water salinity varies considerably throughout the world, within a local area of sea it remains extremely constant. This means that most marine fishes can rely on very stable conditions.

FRESH WATER

In contrast to the stability of sea water, the chemical content of fresh water is extremely variable, both seasonally and between individual bodies of water.

Water has been described as "the universal solvent". This description is not strictly accurate, but water does in fact dissolve almost everything, albeit often in minute amounts only. This means that, as fresh water moves through and over the land, it often dissolves a proportion of whatever minerals are contained in it, so that the composition of the water is altered slightly. Where the land is impervious (granite rock, for example), water flows over it in virtually the same pure condition as it fell.

Water may remain underground for long periods, gradually dissolving more of the surrounding rock, and in doing so, usually becoming harder. Spa resorts around the world commercially exploit water which has spent time underground, and which may have an extra natural "sparkle", due to having become heavily saturated with carbon dioxide.

In some parts of the world, the phenomenon known as acid rain – the result of waste gas emissions from chimneys, factories, or cars, which introduce minerals into water at the vapour stage – makes the water highly acidic, even before it falls to earth. As acid rain falls it causes great damage to the land's vegetation, and as it passes through the earth, it picks up toxic metals from the soil that make the water dangerous to animal and plant life.

THE UNIVERSAL SOLVENT *The waters of the river continually splashing down these rocks have produced a group of natural potholes.*

FRESHWATER HABITATS

Despite the fact that the fresh water of rivers and lakes is a minute proportion of the world's water, it does play host to a substantial percentage of the fish population. Warmer waters produce more food for fishes, and the fishes themselves reproduce at a greater rate than those in temperate waters. As you would expect, they have more species of fish: the Amazon River alone has more than 1,300 species, the Zaire River almost 700, and the Mississippi system 250. In contrast, the cooler fresh waters of the whole of Europe have no more than 192 species.

RIVERS AND STREAMS

Although rivers and streams account for only a tiny percentage of the world's water, conditions in them are far more varied than in lakes or seas. The altitude, the slope of the riverbed, water temperature, local geology and vegetation, and water supply, as well as industrial pollution, all have an effect on the nature of rivers and streams. This huge variety of habitats provides endless opportunities for the aquarist to imitate them in tanks.

TROPICAL RIVERS AND STREAMS

Despite the wealth of different environments in the rivers and streams of the world, there is one consistent factor in the tropics: the high temperatures and the constant number of daylight hours found in these regions create a stable and warm environment that provides great productivity at all levels of life in these waters.

THE RIVERS OF THE TROPICAL RAIN FORESTS

Over the whole equatorial region, that is, between the Tropics of Cancer and Capricorn, more than $1\frac{1}{2}$ m (5 ft) of rain falls annually. This rain causes forest habitats to undergo enormous changes throughout the year, most notably from seasonal flooding. Along the equator itself, the rainfall is distributed evenly throughout the year, except for peaks in March and September. But to the north and south of the equator there is considerable seasonal variation. In the tropics north of the equator most of the rain falls from May to July, and in the tropics south of the equator, it falls from November to January.

The rain forests of the Amazon and Zaire Rivers both straddle the equator, which means that different regions of these forests have peak rainfalls and floods at different times of the year. In addition, because of their great size, it is almost always raining somewhere in these rain forests, and so the two rivers have exceptionally long highwater seasons. Along their courses there are lakes, swamps, falls, and rapids; each of these environments is quite different and home to an amazing variety of fish species.

THE RAIN FOREST *A Guyanan rain forest with morning mist clearing. The world's rain forests, now under threat due to man's influence (see p. 22), provide a diverse habitat for many fishes.*

RIVERS IN THE RAIN FOREST *A section of the Mazaruni River in Guyana. The small forest streams running into it teem with aquatic life.*

The animal and plant life in the dense, lush jungles and the rivers, streams, and pools of the rain forests is balanced in a delicate and extremely fruitful relationship. Although the growth of the forest above the streams that feed the main river reduces the light levels and so inhibits the growth of aquatic plants, the high temperatures and sheer plenitude of life on the forest floor means that there is plenty of food for the fishes and the rivers are highly productive (*see* Amazon rain forest stream tank, p. 54).

In the plains or marshes downstream and away from the rain forest itself, the massive rate of flow caused by floods breaks the river's banks. In time this causes a change in the course of the river. In addition, silt that is washed downriver creates large deposits in the area of the estuary. Here the shallow waters are fully exposed to the sun, and aquatic plants grow in abundance, providing a home for many interesting species. Fishes that eat from the bottom, such as catfish, are common in estuaries as these freshen during the floods, while some marine fish species may retreat into the estuaries to avoid the blooms of toxic plankton that can occur offshore following rain.

FERTILE HABITAT *This Amazon floodplain at Marajo Island, Para State in north Brazil is criss-crossed by small streams and pools.*

—————— THE RIVERS OF TROPICAL SOUTH AMERICA ——————
The drainage basin of the mighty Amazon River is the largest in the world; and the network of rivers that drain into it extends over most of the subcontinent. There are three basic types. From the Andes come whitewater rivers fed by the melting snows; these carry suspended material that discourages aquatic plant life, so the fishes tend to live on food that falls from the land. From Guyana and Colombia flow inhospitable, acidic blackwater rivers like the Rio Negro; many of these have little life in them, although the least acid pools and streams do support fishes such as the *Apistogramma*. The third type of river is the clearwater; also fairly acidic but with good visibility, these rivers support plants, algae, and plankton-eating fishes.

MEETING OF THE WATERS *Where the muddy Amazon meets the silty, black Rio Negro, the waters run downstream for several miles before mixing.*

THE FLOODED RIVER

In the Amazon the seasonal floods begin with heavy rains, building up in December and January when the rain clouds are above the equator. Depending on local conditions, the floods can last for between three to eleven months, and the water that builds up can create a floodplain of as much as 100,000 square kilometres (38,564 square miles) in area.

As the Amazon River floods, it becomes stained with decomposing plant matter that it has picked up from the forest floor; when the flood water recedes, the streams and isolated pools that are left are filled with these "contaminated" waters. This type of water is acidic, with a low oxygen level (*see* Amazon rain forest acid pool tank, p. 60).

The fishes that normally live in the true river respond to floods by moving into new, flooded areas to find additional food. The Amazon is home to fishes that live off the seeds and fruits of the rubber tree, such as the species known locally as the tambaqui, the black pacu (*Colossoma macropomum*). During the period of flooding, this food supply is plentiful; between floods these fishes eat very little.

THE AMAZON IN FLOOD *When the Amazon bursts its banks, thousands of kilometres of the river's margins are submerged.*

THE RIVERS OF TROPICAL AFRICA

The huge continent of Africa is drained by four major river systems – the Zaire, the Niger, the Nile, and the Zambezi – as well as by a network of inland rivers that drain into the great lakes like Lake Victoria and Lake Tanganyika.

The Zaire rain forest river system is extraordinarily fertile (*see* Zaire River rapids tank, p. 66). Although 80 per cent of the species there are unique to the region, the families to which they belong have, over millions of years, produced thousands of descendants which became established in other systems when these met the Zaire. The rather unproductive, acidic waters of the Niger River's upper reaches dictate that

TREASURE TROVE OF FISHES *The networks of African fresh waters like this are a rich source of aquarium fishes.*

many of the fishes depend on the floodplains of the lower river for their food. The lakes within the floodplains are dense with aquatic plants and support a rich fish life.

Although the Nile has a smaller range of habitats and seasonal changes than are found in the rivers of the west, millions of years ago it was linked with the Zaire system. This allowed a wide spread of new species, such as the marbled leopard lungfish (*Protopterus aethiopicus*) and the bichir (*Polypterus bichir*).

The Zambezi River system has the high land and cooler waters that are favoured by cyprinids. Many of these fishes migrated to Africa from Asia before the two continents divided (*see* p. 27). The Zambezi is home to a quite different collection of species to those in other African rivers. Some fishes do, however, move between the Zambezi and the Zaire systems when these rivers flood and meet.

THE RIVERS OF TROPICAL ASIA

Tropical Asia is a particularly rich source of freshwater fishes for aquaria, and these include many different cyprinids. Although there is an enormous diversity of fish species, these are well distributed across the whole region. This is because the rivers of the smaller islands like Sumatra and Borneo, together with those of Thailand and India, were once all part of one large river system.

River environments throughout Asia are many and varied. In India, for example, rivers are often short and they dry up seasonally. However in the east, some of these rivers have huge deltas into which the fishes can swim in the dry season. Other rivers, such as the Brahmaputra and the Ganges, fed by the melting snows of the Himalayas, do not dry up – in fact, these rivers are well known for the problems of flooding they cause for the people of Bangladesh.

One of the biggest world exporters of freshwater aquarium fishes is Malaysia. Many of these fishes originate in the blackwaters (stained by iron and by rotting organic matter) and the riceland waters of the paddyfields (*see* Southeast Asia back-water tank, p. 72). Forest streams and established rivers of this region (*see* Southeast Asia river tank, p. 78) have a different and equally wide range of fishes.

THE RIVERS OF TROPICAL AUSTRALASIA

Although it is close to tropical Asia, Australasia is home to strikingly different fish species – rainbowfish, for example. This is because the lands that are now Australia and Papua New Guinea became separated from the Gondwanaland landmass very early in the history of fish life. There are actually no more than three species in Australasia with evolutionary links to Asia. The rest of the freshwater fishes of Australia and Papua New Guinea originated in the primitive seas of the region, and today remain distinct to it.

Papua New Guinea is the source of some particularly attractive and interesting species for the aquarist (*see* Papua New Guinea sandy river tank, p. 84). It has two distinct sets of fish inhabitants – one on either side of the Central Highlands, which are high enough to prevent substantial mixing of species. A number of the fishes in the south, such as McCulloch's rainbowfish (*Melanotaenia maccullochi*), are common with those in northern Australia, while those in the north, such as the New Guinea rainbowfish (*M. affinis*), are unique to their region. Many of the fishes of Papua New Guinea are large; almost half the species found there – barramundi, snappers, and grunters, for example – grow to over 30 cm (12 in), while the smaller species inhabit mainly the smaller side streams.

ABUNDANT WATERS *The Annapurna mountain range dominates the Nepalese plain where the snow-fed Beti River carves its route.*

FOREST BLACKWATER *A mass of fallen leaves turns the waters of this small Javanese river dark and acid.*

TEMPERATE RIVERS AND STREAMS

In temperate regions – those that lie between the tropics and the Arctic – the productivity of life in rivers and streams is dictated by the changing of the seasons. Cold winters and hot summers may bring deluge, or they may bring drought. The further inland, the more dramatic the variation in climate. This is because the ocean acts as a moderating influence on climatic extremes.

The growth of insects and plants – what is called primary production – is not so great in temperate regions as in the tropics. As a result, the range and abundance of aquatic life are correspondingly limited. Nevertheless, by exploiting foods available in summer, and by developing seasonal cycles of reproduction, fishes have evolved to make use of the changes that take place over a year. In fact, throughout the world, wherever an aquatic habitat has existed for a considerable period of time, fishes will have found a way of living in it and of exploiting the food that is available there.

Rivers in temperate regions tend to follow a more predictable pattern than those in the tropics. Many have fast, steep upper reaches running over rocks. Here the plants and fishes are adapted to avoid being swept away. Further downstream, the rivers run more gently across flatter areas.

Since the rainfall is not so great as in tropical regions, the rivers carry less water and their courses tend to be guided by the geography of the land; even upland rivers may meander across country, rather than carving it out. As they cross the country, the rivers deposit silt and pick up organic material. Fishes that prefer high oxygen levels, such as trout, live in the upper waters of the rivers, where the flow is fast and aeration good, while coarse fishes, such as cyprinids, dominate the lower, slower-moving parts.

RAINY SEASON RIVER *From the Central Highlands of Papua New Guinea spring streams that are home to rainbowfish.*

MEANDERING TEMPERATE RIVER *The Nenana River finds its way through the conifer forests of the Alaskan mountains.*

LAKES AND INLAND SWAMPS

A lake can be formed in a variety of ways – perhaps from a crack in the earth or from the scouring action of a glacier. The way a lake is formed, together with its depth, the source and inflow of the water, and the climate, dictate the kind of life it plays host to.

Unlike a river, which may be linked to other rivers, so that species can spread, a lake may be a relatively isolated type of habitat, where the fishes have become highly specialized.

TROPICAL AND TEMPERATE LAKES

Tropical lakes enjoy more sunlight and higher temperatures than temperate lakes, so they are often more productive. Some lakes, such as those in the floodplains of the Amazon, are regularly flushed out. In others, particularly large tropical lakes with a small inflow, the productivity of life is dependent on the amount of recycling that occurs in the shallows. This is because, like the sea, such large lakes can develop zones in which warm, lower-density surface waters float on cold, higher-density deep waters, and very little mixing occurs. The division between the two is called a thermocline. As a result of this, dead fishes, waste, and other nutrients become locked up in the depths, and in some cases can only be released where water wells up from below, perhaps when two currents meet. Many shallow tropical lakes have no thermocline, since winds ensure that the water is overturned throughout the year, releasing nutrients at all levels. In some deeper tropical lakes, however, there is no overturn; the loss of nutrients from the production cycle can be permanent and there is almost no plant growth. The fish inhabitants have to live on the small amount of vegetation that does exist and on other fishes.

A satisfactory system exists in many temperate lakes, where the thermocline is overturned seasonally. In winter, when the temperature differences between the water layers become minor enough, the wind, rain, and incoming streams all serve to mix the water and cause an overturn. This releases nutrients that have been lying dormant, leading to blooms of algae on the surface. The algae provide food for young fishes, making the spring an ideal breeding time.

LAKE MALAWI CICHLID *A fish that has adapted to the demands of its habitat.*

THE LAKES OF TROPICAL AFRICA AND SOUTH AMERICA
Africa's Rift Valley comprises the area lying between two rift lines in the earth running through East Africa. Lakes Albert and Malawi lie along the western rift, while those along the eastern rift include Lakes Turkana and Nyasa. Lake Victoria straddles the rifts, so it is shallower than the others. These habitats are dominated by cichlids, which have come to exploit every possible food source – an amazing range of species has developed, with many unique to a particular lake. The lakes are generally fairly inhospitable with hard, alkaline water (*see* East Africa rocky lake tank, p. 96).

Lakes Tanganyika and Nyasa are so deep that they do not overturn. Despite this, however, the lakes are productive; algae on the many rocks and aquatic plants in sandy areas provide food for fishes and for the aquatic invertebrates on which some of the fishes feed.

The tropical lakes of Central and South America (*see* Central America rocky lake tank, p. 90) do not generally boast the same variety of fishes as those in Africa. Since each continent was derived from the supercontinent Gondwanaland, the cichlid communities of South America parallel those in African lakes. The species are not the same, however, each group having evolved to suit its particular environment.

TROPICAL INLAND SWAMPS

Swamps – temporary or permanent wetlands – are a common feature of the tropics around the world (*see* West Africa floodplain swamp tank, p. 102). These swamps may shrink in the dry season and become stagnant and starved of oxygen. The fishes that inhabit the swamps have therefore needed to develop modifications for survival and successful reproduction. The African lungfish, for example, may spend the summer in a state of torpidity in the mud at the bottom of the swamp, while it breathes atmospheric air. Some killifish, on the other hand, may die in the dry season, but they leave behind eggs that are resistant to the conditions. These eggs lie dormant and often completely dehydrated, and hatch when the next rains come to flood their home.

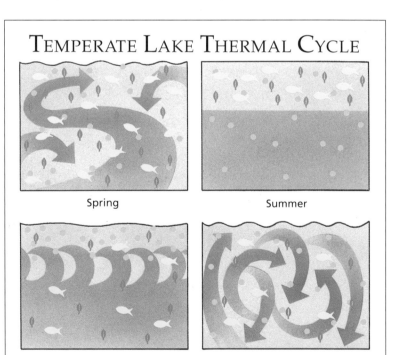

TEMPERATE LAKE THERMAL CYCLE

Spring

Summer

Autumn

Winter

In spring, nutrients, plants, and tiny animals are plentiful. In summer the thermocline locks nutrients in the depths, while autumn brings an overturn of water that lifts them to the surface. Winter weather stirs the waters thoroughly, mixing once again the contents of the water.

- ⬭ Tiny animals
- ⬩ Planktonic plants
- ⬤ Nutrients

BRACKISH HABITATS

Where fresh water meets the sea, an endless variety of brackish habitats is created, governed by the rise and fall of the tide and by ceaseless wave activity.

The salinity of the water can vary from 1 ppt to 36 ppt (*see* Sea water, p. 12) at various points on a coastal stream or estuary. This huge variation means that there is a very cosmopolitan plant and animal life in these habitats.

Brackish areas are rich in sediments, which are washed down and deposited in sheltered areas. Often loaded with food and detritus, these encourage plant and animal life to settle in the estuary. Not surprisingly, considering the assorted carrion that arrives in the water, many inhabitants of brackish waters are scavengers. The plants have dense roots for clinging to the deposited mud.

JAVANESE MANGROVE SWAMP *Forests of trees and plants with shallow, spreading roots are typical of these brackish salt marshes where the waters flow sluggishly.*

TROPICAL ESTUARY *The estuary provides a calm habitat for some marine species, and a fertile feeding-ground for some river fishes.*

TROPICAL ESTUARIES

The estuaries of Central and South American and Asian rivers (*see* Central America coastal stream tank, p. 110 and Southeast Asia estuary tank, p. 122) are generally shallow, and huge amounts of river waters have made them wide. They have large, brackish areas where the sea encroaches into the estuary. Depending on the type of river that is meeting the sea, the estuaries may or may not be bordered by areas of brackish mangrove swamp with varying levels of salinity. These are found in the sheltered waters of muddy tropical estuaries, especially if the river is large and slow-flowing (*see* East Africa mangrove swamp tank, p. 116). In the Niger River system, almost 9,000 square kilometres (3,470 square miles) are covered with mangrove swamp. The habitat is also a particular feature of the deltas of the Mekong, Amazon, Congo, and Ganges Rivers, as well as the coasts of Sumatra and northeast Australia.

"Mangrove" is a generic term that includes several different plants characteristic of saltwater swamps; all have a wide spread of shallow roots, sometimes the stilt roots that rise clear of the water or mud. As in most brackish waters, few freshwater fish species spawn here, but many use them as nursery feeding areas. Many marine species of fish also penetrate well into the swamps.

CARIBBEAN LAND CRAB *A Costa Rican crab whose food is washed downriver to the coast.*

MARINE HABITATS

The nature and flow of water in the world's oceans is dictated by global heating and cooling, by the pull of the moon and the sun, by the Earth's rotation, and, more locally, by the effects of winds and currents.

Currents on the surface of the ocean are created by the expansion of the waters under sunlight. Warm waters expand and move into the place of cooler waters, which, because of their greater density, sink towards the bottom of the ocean. This sinking mass of water replaces existing deep water, causing the more major currents that are known to occur in the ocean depths.

TROPICAL SEAS

As with fresh water, warm marine waters are more productive of food, and contain more fish species than cool waters. As an illustration, of over 20,000 species of fish in the world, around 8,000 live on the continental shelves of tropical seas, compared to 1,150 on the continental shelves of colder waters. Over 100 species can be found in tropical seas anywhere in the world; 14 of these inhabit the shorelines, the rest are ocean-going, or pelagic.

Plant life in the sea only survives to a depth at which light still penetrates – in many seas this is only a small fraction of the total depth. As in lakes, there is greater local productivity of food and fishes in warm, shallow waters than in the deep. In deeper waters, a permanent thermocline may be formed (*see* p. 18), the position of which varies with currents and seasonal wind changes. Life-supporting nutrients may be locked away in the deep. In some of these waters, however, the thermocline is not very deep – off West Africa, for example, it can be at less than 20 m (65 ft), and since local currents and winds in this region are strong enough to mix the waters to some extent, although there is no overturn, the productivity in these waters is quite high.

The tropical Indian Ocean supplies many of the fishes for the marine aquarist. These come mainly from the Philippines, Kenya, Sri Lanka, and the Maldives, where the seas are rich in species of fish that are exported in great numbers. The majority of the more colourful and popular aquarium species – damselfish, clownfish, anemonefish, angelfish, and butterflyfish, for example – are natives of these areas, as well as of the Red Sea and the Caribbean. For many aquarists, setting up a marine tank involves the recreation of one of the many spectacular coral reefs that are found in tropical seas around the world.

IN THE SHADE *This sun coral* (Tubastrea aurea) *prefers low light conditions beneath rocky overhangs of Indo-Pacific reefs.*

TROPICAL CORAL REEFS

Coral reefs provide a home for the most fantastic of shallow water marine communities. Reefs are formed over thousands of years from the skeletons of calcium-containing corals that build up, generation after generation, on the sea bed. The waters above the coral reef are clear, shallow, warm, well oxygenated, and very stable. The sunlight penetrates easily into the surface of the reef. An enormous variety of species and types of marine animal, many of them colourful and exotic, has evolved to exploit the holes, cracks, and ledges provided by reefs.

DELICATE SEA FAN *This beautiful Gorgonian soft coral (*Gorgonacea*) is one of the horny corals that usually have a plant-like appearance.*

HAND-LIKE CORAL *Dead men's fingers (*Alcyonium palmatum*) grows on the Mediterranean and northeast Atlantic seabeds.*

TYPES OF REEF

Reefs develop naturally in several different ways, depending on their location. Close to the shore, on the continental shelf that slopes away from the land before the sea-bed falls away abruptly, fringing reefs may develop. The very edge of the continental shelf may possibly throw up a barrier reef, while those reefs that lie between these two boundaries are known as either patch, or platform reefs. All these reefs occur in shallow water, often breaking the surface. Bank reefs, which are known to grow either on the continental shelf or actually in the middle of the ocean may, in complete contrast, be up to 40 m (130 ft) deep, and an oceanic reef can build up many thousands of kilometres from land.

SOUTH PACIFIC REEF *An aerial view clearly shows the fringing reef around Fiji's volcanic Monuriki Island.*

Inshore reefs lie close to the water's surface, so they are well warmed by the sun, while the washing action of the tide keeps them generally clear of sediments emanating from the land. Marine life on fringing reefs is particularly rich on the seaward side; the landward side is often too shallow, hot, or exposed to the air. Further out to sea, on barrier reefs, the spread of life extends from soft corals on the landward side (these are protected from some of the direct wave action), to hard corals on the seaward side. The different types of coral attract different inhabitants. Oceanic reefs are much deeper and less hospitable to life than shoreline reefs. They tend to be home to larger, pelagic fishes.

Indian Ocean reefs Some spectacular fringing reefs have developed along the Kenyan and Tanzanian coasts and off the island groups of the Comoros, the Seychelles, the Maldives, and Madagascar. Between the islands are patch reefs that have grown up on the ocean ridges, while large oceanic reefs lie in the central Indian Ocean.

Hawaii too has spectacular reefs (*see* Hawaii coral reef tank, p. 138). Supplied by warm sea currents from the equator, these reefs are among the most northerly in the world. As a result, the fish fauna there is somewhat isolated from the rest of the Indo-Pacific and includes some unique fishes such as the Hawaiian sharpnosed puffer (*Canthigaster jactator*), Fisher's pygmy angelfish (*Centropyge fisheri*), and the Hawaiian pygmy lionfish (*Pterois sphex*).

Other reefs Coral reefs that support a unique marine life are dotted all over the Caribbean, particularly along the eastern coasts of the Bahamas and the Leeward Islands, as well as the coast of mainland U.S.A. Some islands, such as Jamaica, are almost completely ringed by reefs.

The Great Barrier Reef lies off the east coast of Queensland, Australia. It is the most well-known and impressive reef of all. Built up mainly from the strong coral Scleratinia over 600 million years, it covers 208,000 square kilometres (80,000 square miles).

Red Sea coral reefs are host to over 1,000 species of fish.

BARRIER REEF INHABITANTS
A common clownfish (Amphiprion ocellaris) *swims among the tentacles of a Heteractis anemone.*

TEMPERATE SEAS

Temperate sea waters also harbour life that is suitable for the aquarium. Particularly in coastal waters, the waves and the movement of the tide provide a constantly changing home for the life on the rocks or among the sediments of the shoreline (*see* British rock pool tank, p. 146).

In general there is not enough constant light to generate the amount of life found on tropical reefs, for example, and species tend to be less brightly coloured. In addition the water is less clear, and mud and coastal pollutants are often stirred up. Nevertheless temperate marine fishes and invertebrates come in shapes as extraordinary, and sizes as varied, as their tropical relatives. The inhabitants include many types of shellfish, crab, prawn, sponge, and filter-feeders such as anemones.

MAN'S INFLUENCE

Numerous species of fish are endangered around the world today. Sadly, the chief reason for this is the influence of man. The destruction of fish habitats, pollution, and the introduction of competitors in the interests of fishing have created countless problems.

DESTRUCTION OF THE RAIN FORESTS

A key influence on the aquatic environment of the tropics, which is home to so many aquarium fishes, is the massive deforestation of the world's rain forest areas. One-third of these forests are in Brazil, where huge tracts have been cut down for short-term farming projects financed by the government. As part of a deliberate "slash and burn" policy, the land is used for a couple of years until it becomes

MAN-MADE FIRE *The deliberate destruction of huge areas of valuable rain forest has become an all-too-frequent sight in the tropics.*

exhausted, then it is left idle and useless while the farmer moves on to the next area. The increase in carbon dioxide levels in the atmosphere, said to be partly due to this burning of rain forest trees, is believed to be the cause of global warming and the appearance of abnormal weather patterns throughout the world.

Deforestation also has a very specific effect on waters in the rain forest. With the disappearance of the forest, a new floodplain is often produced. When water flows across this newly exposed land, it takes with it the store of nutrients that was held in the topsoil. In the short term, this provides food for fishes, but ultimately the nutrients are washed away. As timber-collecting and iron-ore mining have increased in order to satisfy demand in the developed world, they, too, have caused massive soil erosion. A side effect of these industries is that soil may be washed down the rivers, where it can smother fishes' habitats, even affecting fishes living on coral reefs right out to sea.

THE DANGERS OF DAMMING

The construction of large hydro-electric plants and dams is another factor that will alter the floodplains of the tropics forever. Dams can alter habitats until they become unrecognizable – quiet streams and rivers may be replaced by great lakes. Some river- and stream-living species with particular feeding habits will not be able to adapt and will die off, or they may be driven out when new species are added to the newly formed lake for fishing. And the appearance of a dam may mean that migrating fishes may no longer be able to swim upriver to spawn.

In some parts of the world, compromises have, however, been made to avoid the worst effects of damming. In the U.S.A. the Dexter National Fish Hatchery was established in an attempt to preserve species that were threatened as a

THE DEVIL'S HOLE PUPFISH

Among the species in greatest danger from the activities of man are the desert pupfish of the U.S.A., the best known of which is the Devil's Hole pupfish (*Cyprinodon diabolis*). Climatic changes have caused the lakes that once covered a large part of southwest America to dry up, and the pupfish have been left isolated.

The homes of the Devil's Hole pupfish have all disappeared, except for one, at Ash Meadows, Nye County, Nevada – a pool 15 m (50 ft) long by 3 m (9 ft) wide, which lies some 18 m (60 ft) below ground. This tiny pupfish lives off

Devil's Hole pupfish (*Cyprinodon diabolis*)

the invertebrates that eat the algae growing on a rock shelf just below the surface of the pool, and the population rises or falls as the algae comes and goes. Although the pool is within the protected part of the Death Valley National Monument, pumping for drinking water at another location was threatening to expose the rock shelf on which the food is produced. An action was eventually brought in the United States Supreme Court by environmentalists, who succeeded in putting a halt to the pumping of the water and saving the pupfish from extinction.

FLOODED FOREST *The result of building a new dam in Sri Lanka is a floodplain covering an area of precious forest.*

RAVAGES OF DAM-BUILDING *The world's largest dam-site is at Itaipu in Brazil. Apart from creating enormous lakes where there were none, such constructions lay waste to land that previously provided foodstuffs for the river fishes.*

result of the new Amistad Dam, built on the Colorado River. One of the fishes whose habitat was totally lost, but which was saved by the hatchery, was a rare mosquito fish (*Gambusia amistadensis*), a native of the Goodenough Spring.

THE ROLE OF THE AQUARIST

Aquarists themselves are often accused of exploiting coral reefs and pillaging the life there. In fact the productive capacity of reefs around the world is so great that exports of fishes for aquaria are insignificant in comparison with the havoc wreaked by man in other areas. A single square kilometre (0.386 square mile) of reef could potentially produce up to 40 tonnes of fishes per year – or more than a year's exports from Sri Lanka, one of the world's major suppliers.

Some governments, such as that of the Maldives, regard their reef fishes as a precious resource, encouraging tourists and boosting international trade. Marine parks, in which fish-collecting is forbidden, have been established off the islands, and studies to assess the level of harvesting that can be sustained without harming the reef are underway.

Some fishes have had high mortality rates in transportation over the years, but the situation is now much improved with the trade association Ornamental Fish International (O.F.I.) placing embargoes on trade in species known to be endangered, and which do not thrive in aquaria.

The use of living rock (*see* p. 134) for aquaria has caused concern over recent years, and embargoes are now in place in some countries. Much of this rock, which is colonized by marine animals, has been taken from reefs, causing serious damage. This human erosion has prompted collectors to seed areas between the reef and the shore with suitable rock;

the mature rock can be gathered several years later. Major sources of living rock for the aquarium trade are the Caribbean, Indonesia, the Gulf of Mexico, and California.

MISMANAGEMENT

Mismanagement of water resources – usually in the cause of successful fishing – can lead to the introduction of new fish species in unsuitable environments that were previously stable fish habitats. The practice has been especially damaging in East Africa, where numerous species are in danger, or have already been lost. Lake Victoria is a good example of the damage this practice can cause (*see* below).

LAKE VICTORIA *Since the Nile perch (*Lates niloticus*) was introduced for fishing, many species of* Haplochromis *have disappeared.*

African glass catfish
Eutropiellus "debauwi"

Tiger barb
Barbus tetrazona tetrazona

THE FISH

Over the hundreds of millions of years that fishes have been evolving, they have adapted to live, feed, and breed in a fascinating variety of ways. So tenacious is their instinct for survival that there are fishes alive today virtually identical to species that we know from fossil evidence swam the oceans unhindered more than 70 million years ago. It is the very diversity of habitats in which we find fishes that largely accounts for their astonishing range of body shapes – slim and deep, for example, to glide easily through reeds and other plants, more barrel-like to give maximum stability in rushing

Harlequin
Rasbora heteromorpha

Angelfish
Pterophyllum scalare

water, or flat with eyes situated on top of the head to provide
virtual invisibility on the silty sea bottom. Other adaptations
are the results of feeding habits, and from the shape of a fish's
mouth it is usually possible to tell whether it is a surface-,
mid-water, or bottom-feeder. For mobility and stability in
different habitats, fishes have an astonishing variety of fin
shapes. Within this chapter you will see how fishes sense and
react to their environment; how colour and markings are
used by them for both camouflage and courtship; and how
different species of fish reproduce and spawn.

Scat
Scatophagus argus

Adolph's corydoras
Corydoras adolfoi

THE ORIGINS OF THE FISH

Life in all the myriad forms we know it in today, began in the seas some 4,000 million years ago. The earliest fossil evidence we have is of very simple organisms consisting of thread-like chains of cells, dating back about 3,500 million years.

Fossil evidence covering much of the early geological history of the development of fishes is scanty. Some comes from the Cambrian period of about 500 million years ago – with fossil remains of invertebrate molluscs, the immensely prolific trilobites, and the clamlike brachiopods – but more importantly it comes from the Devonian period. During this period, between 360 and 410 million years ago, the placoderms (plate-skinned fishes) were by far the most abundant.

THE EVOLUTION OF FISHES

The crucial evolutionary link between invertebrates, such as Cephalaspis – a small, bony, fishlike creature – and the first vertebrate fishes, is thought to have come with rhipidistians, large fishes with lobe-shaped fins related to coelacanths (*Latimeria chalumnae*). Coelacanths themselves are of pivotal importance to the evolution of fishes, since they are thought to be a direct ancestor of all fishes as we know them today.

Over millions of years of evolution, fishes colonized the fresh waters of the land. During this period, geological upheavals, climate changes, and land-mass movements cut many of them off from their home waters; whereas countless

ADAPTATIONS TO THE CHANGING SEA

In the time of Pangaea (*see* opposite), the Tethys Sea, thought to be the original sea, had a lower level of salinity than the seas we know today. The level of minerals, consisting primarily of salt, in the living cells of the life that developed in these waters was close to that of the surrounding sea. This meant that there was little problem with osmosis (*see* p. 37) since water passed neither in nor out of these creatures' bodies.

Since then, however, water from the seas has been lost to clouds to fall as rain on the land, bringing with it, on its return to the seas, dissolved minerals from the land. Additionally, water from the sea was lost to the icecaps as the planet cooled. This meant that the level of minerals in the sea increased (*see* p. 13). The higher mineral levels outside the bodies of marine fishes tended to draw water out of them, forcing them to drink to prevent dehydration. Conversely, as the migration of fishes to fresh water began, the kidneys of those species that made the transition to these waters had to develop to cope with the elimination of water drawn into them by the higher concentrations of minerals in their bodies.

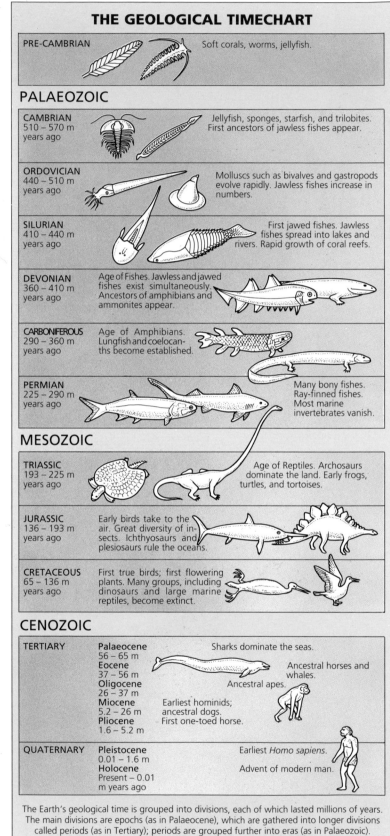

THE GEOLOGICAL TIMECHART

PRE-CAMBRIAN	Soft corals, worms, jellyfish.

PALAEOZOIC

CAMBRIAN 510 – 570 m years ago	Jellyfish, sponges, starfish, and trilobites. First ancestors of jawless fishes appear.
ORDOVICIAN 440 – 510 m years ago	Molluscs such as bivalves and gastropods evolve rapidly. Jawless fishes increase in numbers.
SILURIAN 410 – 440 m years ago	First jawed fishes. Jawless fishes spread into lakes and rivers. Rapid growth of coral reefs.
DEVONIAN 360 – 410 m years ago	Age of Fishes. Jawless and jawed fishes exist simultaneously. Ancestors of amphibians and ammonites appear.
CARBONIFEROUS 290 – 360 m years ago	Age of Amphibians. Lungfish and coelocanths become established.
PERMIAN 225 – 290 m years ago	Many bony fishes. Ray-finned fishes. Most marine invertebrates vanish.

MESOZOIC

TRIASSIC 193 – 225 m years ago	Age of Reptiles. Archosaurs dominate the land. Early frogs, turtles, and tortoises.
JURASSIC 136 – 193 m years ago	Early birds take to the air. Great diversity of insects. Ichthyosaurs and plesiosaurs rule the oceans.
CRETACEOUS 65 – 136 m years ago	First true birds; first flowering plants. Many groups, including dinosaurs and large marine reptiles, become extinct.

CENOZOIC

TERTIARY	Palaeocene 56 – 65 m	Sharks dominate the seas.
	Eocene 37 – 56 m	Ancestral horses and whales.
	Oligocene 26 – 37 m	Ancestral apes.
	Miocene 5.2 – 26 m	Earliest hominids; ancestral dogs.
	Pliocene 1.6 – 5.2 m	First one-toed horse.
QUATERNARY	Pleistocene 0.01 – 1.6 m	Earliest *Homo sapiens*.
	Holocene Present – 0.01 m years ago	Advent of modern man.

The Earth's geological time is grouped into divisions, each of which lasted millions of years. The main divisions are epochs (as in Palaeocene), which are gathered into longer divisions called periods (as in Tertiary); periods are grouped further into eras (as in Palaeozoic).

THE LIVING FOSSIL

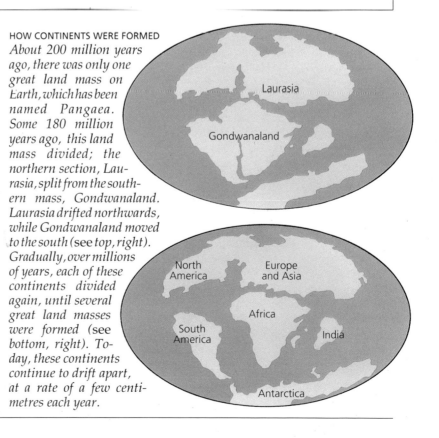

THE COELACANTH *Just under the surface of the coelacanth's head lie massive bones, while scales in its extremely oily skin overlap to such an extent that they form formidable armour.*

About 360 million years ago, primitive vertebrate fishes swam in swamps and deeper waters around the world. Among them was the coelacanth, a fish that was until recently believed to have been extinct for 70 million years. In 1939, however, a curator at the East London Museum in South Africa wrote to the British Museum stating that she had seen in the catch of some local fishermen a very large,

heavily scaled fish, with fleshy fins and tail, the like of which she had never seen before. She enclosed samples of its scales with her letter to the museum, and these were positively identified as having come from a "long-extinct" coelacanth. On investigation it was discovered that this species had been for centuries part of the catch of the fishermen around the Comoros, off southeast Africa.

species became extinct, others managed to survive and slowly adapt, often even learning to thrive in completely new environments. Some of these adaptations were so successful that they still live on, all these millions of years later, as with the agnathas and cyclostomes, two of the most primitive of all living fishes today.

THE ECOLOGICAL NICHE

There is evidence to suggest that for most of the Earth's geological history there was only one supercontinent, which has been named Pangaea. Between 180 and 120 million years ago, Pangaea began to fragment and drift apart, a process that is still continuing. As a result of this continental drift, fish families became divided and, over the course of time, adapted to new ecological niches.

The cichlid family provides an excellent example of how just a small number of original species can diversify and produce many new species to exploit different habitats and food sources. Similarities between the cichlids that inhabit the various lakes of both Africa and South America are strong, indicating that before the land masses split, these fishes shared the same home waters. As the continents drifted apart (*see* right) the fish evolved in numerous different ways, each within its own land mass.

HOW CONTINENTS WERE FORMED
About 200 million years ago, there was only one great land mass on Earth, which has been named Pangaea. Some 180 million years ago, this land mass divided; the northern section, Laurasia, split from the southern mass, Gondwanaland. Laurasia drifted northwards, while Gondwanaland moved to the south (see top, right). Gradually, over millions of years, each of these continents divided again, until several great land masses were formed (see bottom, right). Today, these continents continue to drift apart, at a rate of a few centimetres each year.

THE CLASSIFICATION OF FISHES

Aquarium hobbyists soon discover that there is a bewildering range of common names for fishes. Often one species seems to have several different names; sometimes the same name is actually used for different species in different countries. The definitive, worldwide name for a fish is its latin name, usually shown in italic print. The latin name is the most reliable name to use for identification purposes. Some fishes do not even have common names.

In the eighteenth century, the Swedish naturalist Carl von Linné, also known as Karl Linnaeus, devised a system for classifying plants and animals that laid the groundwork for today's system. Linnaeus established the system by which a single specimen (the holotype) held in one of the world's national museums is universally acknowledged as the standard for the whole species. He set up the format for latin names that is used today, although the original system has been modified in minor ways over the years. An international committee now sits to lay down the rules for classification. Various levels of classification are set so that a species can be filed in one group, as well as being grouped with others in another file, and so on.

THE NAMES OF SPECIES

A fish's latin name is composed of two, or even three parts. The first part of the name is the generic name and gives the genus. The second part is the species name, which invariably begins with a small letter. This may be a latinized form of the name of the discoverer – for example, *Corydoras rabauti* and *Corydoras natterei*, named after Messrs. Rabaut and Natterer respectively. Species may also be named in honour of an individual: *Corydoras davidsandsi* is, for instance, named after David Sands. Often the species name reflects a particularly salient characteristic of the fish, as in *Corydoras trilineatus*, the three line catfish. In a number of instances, it may also relate to a fish's geographical origin.

Where forms of the same species are distinct enough to be considered as subspecies, but not different enough to constitute a species in their own right, a third name may be added. Classifications like this are often in a state of flux, with fishes being reclassified several times. *Corydoras hastatus australe*, a subspecies of *Corydoras hastatus*, for instance, has recently been reclassified as a distinct species.

FRESHWATER FISH GROUPS

Fishes can be divided up into certain groups, each one made up of various genera, that are useful categories for aquarists. On looking at most freshwater fishes, there are certain simple external characteristics that allow you to make a tentative identification of the fish's group. These include body shape, fins, mouth and teeth, colouration, plus other specialized traits. Based on these features, the majority of freshwater fishes can be divided into seven broad groups.

Catfish These fishes have between four and eight barbels around the mouth; sometimes these are long and whiskery. Often a rayless adipose fin sits behind the dorsal fin. The dorsal fin may have very strong fin rays, which are sometimes serrated. The colouration is quite dull, and some species have no scales.

Loaches Similar in some ways to catfish, loaches have no adipose fin. They are generally small fishes; many have long, snake-like bodies. They have six short barbels around the mouth. The dorsal fin is often close to the middle of the body, which may be brightly coloured.

Characins These have the true fish-shaped body, scaled and often with a metallic colouration; some are almost fluorescent. The fins may be coloured and there is a small adipose fin. The males of some of the species in this group also have a tiny hook on their anal fin. The mouth is always terminal, and contains teeth. The majority of fishes in this group originate in South America.

Barbs and Rasboras Members of this group are classically fish-shaped, and are obviously scaled and often brightly coloured. The dorsal fin is often set back on the body and there is no adipose fin. Most have barbels, although these are inconspicuous. The mouth, which is usually terminal, has no teeth.

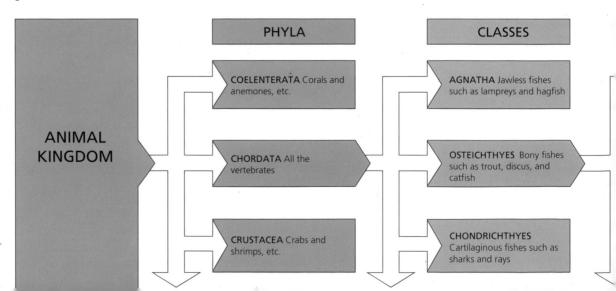

FISHES IN THE ANIMAL KINGDOM
This chart gives examples of how fishes fit into the vast classification system of animals pioneered by Linnaeus. Each species belongs to a genus, as in Corydoras. *The genera (plural of genus) are grouped into families with similar characteristics, and these families are grouped into orders. The orders are gathered into classes; each class is part of of a phylum (plural phyla) – one of the major divisions of the Animal Kingdom.*

ANIMAL KINGDOM

PHYLA

COELENTERATA Corals and anemones, etc.

CHORDATA All the vertebrates

CRUSTACEA Crabs and shrimps, etc.

CLASSES

AGNATHA Jawless fishes such as lampreys and hagfish

OSTEICHTHYES Bony fishes such as trout, discus, and catfish

CHONDRICHTHYES Cartilaginous fishes such as sharks and rays

FISH GROUPS

Livebearing and egg-laying toothcarps
Usually less than 2 in (6 cm) long, these have a flat-topped head with a small, upward-facing mouth. The dorsal fin is often set well back on the body.

Cichlids Often brightly coloured and with bands and bars as markings, these fishes have a terminal mouth. Many of them also have a large dorsal fin and/or a deep body.

Labyrinth fishes Externally similar to the cichlids; the anal fin of Asiatic species trails to the level of the dorsal fin or beyond it. In the African species this feature is not as prominent; instead look for a serrated edge to the top of the gill cover. Labyrinth fishes often have marbled body markings.

COMMON MARINE FISH GROUPS

Since there are many more marine species, it is not so easy to identify them using the same kind of distinctions as for freshwater fishes, but basic visual descriptions can be given for ten of the groups most commonly seen in aquaria.

Surgeonfish and Tangs Deep-bodied fishes with compressed sides and a high profile. They have sharp spines protruding from the "neck" of the tail (caudal peduncle); these spines can be erected or left flat.

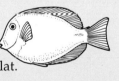

Angelfish and Butterflyfish This group is similar to the surgeons and tangs but there are no spines on the caudal peduncle, although angelfish have a spine protruding from the lower part of their gill cover. The colours and patterns of these fishes are designed primarily for camouflage or species recognition.

Cardinalfish These have two obvious, erect dorsal fins and a large mouth. Being nocturnal, they have large eyes.

Squirrelfish Another group with large eyes due to their nocturnal habits. The dorsal fin has a strongly rayed front section and a high-standing back section with softer rays.

Wrasse and Rainbowfish Most members of this group have the classic fish body shape, but some are deep-bodied. There is a single, extended dorsal fin and a terminal or slightly downward-facing mouth.

Triggerfish These reef-dwellers have a double dorsal fin. Although the front one is carried folded, it can be erected and locked in place. Their long faces and terminal mouths are designed for picking invertebrates off the reef.

Blennies Although long in the body, these have a flattened, bulldog-type face. The eyes are set high, often with whiskery "eyelashes".

Gobies Distinguished by their fairly elongated, brightly coloured bodies, gobies have pelvic fins modified for grasping rocks. Although they may resemble blennies, they have no "eyelashes".

Mandarinfish Similar to blennies, but shorter-bodied, these fishes have a double dorsal fin with the leading edge extended. They include some extremely brightly coloured species.

Anemonefish (Clownfish) and Damselfish Fishes in this group have a classic, unremarkable body shape (some damselfish are deep-bodied). Clownfish are so-called because of their jerky swimming pattern and often brightly coloured markings.

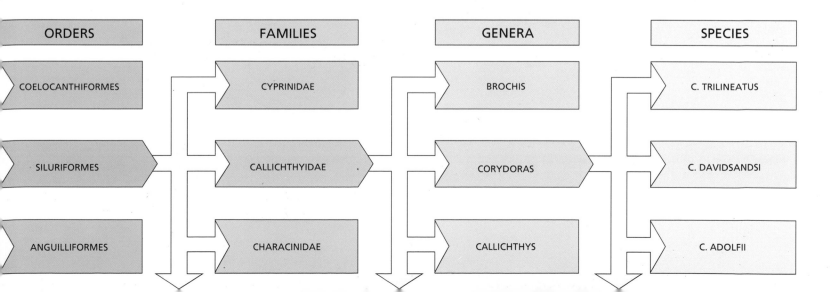

ORDERS	FAMILIES	GENERA	SPECIES
COELOCANTHIFORMES	CYPRINIDAE	BROCHIS	C. TRILINEATUS
SILURIFORMES	CALLICHTHYIDAE	CORYDORAS	C. DAVIDSANDSI
ANGUILLIFORMES	CHARACINIDAE	CALLICHTHYS	C. ADOLFII

THE DESIGN OF THE FISH

Within a certain "blueprint", fishes have evolved to a very high degree to suit the environment in which they live, both in their structure and their behaviour. As a result, they are more vulnerable than many other forms of life to changes in their surroundings. This is why successful fishkeeping requires a good basic knowledge of how the fish's body works, and of why fishes can look so different.

The overall body shape of each species reflects certain features of the fish's lifestyle, such as the speed at which it needs to swim. Body shape also depends on the flow of water experienced by the fish in its habitat.

The shape of the fish's mouth indicates where it feeds, and on what. The body colour of the fish is also significant; for instance, it can act as a bright beacon to attract a mate, or as a camouflage to protect the fish from predators.

Like other creatures, the fish is endowed with certain senses. These promote its survival, by helping it to recognize its own habitat or territory, to identify other fishes, and to find food. The various physiological functions of the fish, such as breathing and breeding, are similarly tailored to life in the water.

BODY SHAPE

The shape of fishes depends mainly on the kind of swimming that they are required to do. Some fishes swim at speed because of the way they feed, to avoid predators, for migration, or to hold their own against fast currents.

Some fishes have streamlined, torpedo-shaped bodies, that exploit fully the laws of hydrodynamics. The tails of these fast-moving fishes provide the necessary power, but have a narrow area at the base to minimize side-to-side drag.

Fishes not requiring bursts of speed have evolved into less streamlined forms. Deep-bodied, laterally compressed fishes swim between plants with ease, while fishes with fatter, cylindrical bodies are stable in fast-flowing waters.

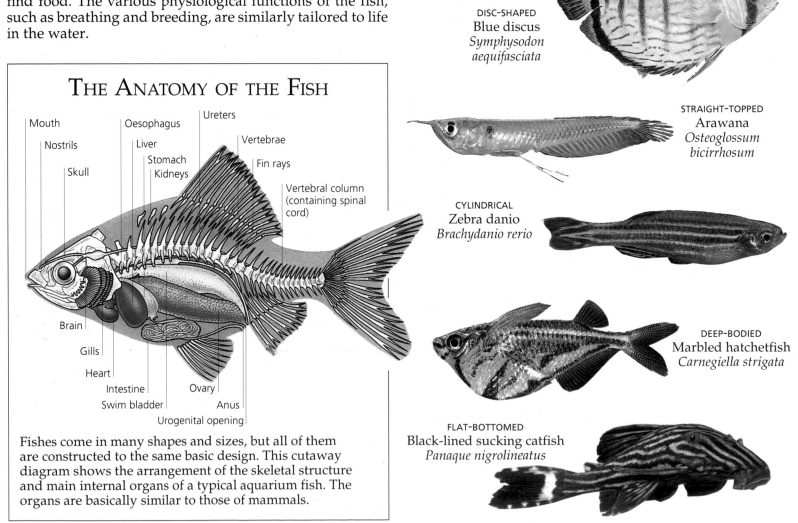

FIVE BASIC BODY SHAPES
The shape of each fish has evolved to suit the environment in which it lives.

DISC-SHAPED
Blue discus
Symphysodon aequifasciata

STRAIGHT-TOPPED
Arawana
Osteoglossum bicirrhosum

CYLINDRICAL
Zebra danio
Brachydanio rerio

DEEP-BODIED
Marbled hatchetfish
Carnegiella strigata

FLAT-BOTTOMED
Black-lined sucking catfish
Panaque nigrolineatus

THE ANATOMY OF THE FISH

Mouth
Nostrils
Skull
Oesophagus
Liver
Stomach
Kidneys
Ureters
Vertebrae
Fin rays
Vertebral column (containing spinal cord)
Brain
Gills
Heart
Intestine
Swim bladder
Ovary
Anus
Urogenital opening

Fishes come in many shapes and sizes, but all of them are constructed to the same basic design. This cutaway diagram shows the arrangement of the skeletal structure and main internal organs of a typical aquarium fish. The organs are basically similar to those of mammals.

THE FINS AND TAIL

Fins, including the fish's tail, are rays of cartilage or bone, webbed with tissue. The fin rays can be rigid or soft, and may have articulations or branches. By flexing small muscles, the fish is able to fold or extend its fins.

Most fishes have three single fins and two sets of paired fins. The single fins are the caudal (the tail), dorsal (on the back), and anal (on the rear underside); the paired fins are the pelvic (or "ventral", on the underbelly) and pectoral (behind and beneath the gills). Some fishes also have a small, apparently useless extra fin: the adipose fin. Other fishes

FIN TYPES *The rainbow characin (*Exodon paradoxus) *boasts six different types of fin, including the apparently redundant adipose fin. Fins are used for locomotion, direction, and to stabilize the fish. On some fishes, fins may be modified, or missing, always with some reason for such a departure from this basic plan.*

Dorsal fin
Adipose fin
Caudal fin
Anal fin
Pelvic fins
Pectoral fins

FINS FOR PRECISE MOVEMENT *Coral dwellers like the porcupinefish (*Diodon holocanthus) *– here inflated and as normal – make fine movements with their fins to manoeuvre around a coral head.*

may require fewer fins than the normal quota for effective movement. Knifefish (Gymnotidae), for example, have only a long anal fin for propulsion.

Fins are used to control direction, position and attitude in the water. The caudal fin propels the fish through the water, transferring power into wave-like motions of the body; the dorsal and anal fins stabilize the fish in the water; the pelvic fins are used for turning, and as brakes; and the pectoral fins can lift or lower the fish, feel for food, or gesture to rivals.

Deeper-bodied fishes need large fins and a wide tail to maintain the correct attitude, while fast-swimming fishes may have narrower fins and a crescent-shaped tail to provide power. Larger, sensitive fins are important to fishes that travel using fine, precise movements, for example around coral heads or rock. Some fishes propel themselves by means of their fins alone, without making any other bodily movements. Pufferfish (*Tetraodon* spp.) for instance, use their dorsal and paired fins for delicate manoeuvres. The hatchetfish (*Gasteropelacus* spp.) has a very deep chest, and can fly from the water by beating its large pectoral fins.

NEUTRAL BUOYANCY

Most fishes have developed a swim bladder, an air-filled bladder designed to exploit the supportive action of the water. This makes them effectively weightless or "of neutral buoyancy"; therefore, they neither float nor sink.

The swim bladder can help the fish in surprising ways. In the upside-down catfish (*Synodontis nigriventris*), for example, it is situated off-centre, so that the fish swims upside-down and can exploit unusual food sources. In physostomatous fishes, air is swallowed and passed through a duct to inflate the swim bladder. In physoclistous fishes, on the other hand, the swim bladder is closed, the gas that fills it being introduced via the bloodstream.

UPSIDE-DOWN SWIMMER *Eight weeks after birth, the false upside-down catfish (*Synodontis nigrita) *begins to swim belly upwards.*

Some species, like sharks, lack a swim bladder, but store huge amounts of oil in their livers to give them almost neutral buoyancy. In species that never rest long enough to need so much buoyancy, the swim bladder is small.

SPECIAL FINS

In some species the anal fin is a tube that delivers sperm during spawning. Other fishes use their fins for self-defence (*see* right). Angelfish (*Pterophyllum* spp.) and killifish (Cyprinodontidae) have ornate fins and tails for display purposes. Fishes like Gurnards (Triglidae), and anglerfish (Lophiidae) even have fins which are used for "walking".

DEFENSIVE FINS *The white fin lionfish has venomous spines.*

THE DESIGN OF THE MOUTH

As with the fins, the shape of a fish's mouth depends strictly on the job that it needs to do. There are three basic mouth types in fishes. The superior mouth is upturned for surface feeding, particularly for gathering floating insects; the terminal (forward-facing) mouth is situated at the tip of the snout to assist midwater swimmers and feeders; and the inferior mouth is directed downwards for feeding on the bottom, and browsing on rocks or plants. An extreme example of this last type of fish is the spiny eel (*Macrognathus aculeatus*), which may actually bury itself in the substrate, leaving only its head exposed for feeding.

Some fishes have mouths of unique design. As its name suggests, the unusual elephant-nosed fish (*Gnathonemus petersi*) has a long "trunk" with which to search the bottom. Many of the fishes with downward-turned mouths – catfish, for example – have fleshy, tactile whiskers called barbels; some species rely on these to feel their way and to detect food. The broad mouth of the bristle-nosed catfish (*Ancistrus* spp.) razes algae from the substrate, and can also be used to cling on to rock surfaces.

SUPERIOR MOUTH
East African killifish
Nothobranchius guentheri

TERMINAL MOUTH
Angelfish
Pterophyllum scalare

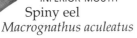

INFERIOR MOUTH
Spiny eel
Macrognathus aculeatus

FEELING FOR FOOD *The black-spotted corydoras (Corydoras melanistius) has two pairs of barbels for probing the bottom.*

TACTILE SNOUT *As it has poor eyesight, the elephant-nosed fish (Gnathonemus petersi) finds food using a trunk-like jaw extension.*

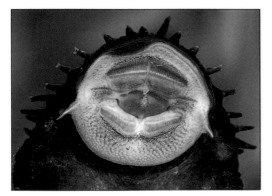

SUCKING MOUTH *The broad mouth of the bristle-nosed catfish (Ancistrus spp.).*

CARNIVOROUS FISHES

TEETH FOR TEARING *A shoal of red piranha (Serrasalmus nattererei) can rapidly strip a large animal to the bone.*

Fishes that are carnivorous need a combination of powerful jaws and teeth. Although some Serrasalmidae are vegetarian, those species that eat meat, such as the red piranha (*Serrasalmus nattererei*), have pronounced and powerful lower jaws and sharp, cutting teeth that enable them to tear pieces from their prey. Only young red piranhas may be kept in a domestic aquarium, for obvious reasons.

The triangular teeth of predatory sharks like the carcharinids, which include the great white shark (*Carcharodon carcharias*), are pointed and serrated. They need to be razor-sharp, and are renewed every ten to fourteen days.

BODY COLOUR

It is the colour of a fish by which its species and its sex can often be most easily determined, many species being of very similar shape. The colour of a fish is produced by both reflection of light and by pigmentation; the scales themselves are in fact almost transparent. There are many good reasons for particular colourations of certain fishes.

Some fishes living in dark or muddy waters are brightly coloured, so that they are able to be seen and can attract a mate. Other fishes may need camouflage. Some freshwater species have silver undersides that hide them from fishes below by camouflaging them against the surface of the water. This effect is created by a reflective metabolic waste product called guanin, which is carried within the skin. Similarly, a dark green or black upper body, seen from above, can appear to merge into mud or a mass of vegetation. Many fishes have camouflage related even more specifically to their habitat. The discus (*Symphysodon* spp.), for example, has stripes that allow it to blend in with reeds.

Most fishes are able to lighten or darken their colour, or even to change it. Pencilfish (*Nannostomus* spp.) alter their colour to suit their daytime or nocturnal activities. The colour of a fish can indicate whether it is excited, angry, ill, or frightened, while the colour of male fishes tends to be intensified during the breeding season.

Often eye-catching body colour warns predators that a fish is poisonous, while some marine species mimic the patterns of their prey. A black area that looks like an eye (eye spot) may deceive predators about the orientation of the body and the likely direction of escape.

HIDDEN HORROR *The highly venomous false stonefish (*Synanceia horrida*) lies superbly camouflaged against the ocean floor.*

THE SCALES

A fish's scales grow within the outer layer of its skin, which is covered in a layer of mucus that allows the fish to slip easily through the water and also repels parasites. Apart from this streamlining, the scales also help to protect the body from damage by rocks or predators.

The majority of fishes have non-placoid scales. These are thin, often smooth, and usually have many fine ridges across their surface, giving an effect rather like a fingerprint. As the fish matures, these ridges increase, much as rings develop around a tree trunk. Placoid scales, which are tooth-like and usually have an enamel cap, appear on sharks and rays. There are several special cases where scales are specifically modified for a particular species. Eels (*Anguilla* spp.) have very small, deeply embedded scales, which are almost invisible, while other fishes, such as sturgeons, have a few rows of large, flat, hard external scales called scutes. Naked catfish (Mochokoidae) from Africa have no scales at all. Instead they rely on the toughness of their skins for protection. A small number of the scales on the stingray (Dasyatidae) carry a venomous sting powerful enough to kill a human being.

REED DWELLER *The discus (*Symphysodon *spp.) is found in a number of colour varieties; these help it to blend in with the reeds of its preferred habitat.*

HUNT THE "REAL" EYE *A one-spot butterflyfish (*Chaetodon unimaculatus*).*

THE BODY SENSES

Most fishes have the same five senses as humans: sight, touch, taste, smell, and hearing. The latter two are more highly developed in fishes than in humans. In addition, the fish has a sixth sense made possible by its lateral line system.

THE SENSE OF SMELL

In most fishes, the sense of smell is more acute than the sense of taste. This is because it is far more important to their survival, being used to actually find food. Fishes can usually detect food by smell from a great distance, using their nostrils. The nostrils are generally visible on the snout of the fish; they are not often connected to the mouth. In most cases, the nostrils are simply two shallow pits, each covered by a flap to control the flow of water through them. Sharks and

GUIDED BY SMELL *Highly visible close to the eye, the nostrils of the European eel* (Anguilla anguilla) *help it follow its course from Europe, all the way to the Sargasso Sea (between the West Indies and the Azores), where it breeds in the depths.*

eels have particularly well-developed nostrils. Because they are blind-ending, the nostrils of fishes are not involved in the movement of water across the gills (*see* p. 36).

Apart from using scent to find food, several species of fish can detect their own home zones in rivers by smell alone. Salmon (Salmonidae) have especially sensitive nostrils, and can recognize the river of their birth by its scent when they return from the feeding ground to spawn.

Some fishes, such as minnows (Cyprinidae), are capable of releasing an "alarm substance" into the water from the mucus on their skins. Other fishes in the shoal detect this by smell, and are warned of danger.

HOW THE FISH HEARS

Since water is a very dense medium, sounds are detected through it much more easily than through air. In fact the pressure waves that sounds produce travel through it five times faster. Because of this, the inner ear of a fish is able to pick up a wide range of sound waves, and so it needs no outer or middle ear such as humans have; in fact fishes have no visible ears of any kind.

To supplement their basic method of hearing, many fish species can also use the swim bladder to receive sound vibrations. These are able to be transmitted to the inner ear via a series of interconnecting tubes and bones.

HOW THE FISH SEES

The majority of fishes have what is known as monocular vision. They can see in two directions at once, but they cannot focus both eyes on the same object. The eyes of fishes are not so well developed as human eyes, and the fact that they see everything through water causes extra loss of resolution in their vision, so that objects look slightly out of focus to them. Fishes cannot focus over very long distances – 45 cm (18 in) is about their limit for clear vision; however, this apparent defect is compensated for by their highly sophisticated lateral line system (*see* opposite).

In more advanced fish species like cyprinids, the eyes can move completely independently of each other. In stream-living species, they are used to help maintain the fish's station in the water, one eye being fixed on a stone or other stationary object.

SOUND-MAKING

Most fishes are silent. However, a few species are mysteriously able to make various sounds. Squirrelfish (Holocentridae) grind their pharyngeal, or throat teeth, probably for communication, while in triggerfish (Balistidae), movements of the pelvic bones and the muscles that support the swim bladder cause the bladder to vibrate, producing a drum-like sound.

GRINDING SOUND *The squirrelfish* (Adioryx caudimaculatus) *makes a grinding sound with its teeth.*

DRUMMING FISH *The Picasso triggerfish* (Rhinecanthus aculeatus) *uses its swim bladder as a "drum"*

OPTIMUM TEMPERATURE

Although the skin of fishes is relatively insensitive to touch, it can detect small changes in temperature. Given a gradient of temperatures, fishes are able to choose water at their optimum temperature to within one degree. As they are cold-blooded, this is their only means of regulating body temperature.

To enhance their awareness of their environment, fishes that live in well-illuminated, shallow waters have evolved a superior perception of contrast – the difference between light and dark. In addition, these fishes see more shades in the violet part of the colour spectrum. Fishes that live in deeper waters are likely to have less well-developed colour vision, or even none at all, since they essentially have little need for it.

"Double vision" Some fishes have both eyes raised high on their heads, which gives them a certain degree of binocular vision (the ability to focus both eyes on the same object at the same time). A very highly developed example of this is the four-eyed fish (*Anableps anableps*). The cornea, pupil, and retina of its eyes are each divided in two by a horizontal layer of tissue. This allows the fish, when swimming at the surface of the water, to see both above and below the water-line simultaneously. Images out of the water are perceived by the upper eye, while objects underwater are seen by the lower eye.

TOUCH AND TASTE

We tend to consider fishes as being relatively insensitive, but some of them are extraordinarily sensitive to a variety of stimuli. Carp (*Cyprinus carpio*), for instance, are thought to have senses very similar to those of mammals. Most fishes have a reasonable sense of taste, with taste-buds located around the mouth and lips.

The majority of fishes are not very sensitive to touch, although this varies considerably. Structures similar to the touch-cells and nerve endings that serve the human sense of touch have been found in certain specific areas such as the pectoral fin rays of gurnards (Triglidae). The bullhead (*Cottus gobio*) possesses nerve endings, but is without touch-cells; nevertheless it is extremely sensitive around the head and barbels. Bullheads are also endowed with a much better sense of taste than most fishes.

"FOUR EYES" *The large, protruding eyes of the four-eyed fish* (Anableps anableps) *allow it to see above and below the waterline simultaneously.*

THE LATERAL LINE COMPLEX

Lateral line

The fish's lateral line complex is like a personal radar system. Its main function is to detect pressure changes in the immediate vicinity, from the movement of currents or from other fishes, and it is invaluable for navigation, finding food, and avoiding predators. As water carries pressure waves (vibrations) very well, fishes are able to sense pressure changes acutely. The lateral line is unique to fishes (and to amphibians when in water). It is made up of a system of interconnected, fluid-filled ducts under the scales. These ducts are visible as a horizontal line of perforations along the fish's body. They contain cells called neuromasts, which can detect movement of the fluid within the ducts, caused

Finger fish
(*Monodactylus argenteus*)

A cross-section of part of the system. Water enters through the pores to keep the ducts filled. When this water moves, the neuromasts feed data to the brain.

THE NEUROMAST SYSTEM

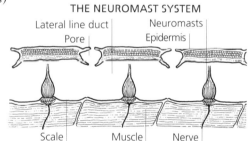

by vibrations. In specific fishes, there are, within the lateral line complex, a variety of associated organs, most of which are sensory. Knifefish (Gymnotidae), the electric eel (*Electrophorus electricus*), and the elephant-nosed fish (*Gnathonemus petersi*), for example, can detect electrical changes in the water. The blind cave fish (*Astyanax mexicanus*) inhabits South American caves, where little light penetrates, and so it need never see. As a result, it has eyes overgrown by skin, and navigates perfectly well using its lateral line alone.

CAVE DWELLER *The lateral line of the blind cave fish* (Astyanax mexicanus) *provides the data it needs to navigate.*

RESPIRATION

With very few exceptions, living organisms need oxygen to survive. While humans live in air, which is approximately 21 per cent oxygen, fishes live in an environment that, in addition to being 800 times as dense as air, contains only one thousandth of one per cent of oxygen. So they need a very efficient system for extracting oxygen from the water.

HOW THE GILLS WORK

Most fishes breathe by taking in water through the mouth and over the gills, pushing it out through the operculum (gill cover). This process enables the fish to take up oxygen and to eliminate waste carbon dioxide and ammonia.

Gills consist of frameworks of cartilage (gill arches), on which there are finger-like projections called filaments. These themselves have plate-like lamellae – carriers of copious amounts of blood – on their surfaces. As the fish swims, the direction of the blood-flow within the lamellae is opposite to the direction of waterflow between them and, when water passes over the lamellae, oxygen is taken from the water by the blood and carbon dioxide is expelled. After this process of "gas transfer", the oxygen taken by the fish is distributed throughout its body.

Active fishes may have a gill surface area up to five times as great as those of sedentary, slow-moving species, because they need to obtain more oxygen to sustain their activity.

Lamellae are very thin-walled and are easily damaged, particularly by suspended matter, so fishes that live in water with a high level of suspended solids may have fine gill rakers that act as prefilters to protect them. Fishes can also "cough", bringing up water to backwash the gills.

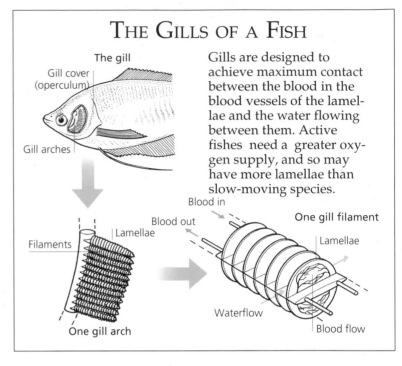

THE GILLS OF A FISH

Gills are designed to achieve maximum contact between the blood in the blood vessels of the lamellae and the water flowing between them. Active fishes need a greater oxygen supply, and so may have more lamellae than slow-moving species.

The gill
Gill cover (operculum)
Gill arches
Filaments
Lamellae
Blood out
One gill arch
Blood in
One gill filament
Lamellae
Waterflow
Blood flow

SPECIALIZED GILLS

In many fishes the gills have adapted in special ways to ensure that they can take in enough oxygen, even when levels are low. These are generally fishes that live either in pools that dry out, or in water in which waste material is not properly broken down and there is little movement. The spiny eel (*Macrognathus aculeatus*), which hides during the day with its body covered in sand, produces a mucus over its

FISHES THAT BREATHE AIR

Twenty-four genera of fish contain species that can actually breathe air directly from the surrounding atmosphere. Lungfish are well known for this ability to breathe air. They usually do this at the surface of the water when the water level is low. As well as gills, they have two lungs, and rely on them to a considerable extent. The lungfish from Africa (*Protopterus* spp.), which developed very early in the evolution of fishes, has the most advanced structure. When its home pool dries out, the fish buries itself, then wraps itself in a mucus cocoon, leaving a breathing hole between itself and the open air. When the rains arrive to fill the pool, the fish frees itself from the cocoon so that it can breathe at the surface. Clarias catfish (Clariidae) and anabantids (Anabantidae) such as gouramis have a different method of taking in air at the surface. Instead of lungs, they use sophisticated extensions to their gills (*see* illustration) which means that they can survive in water with very little oxygen.

Cartilagenous connection to gill extension
Filaments
Base of operculum
Barbels
Gill arches
Gill extension
Extension of gill chamber

GILL EXTENSIONS *Clarias catfish (Clariidae) can take an air bubble into a special compartment of their gill chamber. Here oxygen is removed by blood flowing through a bush-like gill extension of the gill arches that helps to trap the air.*

FISH WITH LUNGS *The East African lungfish (Protopterus annectens) can breathe air.*

RAM VENTILATION

Some gills, such as those on yellow-fin tuna (*Thunnus albacora*), rely on ram ventilation, a form of breathing that is possible only when swimming at speed. Such fishes do not need to pump water over their gills in order to breathe, since the pressure of the water produced by the forward movement is enough to pass water over the gills. This need for speed – the yellow-fin tuna can manage sprints of up to 70 km (43 miles) per hour – means that these species can be difficult to maintain in captivity.

gills that keeps them moist enough for gas transfer, while snakeheads (Channidae) and mudskippers (*Periophthalmus* spp.) have a special gill-cover lining with multiple folds that substantially increase the area of the breathing surface. Mudskippers live in pools that drain away when the tide goes out. So long as their gills remain moist they can breathe perfectly well until the tide returns.

Supplements to gills A variety of other fishes have adapted internal organs to allow gas transfer to take place. In most cases, this "breathing" is supplementary to that done by the gills. Some catfish, such as *Saccobranchus* spp., have a sac extending the full length of their body, which is like a swim bladder, but which is used for gas transfer; some armoured catfish, such as Callichthyidae, can use their stomach; some loaches, for example the Cobitidae, use parts of the lower intestine; and the giant redfish (*Arapaima gigas*) uses the swim bladder itself.

STOMACH FOR BREATHING *The peppered corydoras* (Corydoras paleatus) *can adsorb oxygen through its stomach.*

ELABORATE GILL COVER *Multiple folds make the gills of the mudskipper* (Periophthalmus vulgaris) *highly efficient.*

BODY SALTS AND FLUIDS

When salty solutions of different strengths (giving them different osmotic pressures) are separated by something permeable, such as the skin of a fish, water tends to flow from the weaker solution to dilute the stronger one, by the process called osmosis, until they are the same strength. It does this by pulling in surrounding water molecules through the fish's skin and, particularly, the gills.

All fishes need to maintain the correct levels of both water and salts in their bodies, and the natural level of salts in the body is very similar in freshwater and marine fishes. Because the body salts of freshwater fishes are more concentrated than those of their surroundings, water is drawn into their bodies. They have no need to drink any extra water, and their kidneys contain systems for retaining the salts while eliminating quite large amounts of very dilute urine.

In marine fishes the situation is very different. They are surrounded by water that is actually saltier than they are, and so, by osmosis, water is drawn out of their bodies and they dehydrate. To compensate for this, they drink sea water and, having eliminated the salts, which they do not need, their kidneys produce only small amounts of very concentrated urine. In this way the correct fluid levels are maintained in the body.

OSMOSIS

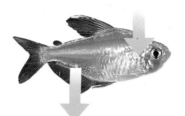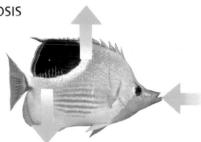

FRESHWATER FISHES *Fresh water is drawn into the fish's body and eliminated by the kidneys.*

MARINE FISHES *In the sea, water is drawn out of the fish's body, so it needs to drink water to survive.*

WASTE AND EXCRETION

The waste produced by fishes is a combination of digested and undigested food, together with metabolic wastes excreted via the kidneys and gills. Other wastes include phosphate in the faeces from the digestion of plant material, and carbon dioxide from respiration.

The wastes that are of most concern to the aquarist are those that are nitrogenous, as they are potentially damaging to the health of fishes. These wastes are the end products of the breakdown of protein from food in the nitrogen cycle (*see* p. 185). In most species, they are composed mainly of ammonia, of which up to 90 per cent is lost through the gills (the kidneys only eliminate small amounts of ammonia and urea). The urine of marine fishes may also contain salts that are extracted from sea water and are not required by the fishes. In an aquarium a filter can be used to help combat the harmful effects of waste and to keep the water clean and fresh at all times (*see* p. 159).

THE REPRODUCTIVE PROCESS

Different groups of fishes reproduce in different ways. An understanding of how the various species go about breeding is indispensable to the fishkeeping hobbyist, especially if you wish to try breeding from your own tank specimens (*see* p. 175).

All fishes are developed from eggs; their production by the female and fertilization by the male is known as spawning. The eggs may either be laid and fertilized outside the female's body (this is the case with most egg-layers), or held in the female's body to be fertilized internally (this is the case with livebearers). The fry (young) are often small and helpless when hatched, and the degree of protection offered by the parents varies greatly.

With the majority of egg-laying fishes, the sperm – or milt – is expelled from the male at the same time as the female ejects her eggs, and fertilization occurs in the water. In livebearers, on the other hand, the male fish introduces sperm directly into the body of the female using its specially modified anal fin, and the eggs develop inside the female.

MATING DISPLAY *In the breeding season, body markings may become pronounced. The bold stripes of this male tiger barb (Barbus tetrazona tetrazona) have deepened and red patches have appeared.*

EGG-LAYERS

Most aquarium species belong in the egg-laying category. Within this group, fishes can be divided into five further groups, according to how they lay and handle their eggs.

The breeding methods of egg-layers may seem diverse, but all are cleverly suited to their habitats. The great fish families of the cichlids and the cyprinids, for example, are particularly associated with lake and river environments respectively. The cichlids produce a relatively small number of eggs. They take very close care of these, and in the stability of the lake, where their eggs are not likely to be washed away, they thrive. The spawning system of cyprinids, on the other hand, is adapted to the rather more hectic life in the river. They benefit from the increased supply of food that becomes available in rivers after seasonal rains. Their large numbers of fry, left unprotected, derive nourishment from this abundant food.

Egg-scatterers This group, which includes the majority of characins, seems to have the most casual approach to egg-laying. The female fish releases a large number of eggs at random; the parents offer no protection for the eggs, and may even eat them. Those eggs that become lodged or hidden in aquatic plants or in the substrate have the best chance of hatching successfully.

Egg-buriers Among the fishes that use this method of egg-laying, savannah killifish (Cyprinodontidae) inhabit shallow pools or streams that dry up every year (this means that in the wild, these fishes only survive for a year). They bury their eggs in substrate sediment, usually mud, having spawned before the onset of the dry season. The eggs lie dormant until the coming of the new rainy season, and it is then that they hatch. The fry must of course grow very rapidly, ready to breed themselves. In permanent pools or swamps, the killifish need not die annually.

SANCTUARY IN THE MOUTH *Mouth-brooders such as this Lake Malawi cichlid may have only a small number of fry, but they often guard them well. When danger appears, one parent (usually the mother) holds the fry in the mouth.*

Egg-depositors Fishes in this group – including catfish, cichlids, and some characins – like to find a safe, clean place for spawning; the splashing tetra (*Copella arnoldi*) even manages to wriggle its body up to lay eggs on the underside of an overhanging leaf. The fry are jealously guarded against predators by one or both parent fishes for the first two or three weeks of their life.

Nest-builders Several species of fish create different kinds of nest in which to lay their eggs. Gouramis, for instance, build a mass of protective bubbles among vegetation. Some cichlids, on the other hand, dig holes in the substrate. The eggs are usually well guarded during the period of incubation, and the parents may wash water over them with their fins to keep them clean.

Mouth-brooders These fishes – which include some cichlids – build a nest in which to lay the eggs. The eggs are picked up, sometimes immediately, for incubation in the mouth or within the throat of the female fish. The fry usually hatch after a few days in the mouth, but they may continue to retire there for safety.

THE DRIVE TO SPAWN

Salmon spend two to three years in the sea, where they feed and mature, before being driven by the urge to return to their home river to spawn. In most species, once this has been achieved, the majority of these fishes will die.

ON A HOME RUN *Sockeye salmon* (Oncorhynchus nerka*).*

BUILDING THE NEST *The male three-spined stickleback (Gasterosteus aculeatus) builds a nest for his potential mate, weaving vegetation which is then glued in place with mucus.*

EGG-LAYING *The female stickleback now enters the nest to lay her eggs, and the male, displaying a bright red breast, rubs her back.*

GUARDING THE NEST *Once the female has laid her eggs, the male drives her out and guards the nest. He moves around it, fanning water through and keeping it clean.*

LIVEBEARERS

In this group, the fry are in a comparatively advanced state of development at birth, and already able to swim independently. Fourteen fish families include livebearers, and there is much diversity in the way that the fry are born. In species referred to as ovoviviparous, the eggs are simply kept in the female's abdomen, where they hatch and are nourished by yolk. In viviparous fishes, on the other hand, the eggs hatch early inside the mother, and she has "placenta-like" contact with the developing young, supplying nourishment directly to the foetuses.

Some species, like the nurse shark (*Ginglymostoma cirratum*), can use either system depending on conditions. In other fish species, like the sand tiger (*Odontaspis taurus*), the hatched foetuses feed on eggs that continue to be produced by the female for several months. Only one pup may finally be born, having eaten all its siblings.

STORING SPERM *Female livebearers like this black molly (Poecilia sphenops), here with day-old fry, may hold sperm in their bodies for months, producing several sets of fry from one mating.*

The Freshwater Aquarium

Black widow
Gymnocorymbus ternetzi

In this chapter, you will find freshwater tanks based on a worldwide range of habitats. If this is your first attempt at establishing an aquarium, or if perhaps you are looking to specialize in keeping fish from a very specific environment, you will find step-by-step instructions, as well as clearly detailed colour photographs, leading you through every aspect of tank design, planning, and stocking. Throughout, cross-referencing directs your attention to other chapters of the book, where you will find comprehensive back-up information on everything from water chemistry and

Yellow cichlid
Neolamprologus leleupi longior

Ram
Apistogramma ramirezi

Deep-water cichlid
Cyphotilapia frontosa

plant maintenance, to lighting and filtration. The first tank looked at is the freshwater community tank. Here, the objective is to include fishes and plants from diverse areas of the globe, and to manage an aquatic population that will live in harmony, as well as colonizing every zone of the aquarium. For those with specialist aspirations, other tanks in this chapter include Amazon rain forest stream and acid pool tanks, a Zaire River rapids tank, a New Guinea sandy river tank, and East Africa and Central America rocky lake tanks.

Red-tailed black shark
Labeo bicolor

SETTING UP AN AQUARIUM

One of the most useful qualities that a prospective aquarist can possess is patience. It is all too easy to rush straight into the task of setting up your aquarium, without first having studied the ground-rules. Take careful note of the following principles and, besides showing suitable respect for the well-being of your future livestock, you will, in the end, save both time and money.

CHOOSING THE SYSTEM

Fishkeeping is usually divided into two categories: freshwater and marine. This book, however, also deals with brackish-water aquaria, for which many fascinating species of fish and invertebrate are available. Among the first things that you will have to decide is which of these aquaria you wish to set up, and whether you intend to keep a tropical or a temperate aquarium. Tropical tanks dominate the aquarium hobby, because of the spectacular species of fish that can be kept in them. You will find, therefore, that all but one of the aquaria in this book recreate tropical environments.

CHOOSING THE RIGHT TANK

As a general rule, the larger the tank you choose, the more stable the water chemistry will be once the aquarium is functioning. You can use any shape of aquarium that you like, but make sure that the glass is clear and free from

distortion. The most popular aquaria are all-glass tanks bonded by silicone sealant, although numerous other models are available, such as one-piece plastic tanks, or the older, less common, metal-framed tanks. The latter are not recommended for marine environments, as the frame may rust.

STOCKING LEVELS

For freshwater and brackish-water aquaria, maximum stocking levels can, as a rule, be calculated by allowing a certain number of fish body lengths for a given surface area of the water. Acceptable freshwater and brackish-water levels are usually considered to be 1 cm of fishes per 30 to 36 sq cm (1 in per 10 to 12 sq in) of water surface. It is wrong, however, to immediately stock your aquarium to these levels. Build up the number of fishes to half this level over two to three

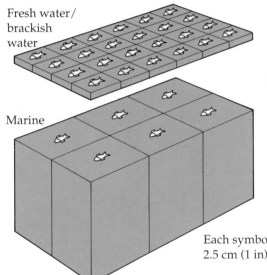

Fresh water/
brackish
water

Marine

FINAL STOCKING LEVELS
An aquarium with a surface area of 1800 sq cm (280 sq in) containing roughly 55 litres (12 gallons) of water, will have a maximum stocking level of 160 cm (24 in) of freshwater fishes or 15 cm (6 in) of marine fishes.

Each symbol represents 2.5 cm (1 in) of fish length.

months, and then continue at a similar rate until the final stocking level is achieved (*see* above). Do not be tempted to accelerate this fundamental process.

Convention dictates that suitable stocking levels for marine aquaria are calculated in relation to the volume of water in a tank, rather than the surface area. The main point to remember when initially stocking marine aquaria, however, is that you are trying to establish a stable society from among delicate, often demanding individuals. Excessive haste can, among other things, easily lead to an outbreak of disease. Aim for a maximum stocking level of 1 cm per 8 litres (1 in per 4 gallons) after six months and, if you wish, double this figure over the following year. Only by adding to your community very slowly, monitoring the progress of each new member to see when it has settled, will you succeed in laying the foundations for a healthy marine aquarium.

Finally, it is worth remembering that aquarium dealers usually sell juvenile fishes. Stocking your tank to its limit with these fishes, before they mature, will only mean having to remove some of them as they increase in size.

A HEALTHY ENVIRONMENT *The ideal combination of attractive, compatible fishes, and a well-planted, thoughtfully aquascaped aquarium.*

SHOALING *These glass catfish* (Kryptopterus bicirrhus) *are best kept in medium-sized shoals of around six or more. They are, by nature, rather nervous fishes.*

LIFESPANS

The lifespan of a fish is greatly determined by its size. Small species, with a high metabolic rate, use up the same number of heartbeats more rapidly than larger animals with slower heartbeats. According, therefore, to the general rule that a heart is designed to beat only a limited number of times, larger fishes will tend to enjoy longer lives than smaller ones. For example, the smaller common freshwater livebearers and gouramis live for between two to three years, and three to four years respectively. Larger corydoras catfish and some cichlids, on the other hand, live for at least eight to twelve years. This principle also extends to marine fishes, where large species, such as batfish or lion fish, may live for over ten years.

THROUGH THE LOOKING GLASS *When creating points of visual interest within the tank, remember to take its inhabitants into account – actively involve them.*

YOUTHFULNESS AND MATURITY *It is sometimes the case that species undergo dramatic colour transformations as they mature. The grey-brown speckles of the juvenile rhamdia catfish* (Rhamdia quelen) *bear no relation to the colouration of the adult individual.*

BUYING FISHES

The best sources of aquarium fishes are aquatic societies and specialist aquarium shops. Look for specimens with appropriately healthy colours and a well-defined example of any distinguishing pattern. They should have well-proportioned bodies, and should appear to swim effortlessly. Be watchful for any evidence of disease, such as ulcers, fin damage, cloudy eyes, and breathing or swimming abnormalities (*see* p. 180). Try to observe the fishes while they are feeding; those that are reluctant to take food may be in poor health.

COMPATIBILITY OF FISH SPECIES

Many species of fish are characteristically extrovert, and will only become aggressive, or unusually reserved, if they are isolated from members of their own species. Some species, on the other hand, are certain to fight with most others, particularly at breeding time. They should only be kept in a species tank, with a mate.

A further problem with a number of species, particularly marine fishes, arises after maturity. In a few cases, only the juveniles of a species may be compatible with the other fishes in an aquarium. Of course, a mature specimen can simply become too large for its tank, and will then also have to be removed. In either case, it is worth remembering that most dealers are often happy to exchange healthy specimens. For the various aquaria discussed in this book, refer to the accompanying charts, which include details on the potential size and compatibility of the fishes that you can keep in specific environments.

TRANSPORTING FISHES

Fishes are usually supplied in a plastic bag. If the journey home is a long one, however, a dealer will usually supply a heat-retaining, expanded polystyrene box, and may add extra oxygen to the water. Do not leave the fishes in these conditions for too long, as transportation can be extremely stressful, and the water may rapidly become either too cool (for tropical fishes), or even too warm (for temperate fishes).

Some aquarists recommend keeping newly bought fishes in a quarantine tank for a few weeks, before adding them to the main tank. Others believe, however, that transferring fishes from one tank to another, and then repeating the procedure, causes more harm than good. It is, in any case, always important to handle fishes gently. Follow the correct procedure when adding a fish to the tank (*see* p. 50).

MAPPING OUT THE TANK

The aquascaping of the aquarium should be decided upon well in advance of gathering any materials. Use the relevant notes for each of the aquaria discussed in this book to discover the ideal conditions for tank inhabitants, but also refer to other sources. These may include specialist magazines, television programmes, other books, or even nature study conducted within the environments themselves. It is always possible to conceive of a thoroughly individual design for your aquarium, whilst remaining faithful to the strict demands of your stock.

MATERIALS FOR AQUASCAPING

Great care needs to be taken in choosing materials for the aquarium, as most materials that are put into the tank are liable to affect the water chemistry in some way.

Many rocks leach chemicals. In the natural environment these chemicals are diluted and made safe, but in the aquarium they can cause poisoning. Sedimentary rocks, such as limestone, sandstone, and shale, may have a great effect upon the chemistry. Igneous rocks and metamorphic rocks, however, affect the water chemistry to a lesser extent.

CLEANLINESS *Thoroughly clean all of the material that you plan to introduce to the aquarium. The slightest oversight in relation to hygiene can very often have the most disastrous results.*

Calcareous rocks should not be used in soft-water tanks, but they are excellent for tanks containing fishes that prefer hard water, such as those based on Rift Valley lakes. In marine tanks, rocks help to maintain the required level of pH and hardness. A good test for calcium is to pour vinegar over the rock. If the rock has a high level of calcium carbonate, the vinegar is likely to froth.

Sand and gravel also have calcareous qualities, and they may harden the water over a period of time. Lime-free sand and gravel, available from specialist dealers, are worthwhile investments when setting up a soft-water tank.

Wood can be collected from rivers or forests. Any pieces that you select must have been dead for a considerable length of time, and should show no sign of rotting. Boil the pieces several times, each time in clean water, before you use them. Alternatively, some aquarists prefer to seal their wood with a suitable varnish.

Always ensure that all of the materials you plan to use in an aquarium are thoroughly cleaned. Do not be surprised if you find yourself amounting a considerable collection of materials for use in the aquarium.

ROUGH SKETCH *A simple but comprehensive pencil sketch, showing the planned locations for rocks and plants within the finished tank, will prove to be an invaluable asset.*

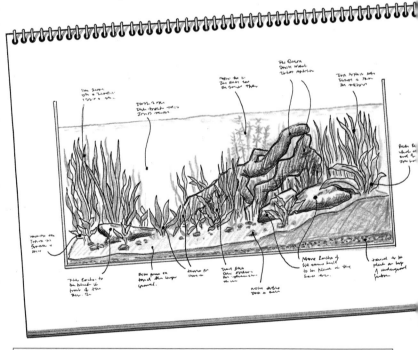

NOTES ON SAFETY

Remember that electricity and water can be a particularly deadly combination. All light fittings should be completely waterproof. Condensation trays (*see* p. 50) should be fitted, as they prevent water from collecting on the electrical fittings. Never switch on electrical equipment until the aquarium is full of water.

Always keep the heater/thermostat (*see* p. 163) completely immersed. If they are removed from the water whilst in operation, the heater will crack.

POSITIONING *There are a number of factors that should be taken into account when deciding upon the site for your aquarium. Aesthetic reasons, although valuable, should never be given priority.*

SETTING UP THE SYSTEM

Once you have decided on the system that you would like to set up, chosen the fishes and materials, and found suitable sources for them, you are ready to build the aquarium.

A tank full of water is extremely heavy, so you must choose its final position before attempting to set it up. The site should be near a power point, and there should be plenty of room above and beside it for access and for maintenance.

Select a strong, level surface – you may choose to buy an aquarium stand from a dealer. So that the tank remains level, it should be positioned on a sheet of expanded polystyrene or cork. You should also make sure that the floor beneath the entire structure will be capable of taking the final weight.

The site should not suffer from substantial variations in temperature, and should be removed from draughts and direct sunlight. Too much sunlight may make the water temperature rise excessively, and will encourage unnecessary algal growth. As long as the tank is correctly lit (*see* p. 164), it is preferable to place it in a dark corner.

Do not locate the tank near a door, as the irregular banging will stress its inhabitants. Knocking on the glass, or any other abnormal noises, are equally undesirable. Although it may not at first seem so, a well-frequented room, with a stable noise level, is a far better site than a room which is only used occasionally. Try to keep atmospheric pollution in the room, such as cigarette smoke, to a minimum. The quality of the air in a room is almost as important to fishes as the quality of the water, since the two interact.

MOVING THE TANK

Never try to move a full aquarium – the glass could crack under the immense stress. If you ever need to alter the position of your tank, observe the following procedure:
Disconnect the electricity supply.
Drain off about half of the water into a clean dustbin.
Remove the plants and put them in a bucket of water.

CLEANING CHECKLIST

Once the tank has been set up, establish a rota of tasks to be carried out every month or two, which will help to keep the aquarium in a good condition. In addition to regular water changes (20 to 25 per cent every 2 to 4 weeks is usual), the tank and its contents will need to be kept clean. When making water changes in marine aquaria, it is important to use water with the correct amount of synthetic minerals added (*see* p. 155).

Clean algae from the glass and the condensation tray (*see* right). Do not, however, become obsessive about this, as some fishes rely upon algae as an important source of fresh food.

Especially in tanks with undergravel filters, rake over the surface of the substrate. "Vacuuming" devices can be bought that have been designed specifically for the removal of dirt from the surface of the gravel. You may want to replace some gravel, but do not remove too much, as this will upset the biological filtration (*see* p. 185). Check the filtration system (*see* p. 159).

Prune back excess plant growth, and cultivate areas of the tank that will benefit from new planting. You can do this with cuttings taken from the existing vegetation (*see* p. 166).

Remove the large stones and wood and store them in a suitably clean place.
Carefully recover the fishes, and place them in another bucket, filled with water from the aquarium.
Drain off the rest of the water into the dustbin.
Clean the tank thoroughly.
Set up the aquarium in the new location as quickly as possible, to avoid causing the fishes too much stress. Use as much of the original water as possible.

DEALING WITH EMERGENCIES

Unfortunately, there is always the chance that circumstances beyond your control may jeopardize the safety of your aquarium inhabitants. If the electricity supply fails, it is vital that you take immediate steps to keep the tank at the correct temperature. Covering the aquarium with a blanket, and adding warm water from another source at suitable intervals, are useful emergency measures for ensuring that the water temperature remains relatively stable.

Verging on another extreme, if the tank begins to overheat, float containers of ice-cubes (*see* p. 146) on the surface of the water. With luck, this will temper the effects of the heat whilst the problem is rectified. Buzzer alarms, that sound if part of the aquarium system has stopped working, are commonly available. It is also wise to always keep a spare heater and, if possible, back-up pumps and filters.

FRESHWATER COMMUNITY AQUARIUM

LIVING TOGETHER *Avoid mixing boisterous fishes with shy ones in the community tank. Bullying fishes are prone to nip the fins of submissive tankmates.*

THE AIM OF most of the tanks in this book is to capture a "living snapshot" of a natural environment that is specific to a particular part of the world. So the types of fish and plant that can be included are normally those that would live in that environment in the wild. The aim of building a community tank is quite different: to bring together a collection of fishes and plants that can thrive in each other's company, but do not necessarily share the same origins. The great attraction of creating such a tank is that species from all over the globe can be mixed, which is why many aquarists never set their sights further than a really good community aquarium.

Before embarking on building a community aquarium, think long and hard about what it is that you wish to accomplish, and ensure that that you are properly prepared (*see* p. 42). The first aim of the community aquarium should be to provide a stable, healthy, and comfortable habitat for a wide range of fish species. Secondary to this aim is the arrangement of the ingredients in the aquarium in an attractive way, so as to produce an impressive and original display.

The traditional way of stocking a community aquarium is to include fishes and plants from a whole range of environments, and species that are likely to colonize different parts of the tank. So long as they will live at peace with each other, many species of fish can be included purely because they are attractive, or because they add particular colours to the aquarium. You may want the tank to contain a selection of bottom-feeders, mid-water feeders, and top-feeders; a combination of lively and sedate fishes; or a mixture of small and large fishes. Remember that many species are nocturnal, so you can expect these fishes to be languid during the day and more lively at night. The increased efficiency and affordability of air transport, and an improvement in the conditions in which fishes are traded, have meant that increasingly exotic species are available to the aquarist. The species of fish featured in this tank (and those found in the vast majority of community tanks) are farmed commercially in Southeast Asia – particularly Singapore, Taiwan, and Thailand. However, a number of other producers, such as Israel, are becoming increasingly important.

Most of these farms produce fishes that can adapt to conditions in the "average" aquarium. As a result, tank-bred tetras, angelfish, and other tropical species may now be more comfortable in the tapwater of Singapore than in the Amazon. For the aquarist, the advantage of this is that such fishes are versatile enough to thrive in anything but the very hardest or softest waters. This, of course, makes them ideal for the beginner.

Fishes are often inbred and hybridized to enhance their colours and shapes, but choosing species in their natural form will produce a more faithful representation of a particular fish community or habitat.

Planning the tank

ANY SIZE OF TANK can be used for the community aquarium, although the greater the volume of water, the less it will be altered by fishes and other elements added to it, and the more stable its chemistry will be.

The water should be kept at a constant temperature of around 24°C (75°F) – a reasonably comfortable temperature for most tropical fishes. Its pH should be maintained at about 7 to 7.6, and it should, ideally, be medium-hard, be-tween 100 and 200 mg/litre $CaCO_3$. A standard lighting level is suitable for a good community tank. Plants are very important to the natural cycle of the aquarium; but they do not thrive in tanks with undergravel filtration. However, since the level of planting in the tank shown here is reasonably low, it can safely be used.

See also Heating, p.163; pH and alkalinity in fresh water, p. 156; Lighting, p.164; Underground filtration, p.160.

Essential equipment

The dimensions of the tank used here are 91 × 46 × 38 cm (36 × 18 × 15 in). This tank will hold 159 litres (35 gallons) of water, and should not be stocked with more than 115 cm (45 in) of fishes. Unless it is very hard or soft, most tapwater will be suitable. The tank should be heated by one 250-watt heater/thermostat, and lit by a fluorescent tube. The filter plate for the undergravel filter used here is 91 cm (36 in) long and 30 cm (12 in) wide, and is driven by a pump.

See also Stocking levels, p. 42; Preparing fresh water, p. 154; Heating, p. 163; Lighting, p. 164; Undergravel filtration, p. 160.

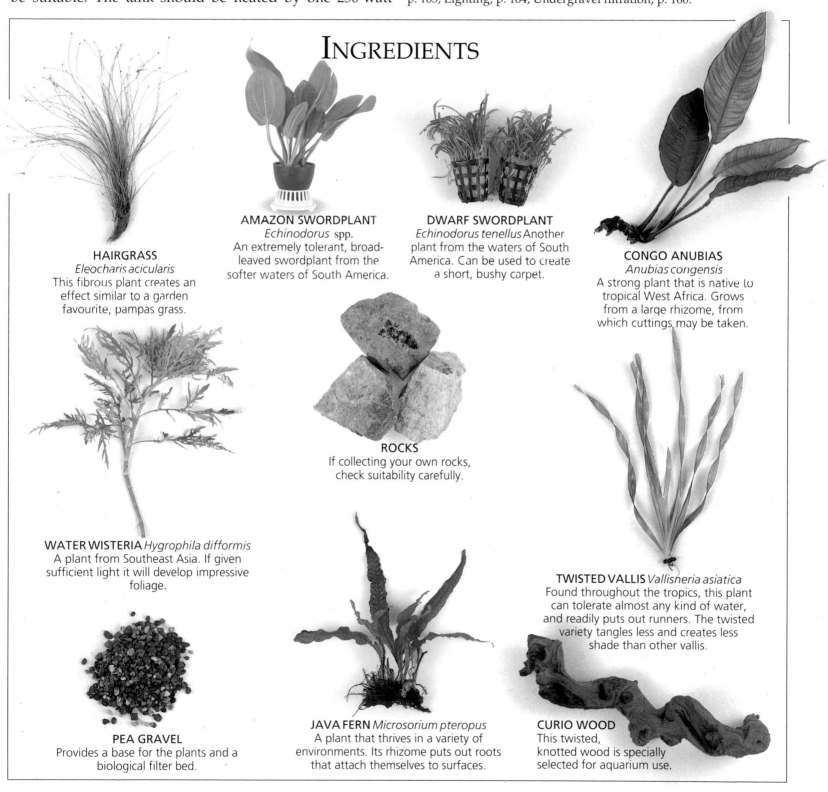

INGREDIENTS

HAIRGRASS
Eleocharis acicularis
This fibrous plant creates an effect similar to a garden favourite, pampas grass.

AMAZON SWORDPLANT
Echinodorus spp.
An extremely tolerant, broad-leaved swordplant from the softer waters of South America.

DWARF SWORDPLANT
Echinodorus tenellus Another plant from the waters of South America. Can be used to create a short, bushy carpet.

CONGO ANUBIAS
Anubias congensis
A strong plant that is native to tropical West Africa. Grows from a large rhizome, from which cuttings may be taken.

ROCKS
If collecting your own rocks, check suitability carefully.

WATER WISTERIA *Hygrophila difformis*
A plant from Southeast Asia. If given sufficient light it will develop impressive foliage.

TWISTED VALLIS *Vallisneria asiatica*
Found throughout the tropics, this plant can tolerate almost any kind of water, and readily puts out runners. The twisted variety tangles less and creates less shade than other vallis.

PEA GRAVEL
Provides a base for the plants and a biological filter bed.

JAVA FERN *Microsorium pteropus*
A plant that thrives in a variety of environments. Its rhizome puts out roots that attach themselves to surfaces.

CURIO WOOD
This twisted, knotted wood is specially selected for aquarium use.

Beginning the aquascaping

Since this tank will not be too heavily planted, an undergravel filter can be used. Standard aquarium pea gravel is an excellent medium for biological filtration. The gravel needs to be deep enough to cover plant roots, but if it is too deep, or if the rocks are too big, the flow through the filter bed and the performance of the filter may be quite seriously affected.

Although bacteria will develop naturally in a new aquarium, it will be some considerable time before there is a stable enough colony to provide an efficient filter (*see* p. 160). If you are able to add pea gravel from an already established, healthy aquarium, this will provide the filtration in the tank with an excellent start.

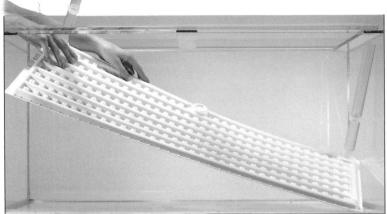

1 Manoeuvre the undergravel filter plate with its uplift tubes into place at the back of the tank, in this case leaving free about 7.5 cm (3 in) at the front of the tank. Make sure that the plate lies perfectly flat.

2 Assemble the filter plate and airlift tube, connecting the airline to its airstone, which should be positioned carefully at the base of the uplift tube. If the airlift tube is too long, trim it with a craft knife or hacksaw.

3 Wash the pea gravel thoroughly, and smooth it across the bed of the tank. Create an even layer with a slight downward slope at the front, where there is no filter. This helps to give an impression of perspective, without disturbing the action of the undergravel filter too much.

4 Carefully select a range of rocks. Planning is vital at this stage, as moving rocks at a later date would cause the waterflow to be cut off from a section of previously active filter bed. This could kill the filter bed in this area, causing it to release poisons. If you do have to move rocks within an established tank, carefully dig out the area for which they are intended, "vacuum" it (see p. 45), then add fresh gravel. Nooks and crannies between the rocks will provide welcome hiding places for catfish and other reclusive species.

5 Since wood may also cover a significant amount of the filter bed, it can cause similar problems to those caused by rocks. Aim to create the effect of a substantial and busy tank, without obscuring too much of the surface of the tank bed. Time spent going through piles of wood in the dealer's shop is well worth the effort, as striking effects can be achieved by good use of bogwood or curio wood. Strategically placed pieces of wood or rockwork can be used to conceal the heater and uplift tubes from view.

6 Add water directly from the tap. Only aquarists in areas of very hard water or very soft water will have problems with the suitability of water for this tank (see p. 154). Run the water over the rocks to avoid disturbing the gravel. A bucketful of hot water from a boiled kettle will give the heating system a good start. Allow the water to reach the correct temperature and let the filter run for a couple of hours, or until the water has settled. Do not fill the tank completely, as you still need to add plants.

Adding the plants

Once the water in the aquarium has reached the required temperature, planting can begin. As with the rocks and wood, you should plan in advance how heavily the tank will be planted and decide on the layout that you consider appropriate. Some plants – particularly those bought as top-cuttings (*see* p. 166), or with short roots – may need to be weighted down with aquarium lead to secure them in the gravel. Be careful not to crush the stems of delicate plants. To give the new plants a good start, you may want to add a water-soluble fertilizer. This creates the yellow tinge to the water seen here, which will disappear into the gravel within a day or two of being added.

1 Spread the roots out in the gravel. Hairgrass, shown here, has a fine rhizome that can be tucked into the gravel and then buried. Ensure that the crown is not buried.

2 Aquarium plants look most natural planted in stands, or clumps. These give the fishes security, and encourage them to behave naturally.

3 Plant from the back and sides first. Build up a background of taller plants, then add individual features towards the front of the tank. Congo anubias makes a fine centrepiece.

THE AQUASCAPED TANK

Pruning runners
Hairgrass puts out runners that produce a fine, matted lawn.

Hiding places
A well-planted aquarium provides plenty of shelter for shy fishes.

Waterflow
The distribution of leaves can be helped by directing the waterflow.

Introducing the fishes

Leave the planted aquarium for about a week, with the filter system running, to allow the plants to settle down. It is much easier to remove plant debris and replant where necessary during this settling down period. The fishes should be introduced a few at a time over the next two to three months, beginning with the hardier species. This allows the filter bed to mature slowly. On its journey from the dealer, the water in which the fishes are carried may cool down considerably. To avoid causing the fishes too much stress there are a number of important steps to follow.

1 Float the bag of fishes in the tank. This allows the temperature of the water in the bag to rise until it is compatible with that of the water in the tank.

2 Open the bag, then gently ease the fishes out with a net. Try to avoid pouring too much water from the bag into the tank, as it may contain undesirable bacteria.

3 Tilt the net gently – but do not tip the fishes out – and be careful not to catch their fins in the net. Allow the fishes to swim away from the net in their own time.

Completing the tank

Once the fishes have been introduced, the tank is ready for completion. This involves adding a condensation tray and a lid with a suitable light. The well-being of the aquarium and the impact of the display depend on the right choice of lighting. In addition to enhancing the effect of the tank and stimulating the fishes, the correct type and amount of light (*see* p. 164) is needed by the plants. Always choose your lighting carefully. Some lights not only enhance the appearance of the fishes, but also provide the correct spectrum of colours for the plants.

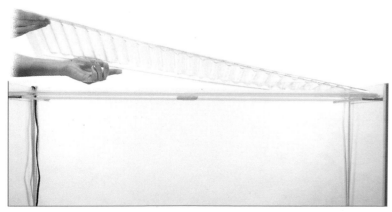 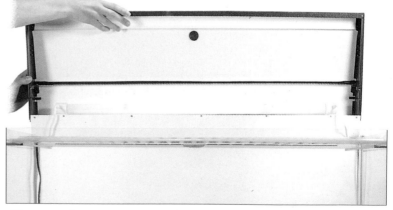

1 Lay a condensation tray – a simple sheet of glass or plastic – across the top of the tank. This prevents condensation from the tank from forming on the electrical equipment. It also stops more agile fishes from jumping out of the aquarium. The tank is now ready for the hood and lighting.

2 Carefully lift the hood and light into position. In this tank a fluorescent tube is used, giving even illumination across the whole tank. Most fluorescent lighting equipment requires a starter. This should be hidden out of sight, securely attached to the rear of the aquarium stand or to a wall.

SUITABLE FISHES

Acanthophthalmus kuhli
COOLIE LOACH
(*see* p. 81)

Balantiocheilus melanopterus
BALA SHARK
Description Silver body; yellow fins with black rear edges.
Length 35 cm (14 in).
Ease of keeping Easy; occasionally grows too large for the aquarium.
Food Accepts most foods.
Breeding Egg-scatterer; difficult in the aquarium.
Swimming level All levels.

Barbus conchonius
ROSY BARB
(*see* p. 81)

Betta splendens
SIAMESE FIGHTING FISH
(*see* p. 75)

Botia macracantha
CLOWN LOACH
(*see* p. 81)

Brachydanio rerio
ZEBRA DANIO
(*see* p. 75)

Cheirodon axelrodi
CARDINAL TETRA
(*see* p. 57)

Colisa lalia
DWARF GOURAMI
(*see* p. 75)

Corydoras aeneus
BRONZE CORYDORAS
Description Bronze body.
Length 8 cm (3 in).
Ease of keeping Easy; best kept in shoals.
Food Pellet; flake.
Breeding Egg-depositor; will lay eggs on broad-leaved plants.
Swimming level Lower levels.

Corydoras julii
LEOPARD CATFISH

Description Silver, black-lined and spotted body.
Length 6 cm (2½ in).
Ease of keeping Easy; best kept in shoals.
Food Pellet; flake.
Breeding Egg-depositor.
Swimming level Lower levels.

Gasteropelecus levis
SILVER HATCHETFISH
(*see* p. 57)

Glossolepis incisus
RED NEW GUINEA RAINBOWFISH
(*see* p. 87)

Gymnocorymbus ternetzi
BLACK WIDOW
(*see* p. 63)

Gyrinocheilus aymonieri
SUCKING LOACH
(*see* p. 81)

Hemigrammus erythrozonus
GLOWLIGHT TETRA
(*see* p. 63)

Hemigrammus ocellifer
BEACONFISH
(*see* p. 63)

Kryptopterus bicirrhus
GLASS CATFISH
(*see* p. 75)

Labeo bicolor
RED-TAILED BLACK SHARK
(*see* p. 81)

Paracheirodon innesi
NEON TETRA
(*see* p. 63)

Pelvicachromis pulcher
KRIBENSIS
Description Gold body; dark, horizontal bands; plum belly; gold edges to dorsal fin; male has egg-spot on tail.
Length Male 10 cm (4 in); female 8 cm (3 in).
Ease of keeping Fairly easy. It is preferable to keep this species in a well-established tank, which should ideally have plenty of hiding places.
Food Accepts most foods.
Breeding Egg-depositor; needs privacy for spawning.
Swimming level Lower levels.

Poecilia reticulata
GUPPY
Description Various colours.
Length Male 4 cm (1½ in); female 6 cm (2½ in).
Ease of keeping Easy.
Food Accepts most foods.
Breeding Livebearer.
Swimming level Midwater.

Poecilia sphenops
BLACK MOLLY

Description Black "velvet" body; much variation in fin shapes.
Length 10 cm (4 in).
Ease of keeping Easy; needs well-filtered aquarium.
Food Vegetable matter; flake.
Breeding Livebearer.
Swimming level Midwater.

Pterophyllum scalare
ANGELFISH
(*see* p. 57)

Rasbora heteromorpha
HARLEQUIN
(*see* p. 81)

Tanichthys albonubes
WHITE CLOUD MOUNTAIN MINNOW
Description Brilliant mauve body, with blue stripes; distinctive bright yellow tips to fins.
Length 4 cm (1½ in).
Ease of keeping Easy.
Food Flake.
Breeding As *Brachydanio rerio*.
Swimming level Upper levels.

Trichogaster leeri
PEARL GOURAMI
(*see* p. 75)

Trichogaster trichopterus sumatranus
GOLDEN GOURAMI
(*see* p. 75)

Trichogaster trichopterus trichopterus
THREE SPOT GOURAMI
(*see* p. 75)

Xiphophorus helleri
GREEN SWORDTAIL

Description Native fish is green, but those commonly available have red body; black marks.
Length Male 10 cm (4 in); female 11 cm (4½ in).
Ease of keeping Easy.
Food Vegetable matter; flake.
Breeding Livebearer.
Swimming level Midwater.

Xiphophorus maculatus
PLATY

Description Various colours; mainly red-bodied. In some cases, both body and fins share same colour. Fishes of this genus are short and stocky.
Length 4 cm (1½ in).
Ease of keeping Easy; a peaceful, hardy fish.
Food Browses on algae; flake.
Breeding Livebearer.
Swimming level Midwater.

Xiphophororus variatus hybrid
VARIATUS PLATY
Description Yellow body; dark-lined vertical markings; distinctive orange-red caudal fin. Other colour varieties often occur, particularly after hybridization with *Xiphophorus helleri*. Although fishes of this genus have upturned mouths (*see* p. 32), they will feed at all levels.
Length 6 cm (2½ in).
Ease of keeping Easy.
Food Accepts most foods, especially vegetable matter.
Breeding Livebearer.
Swimming level All levels.

The finished tank

The freshwater community tank is the most flexible of freshwater aquaria. It contains fishes and plants from the rivers, streams, and lakes of many different countries, each species having been chosen not only for its particular beauty, but also for its resilience. A creative use of plants, rocks, and wood adds to the attraction of such an aquarium, as well as providing hiding places for shy fishes. Monitor the effectiveness of the undergravel filter, ensuring that it does not become blocked by mulm. As it matures, the water may take on the yellow cast caused by organic materials.

HAIRGRASS
Eleocharis acicularis

ANGELFISH
Pterophyllum scalare

PEARL GOURAMI
Trichogaster leeri

KRIBENSIS
Pelvicachromis pulcher

RED NEW GUINEA RAINBOWFISH
Glossolepis incisus

AMAZON SWORDPLANT
Echinodorus spp.

CLOWN LOACH
Botia macracantha
Although nocturnal, these fishes are often active when the aquarium light is on.

GOLDEN GOURAMI
Trichogaster trichopterus sumatranus
The golden gourami constantly changes its body colour during courtship.

RED-TAILED BLACK SHARK
Labeo bicolor
The name of this fish derives from its distinctive dorsal fin.

SUCKING LOACH
Gyrinocheilus aymonieri
With its flat underside and downward-turned mouth (*see* p. 32), the eel-like loach is designed for scavenging.

WATER WISTERIA
Hygrophila difformis

BALA SHARK
Balantiocheilus melanopterus
This is a strong fish, capable of jumping clear of the water.

GUPPY
Poecilia reticulata
The hardy guppy is a prolific breeder.

THREE SPOT GOURAMI
Trichogaster trichopterus trichopterus

TWISTED VALLIS
Vallisneria asiatica

DWARF SWORDPLANT
Echinodorus tenellus

JAVA FERN
Microsorium pteropus

AMAZON RAIN FOREST STREAM

RICH TAPESTRY *The streams that run through the dense jungle of the Brazil-Guyana border harbour an astonishing diversity of life forms.*

THE DEEPER PARTS of the rain forest of the Amazon River are full of smaller rivers and streams (*see* p. 15). These often contain huge amounts of floating plants and other aquatic life, while driftwood, fallen trees, and other plant debris may make the waters acidic and murky. Streams like this play host to some of the most spectacular fish species in the world. The Amazon Basin, which has over 200 tributaries, is the natural habitat of many of the fishes that dominate the aquarium trade. These include the discus (*Symphysodon* spp.), which to many aquarists constitutes the pinnacle of freshwater fishkeeping, being something of a challenge to keep.

While the region contains many true blackwaters (*see* p. 15), such as long stretches of the Rio Negro, the discus tends to choose quiet, less acidic side streams, where it lives among tree roots and plants. The water chemistry is less extreme here, but the fishes may still have to tolerate temporary changes, particularly those caused by minerals that are washed down from the Andes during the rainy seasons. This tank is based on one of these side streams, and the water in it should have a composition as close as possible to that in nature. Debris of all kinds, including insects and fruit, falls from the forest canopy into the streams. As well as altering the water chemistry, this serves as food for fishes. The floating food encourages deep-bodied species like the hatchetfish, which lurk at the surface of the water, and these are included in this tank. The tropical riverbed is an equally superb store of food, and it attracts an endless variety of bottom-dwelling species, such as catfish. Angelfish and smaller, constantly moving "dither" fishes, such as tetras, are also ideal for this tank.

Planning the tank

PLANT MATERIAL *The water in this tank is stained with the humic acids of decaying plant matter.*

SINCE MANY of the fishes that inhabit a small rain forest river can grow to a relatively large size, the tank used to imitate this environment should be large.

Species of discus need warmer water than many freshwater fishes, so keep the tank at around 30°C (85°F), and make sure all your chosen fishes can live comfortably at this temperature. Discus seem to do best with a pH of 6.5 to 7, and a hardness of about 75 mg/litre $CaCO_3$. In fact, the pH of the tank must be monitored regularly, since as the water is comparatively soft, the pH has a tendency to fall below an acceptable level. To control waste nitrate, partial water changes should be carried out regularly. Changing 10 per cent of the water per week should be adequate. Discus are shy, nervous fishes, and need a profusion of plants among which to hide. They also prefer shady conditions, so the lighting level should not be too high. Use a power filter; this is less likely to upset the plant growth than an undergravel filter. Some experts believe that discus should never be kept with other fishes, as life within a community exposes them more easily to disease. In the wild, however, discus do live in areas with the richest fish fauna in the world, and so this fear seems rather over-exaggerated. It is a good idea to set up this aquarium in a room that is not too quiet, as sensitive fishes are happiest once they have become accustomed to a normal, steady level of activity around them.

See also Heating, p. 163; pH and alkalinity in fresh water, p. 156; Lighting, p. 164; Power filters, p. 159.

Essential equipment

The dimensions of the tank used here are 122 × 46 × 38 cm (48 × 18 × 15 in). This tank will hold 212 litres (47 gallons) of water, and should not be stocked with more than 152 cm (60 in) of fishes. Tapwater is acceptable, but use an exchange resin or reverse-osmosis unit to remove unwanted minerals. Heat the tank using two 150-watt heater/thermostats, and light it with two or more fluorescent tubes. Choose a power filter that gives a good flow, but is not too strong. For this tank you will also need pea gravel, bogwood, blackwater extract, and a selection of aquatic plants.

See also Stocking levels, p. 42; Preparing fresh water, p. 154; Heating, p. 163; Lighting, p. 164; Power filters, p. 159.

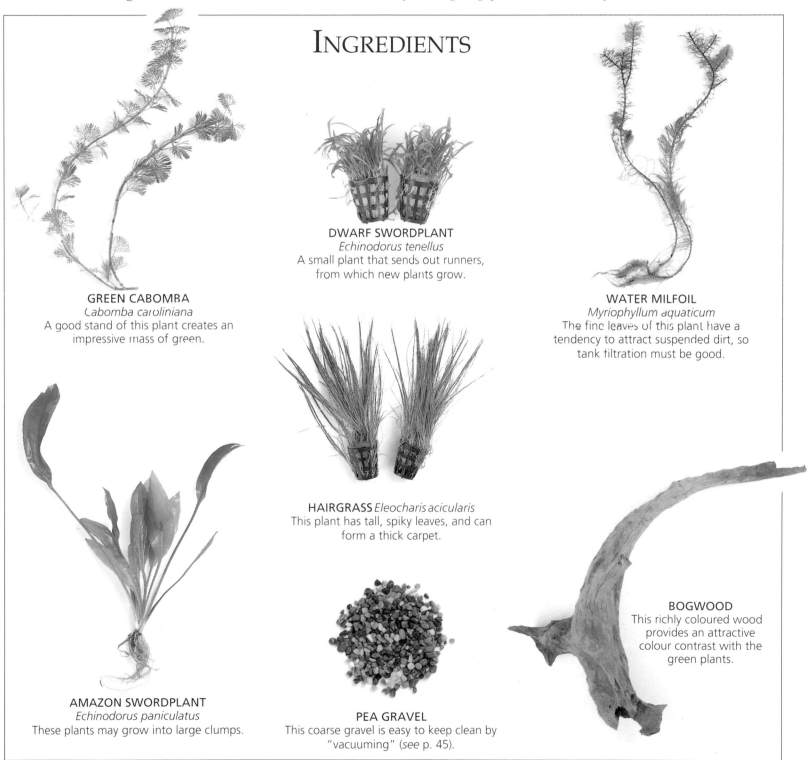

INGREDIENTS

DWARF SWORDPLANT
Echinodorus tenellus
A small plant that sends out runners, from which new plants grow.

GREEN CABOMBA
Cabomba caroliniana
A good stand of this plant creates an impressive mass of green.

WATER MILFOIL
Myriophyllum aquaticum
The fine leaves of this plant have a tendency to attract suspended dirt, so tank filtration must be good.

HAIRGRASS *Eleocharis acicularis*
This plant has tall, spiky leaves, and can form a thick carpet.

AMAZON SWORDPLANT
Echinodorus paniculatus
These plants may grow into large clumps.

PEA GRAVEL
This coarse gravel is easy to keep clean by "vacuuming" (*see* p. 45).

BOGWOOD
This richly coloured wood provides an attractive colour contrast with the green plants.

Building the tank

To reflect the lush vegetation of an Amazonian river and to provide the cover that the fishes need for security, a generous amount of greenery and wood should be added to this tank. Excessive growth can be pruned back later. To give an authentic rich, dark look to the water, blackwater extract can be added before the fishes are introduced. It should be replenished regularly to maintain the colour. Peat added to the power filter will also colour the water, and will soften it too. The fishes should not be introduced until the tank has settled, and the plants require no further arranging.

See also Aquascaping, p. 48; Adding the plants, p. 49; Introducing the fishes, p. 50; Completing the tank, p. 50.

1 Build up a bed of gravel 4 to 5 cm (1½ to 2 in) deep and add the water. Pour in the water over the rocks or other solid objects to ensure that the gravel bed is not disturbed too much.

2 Add plenty of carefully chosen bogwood to create a dense, shadowy labyrinth. The effect should be one of random tangles of roots and driftwood, and other debris that has been washed downstream.

3 Pea gravel is an excellent substrate for tucking in plants, but some may still need to be held down with lead. Take care to bury the roots of the plants only. You may choose to use cuttings from mature plants in another aquarium. Remove existing leaves from the bottoms of the cuttings. This encourages roots to form.

THE AQUASCAPED TANK

Spreading plants
Plant species that spread but stay low have been chosen for the front of the tank.

Creating clearings
Clearings in the middle of stands prevent the plants from choking or blocking out light.

Hiding the hardware
As the plants grow, they will gradually conceal the obtrusive heating equipment.

SUITABLE FISHES

Ancistrus dolichopterus
BRISTLE-NOSED CATFISH

Description Black body; small yellow spots.
Length 12 cm (5 in).
Ease of keeping Easy.
Food Most live foods; pellet; vegetable matter.
Breeding Egg-depositor; female leaves eggs secreted in hollows, guarded by male.
Swimming level Lower levels.

Brochis splendens
EMERALD CATFISH
Description Distinctive, metallic-green body.
Length 8 to 10 cm (3 to 4 in).
Ease of keeping Easy.
Food Pellet; pieces of prawn.
Breeding Egg-depositor.
Swimming level Lower levels.

Cheirodon axelrodi
CARDINAL TETRA
Description Fabulous electric-blue stripe; distinctive, bright red lower body.
Length 4 cm (1½ in).
Ease of keeping Easy; best kept in shoals.
Food Pellet; pieces of prawn.
Breeding Egg-scatterer; needs soft water and gentle lighting.
Swimming level Midwater.

Gasteropelecus levis
SILVER HATCHETFISH
Description Silver body; fine black line running down body.
Length 6 cm (2½ in).
Ease of keeping Easy; requires stable, well-filtered water.
Food Accepts most foods.
Breeding Egg-scatterer.
Swimming level Upper levels.

Hasemania nana
SILVER-TIPPED TETRA
Description Silver-gold body; white-tipped fins.
Length 5 cm (2 in).
Ease of keeping Easy.

Food Accepts most foods.
Breeding Egg-scatterer; difficult in the aquarium.
Swimming level Midwater.

Hemigrammus erythrozonus
GLOWLIGHT TETRA
(*see* p. 63)

Hemigrammus rhodostomus
RUMMY-NOSED TETRA (RED-NOSED TETRA)
Description Silver-gold body; bright red head, colouration spreads slightly to body; alternating black and white horizontal bands on tail.
Length 5 cm (2 in).
Ease of keeping Fairly difficult; nervous fish; sensitive to water chemistry problems.
Food Small live foods; flake.
Breeding Egg-scatterer; difficult in the aquarium.
Swimming level All levels.

Hyphessobrycon erythrostigma
BLEEDING HEART TETRA

Description Pink body; purple tint to flanks; bright pink "heart spot"; red dorsal fin with occasional black rays.
Length 8 cm (3 in).
Ease of keeping Easy; occasionally nervous; prefers shoals. Needs peaceful aquarium, stocked with calm fishes.
Food Accepts most foods.
Breeding Egg-scatterer; difficult in the aquarium.
Swimming level Midwater.

Panaque suttoni
BLUE-EYED PANAQUE
Description Slate grey or black body colour.
Length 45 cm (18 in).
Ease of keeping Easy; should be kept as one of a kind.
Food Pellet; vegetable matter.
Breeding Unknown in the aquarium.
Swimming level Lower levels.

Paracheirodon innesi
NEON TETRA
(*see* p. 63)

Petitella georgiae
FALSE RUMMY-NOSED TETRA
Description As *Hemigrammus rhodostomus*.
Length 5 cm (2 in).
Ease of keeping Fairly difficult.
Food Accepts most foods.
Breeding Egg-scatterer; difficult in the aquarium.
Swimming level All levels.

Pterophyllum altum
ALTUM ANGELFISH
Description Silver-gold body; distinctive black stripes.
Length 33 cm (13 in), from tip of dorsal fin to tip of anal fin.
Ease of keeping Fairly difficult; mature fish requires large, deep aquarium; large specimens may eat smaller tankmates.
Food Crumbs; most fresh foods; flake.
Breeding Egg-depositor; female leaves eggs on leaves; difficult in the aquarium.
Swimming level Midwater.

Pterophyllum scalare
ANGELFISH

Description Generally silver body; darker black stripes than those of *Pterophyllum altum*.
Length 10 cm (4 in).
Ease of keeping Easy, but may menace small fishes.
Food Flake.
Breeding Egg-depositor.
Swimming level Midwater.

Rineloricaria hasemani
WHIPTAIL CATFISH

Description Brown body; dark markings cover body.
Length 15 cm (6 in).
Ease of keeping Easy.
Food Pellet; vegetable matter.
Breeding Egg-depositor; female leaves eggs in caves and hollows, guarded by male.
Swimming level Lower levels.

Symphysodon aequifasciata
GREEN DISCUS
Description Disc-shaped body with nine dark vertical markings; blue veining around head. Green discus always have red spots on at least part of body.
Length 14 cm (5½ in).
Ease of keeping Difficult; very nervous fish; best to begin with juveniles. Some specialists insist on isolating species. Green discus seem to thrive when kept with less nervous species. The chemistry of the water in the aquarium must be carefully monitored and maintained at the level required by this species.
Food Live foods; heart; flake.
Breeding Egg-depositor; fairly easy in the aquarium once fishes settle. Fry initially feed on body mucus produced by female.
Swimming level Midwater.

Symphysodon discus
DISCUS FISH (POMPADOUR)
Description Light brown body; dark brown, vertical stripes; pale blue iridescence.
Length 15 cm (6 in).
Ease of keeping Difficult. As with *Symphysodon aequifascatia*, this delicate species is extremely sensitive to even slight changes in water chemistry.
Food Live, meaty foods.
Breeding Egg-depositor.
Swimming level All levels.

The finished tank

The aim of this aquarium, which is to reproduce the exceptional nature of the streams that flow, teeming with life, down from the Amazon basin, is an ambitious one. These streams usually contain a high level of plant growth, and planting in the finished aquarium should therefore be correspondingly heavy. Peat and blackwater extract can be used to darken the water. A number of the fishes that can be included in this tank are very sensitive to changes in water chemistry, so the filtration system should be checked regularly, and the gravel should never be allowed to develop pockets of dirt. Types of discus, such as the green discus shown in this aquarium, are becoming increasingly popular as aquarium fishes. They are particularly sensitive to water conditions, and will only survive in the aquarium if the water is constantly kept well-filtered, soft, acidic, and at the relatively high temperature of 30°C (85°F).

GREEN CABOMBA
Cabomba caroliniana

DWARF SWORDPLANT
Echinodorus tenellus

GREEN DISCUS
Symphysodon aequifasciata
Encouraging discus to spawn and raise their young in the aquarium is very difficult. Many aquarists regard this as the greatest challenge they can set themselves.

BLUE-EYED PANAQUE
Panaque suttoni
This dark-coloured fish likes to lurk around the bases of the plants in the tank.

ALTUM ANGELFISH
Pterophyllum altum
A fish that appreciates a deep tank with tall plants.

AMAZON SWORDPLANT
Echinodorus paniculatus

HAIRGRASS
Eleocharis acicularis

CARDINAL TETRA
Cheirodon axelrodi
These magnificently coloured
fishes are happiest in a shoal.

EMERALD CATFISH
Brochis splendens
Like all catfish, this is a
peaceful fish.

SILVER-TIPPED TETRA
Hasemania nana
The body colours of these
tetras vary according to
their moods.

WATER MILFOIL
Myriophyllum aquaticum

SILVER HATCHETFISH
Gasteropelecus levis
Although the silver
hatchetfish has built up a
reputation for an insatiable
appetite, take care not to
overfeed it.

GLOWLIGHT TETRA
Hemigrammus erythrozonus
In order to fertilize the
female's eggs, the male and
female glowlight tetra wrap
themselves in an embrace.

AMAZON RAIN FOREST ACID POOL

DEEP WITHIN THE FORESTS of the Amazon River there are thousands of acid-water pools and streams (*see* p. 15). Conditions within each of these bodies of water are unique, and many come and go with the great floods (*see* p. 14) that occur twice a year. The pools and streams are rich in the humic acids that build up in vegetation that has fallen from the trees and plants of the forest, and they support fascinating fish communities. The acids turn the water a darkish brown, and the overhanging trees block out much of the daylight; floating plant debris may block out even more light. Oxygen levels are often low in these pools and streams.

FISHES IN PERIL *Many of the pools and streams of the Amazon rain forest are home to species that are endangered by man.*

Lurking in the brown-stained pools are more than 60 species of dwarf cichlid (*Apistogramma*), and it is these shy fishes, together with the brilliantly coloured tetras and bottom-dwelling catfish, that form the basis of this tank. Many species of *Apistogramma* live in a small area – limited in some cases to the pools that form along a section of river no more than 20 km (30 miles) long. Because many of these pools and streams are inaccessible to man, there are undoubtedly other species of *Apistogramma* in the rain forest that are yet to be discovered. This means that the aquarist has a broad selection of fishes to choose from, but there is of course another effect, namely that some species are highly vulnerable, and may be lost forever due to the detrimental effects of human intervention, such as deforestation (*see* p. 22).

Many of the fish inhabitants of the acid pools hide in the dark shadow of the forest canopy, often milling among the small stands of swordplant and water milfoil by the bank. The very edge of the pool is therefore an excellent spot to depict in a tank.

Planning the tank

TO CREATE an effective and convincing Amazon acid pool aquarium, the size of the tank is not critical. It should not, however, be too small – ideally no less than 60 cm (24 in) long – since many of the fishes that could be included in it are territorial, and each species will need sufficient space to identify as its own precinct. *Apistogramma* in particular are very sensitive to changes in water conditions, so try to make sure that these remain stable. The temperature of the water should be around 24°C (75°F). Soft, acid water is essential, especially if you want the fishes to breed. To soften the water, peat can be added to the filter (*see* p. 157), while the large amount of wood in the tank will also help lower the pH.

GLORIOUS LIVERY *The brilliance of the colours of the fishes included in this tank makes them stand out against the murky water.*

If soft, mature water from another tank can be used, so much the better. A good pH to aim at is 6 to 6.5, with a hardness of no more than 50 mg/litre $CaCO_3$.

So that the tank is able to give the impression of water that in nature is constantly in the shadow of trees and floating debris, the light levels should not be high. Because of the comparatively small number of plants in the tank, and because the water should be relatively still, an undergravel filter is a more appropriate choice than a power filter. This will help to establish a good biological cycle in the aquarium.

See also Heating, p. 163; pH and alkalinity in fresh water, p. 156; Lighting, p. 164; Undergravel filtration, p. 160.

Essential equipment

The dimensions of the tank are 91 × 46 × 38 cm (36 × 18 × 15 in). This tank will hold 159 litres (35 gallons) of water, and should not be stocked with more than 115 cm (45 in) of fishes. Tapwater may be used, but it will usually be necessary to demineralize it with an ion-exchange unit or by reverse osmosis. The tank should be heated by one 250-watt heater / thermostat, and can be lit by a fluorescent tube. The filter plate for the undergravel filter used here is 91 cm (36 in) long and 30 cm (12 in) wide, and is driven by a pump. The airlift tube has been trimmed to suit the intended water depth. Also used in the tank are pea gravel, coal dust, bogwood, blackwater extract, and plants.

See also Stocking levels, p. 42; Preparing fresh water, p. 154; Heating, p. 163; Lighting, p. 164; Undergravel filtration, p. 160.

INGREDIENTS

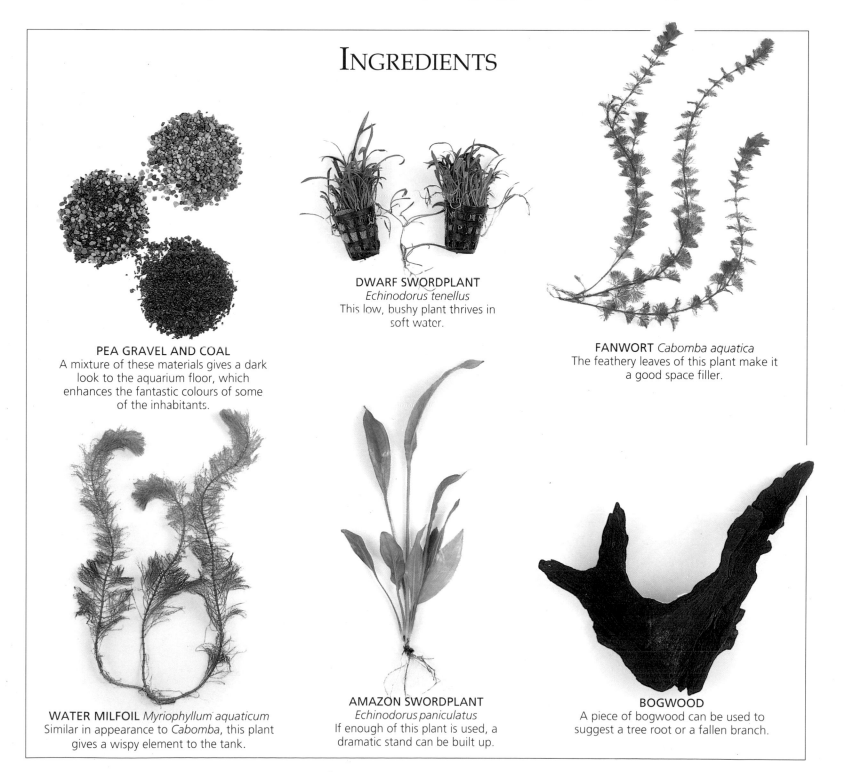

PEA GRAVEL AND COAL
A mixture of these materials gives a dark look to the aquarium floor, which enhances the fantastic colours of some of the inhabitants.

DWARF SWORDPLANT
Echinodorus tenellus
This low, bushy plant thrives in soft water.

FANWORT *Cabomba aquatica*
The feathery leaves of this plant make it a good space filler.

WATER MILFOIL *Myriophyllum aquaticum*
Similar in appearance to *Cabomba*, this plant gives a wispy element to the tank.

AMAZON SWORDPLANT
Echinodorus paniculatus
If enough of this plant is used, a dramatic stand can be built up.

BOGWOOD
A piece of bogwood can be used to suggest a tree root or a fallen branch.

Building the tank

By mixing coal dust with the pea gravel, an interesting shadowy base can be created, and by building up a labyrinth of bogwood, you can give the appearance of a mass of tangled roots. The twisted wood provides hiding places for the fishes, as well as flat areas for egg-laying. Light does not penetrate well through the canopy of the Amazon forest.

Plant growth in many of the pools is therefore limited, so do not overplant the tank. To give a strong, dark brown cast to the water itself, add some blackwater extract before introducing the fishes to the aquarium.

See also Aquascaping, p. 48; Adding the plants, p. 49; Introducing the fishes, p. 50; Completing the tank, p. 50.

1 To recreate the effect of leaf litter and other debris lying at the bottom of the pool, thoroughly wash some coarse coal dust, and add it to the bed of gravel.

2 With your fingers, gently work the coal dust into the upper layer of gravel. You will need to allow the filter some time to clear the water.

3 Carefully arrange pieces of dark bogwood to provide niches and crevices in which the fishes can hide, and to screen the heater/ thermostat from view.

THE AQUASCAPED TANK

Quiet water
The waterflow in the tank should be no greater than is needed to make the filter work.

Room for plants
Water milfoil planted between pieces of bogwood should grow through the gaps.

Nooks and crannies
Crevices encourage fishes to claim territories that are intricate rather than large.

SUITABLE FISHES

Apistogramma agassizi
AGASSIZ'S DWARF CICHLID

Description Various. Generally silver-blue body, with black stripe and orange tint to fins. Wedge-shaped tail.
Length Male 8 cm (3 in); female 5 cm (2 in).
Ease of keeping Fairly easy; prefers well-established tank.
Food Accepts most foods.
Breeding Egg-depositor; eggs prone to fungus. Low pH encourages higher number of males, high pH encourages higher number of females.
Swimming level All, but generally lower levels.

Apistogramma borelli
BORELLI'S DWARF CICHLID
Description Generally pale, metallic-blue body.
Length Male 6 to 8 cm (2½ to 3 in); female 5 cm (2 in).
Ease of keeping Easy.
Food Accepts most foods.
Breeding Egg-depositor; prefers spawning cave. Requires soft, acidic water.
Swimming level All, but generally lower levels.

Apistogramma cacuatoides
COCKATOO DWARF CICHLID
Description Grey or blue body; male often has red spots on tail.
Length Male 8 cm (3 in); female 4 cm (1½ in).
Ease of keeping Easy.
Food Accepts most foods.
Breeding Egg-depositor.
Swimming level All, but generally lower levels.

Apistogramma ramirezi
RAM (BUTTERFLY CICHLID)
Description Blue or purple body with incomplete vertical black banding. Yellow or orange tint to pectoral fins.
Length Varies from 5 to 6 cm (2 to 2½ in).
Ease of keeping Fairly easy; sensitive to nitrite.

Food Accepts most foods.
Breeding Egg-depositor; breeds in open spaces, on round stones; use Artemia (brine shrimp) as food, prefers high temperatures.
Swimming level All, but generally lower levels.

Cheirodon axelrodi
CARDINAL TETRA
(see p. 57)

Corydoras adolfoi
ADOLF'S CORYDORAS

Description Pale gold body, with black base to dorsal fin, over eye, and at rear of body; orange tint beneath gills.
Length 5 cm (2 in).
Ease of keeping Easy.
Food Accepts most foods.
Breeding Egg-scatterer.
Swimming level Lower levels.

Corydoras trilineatus
THREE-LINE CATFISH
Description Silver body, almost entirely covered by black tracery; name derives from distinct black line, and two unpigmented lines on sides.
Length 5 cm (2 in).
Ease of keeping Easy.
Food Live foods; pellet; flake.
Breeding Egg-depositor; leaves eggs attached to undersides of most plants.
Swimming level Lower levels.

Farlowella acus
TWIG CATFISH
Description Tan base; black stripes on sides.
Length 20 cm (8 in).
Ease of keeping Easy.
Food Pellet; vegetable matter.
Breeding Egg-depositor; leaves eggs attached to plants; male guards eggs.
Swimming level Lower levels.

Gymnocorymbus ternetzi
BLACK WIDOW
Description Silver-grey body; dark vertical bands.
Length 5 cm (2 in).
Ease of keeping Easy, prefers mature water.
Food Flake.
Breeding Egg-scatterer.
Swimming level Midwater.

Hemigrammus erythrozonus
GLOWLIGHT TETRA
Description Transparent silver body; bright orange stripe.
Length 5 cm (2 in).
Ease of keeping Easy; generally prefers shoals.
Food Flake.
Breeding Egg-scatterer; needs specially prepared aquarium, with soft, acidic water.
Swimming level Midwater.

Hemigrammus ocellifer
BEACONFISH

Description Silver body; bright red flash over eyes; orange flash at base of tail.
Length 5 cm (2 in).
Ease of keeping Easy.
Food Flake.
Breeding Egg-scatterer; normally prefers specialist tank with soft, acidic water.
Swimming level Midwater.

Hyphessobrycon pulchripinnis
LEMON TETRA
Description Distinctive lemon body; top half of iris of eye bright red; black colouration on anal and dorsal fins.
Length 4 cm (1½ in).
Ease of keeping Easy.
Food Accepts most foods.
Breeding Egg-scatterer; difficult in the aquarium.
Swimming level All levels.

Megalamphodus megalopterus
BLACK PHANTOM TETRA

Description Grey body; female shows some pink; black mark behind gills; black fins. Dorsal fin of male of species occasionally erected like a flag.
Length 5 cm (2 in).
Ease of keeping Easy.
Food Accepts most foods.
Breeding Egg-scatterer.
Swimming level All levels.

Moenkhausia sanctaefilomenae
RED-EYE TETRA
Description Silver body; top half of iris of eye distinctively bright red; light band where black tail meets body.
Length 6 cm (2½ in).
Ease of keeping Easy.
Food Live foods; flake; needs fresh vegetation.
Breeding Egg-scatterer; fairly easy in the aquarium.
Swimming level All levels.

Paracheirodon innesi
NEON TETRA
Description Distinctive electric-blue stripe running along entire length of body. Bright-red underside towards rear. Female is plumper and deeper-bodied than male of the species.
Length 4 cm (1½ in).
Ease of keeping Easy. A peaceful fish, best kept in shoals. Will occasionally fall victim to incurable neon disease (Plistophora), the first sign of which is an expanding pale area beneath the dorsal fin.
Food Flake.
Breeding Egg-scatterer; prefers specially prepared aquarium, with soft, acid water, and plenty of vegetation.
Swimming level Midwater.

The finished tank

Acid pools are an uncompromising type of environment to recreate in the aquarium. The water is dark, acids from rotting plant material are high, and the oxygen level may be low. Only those fishes and plants that can tolerate a low pH are suitable for the tank. The environment of this aquarium, although less harsh than that of an actual acid pool, is nonetheless anything but gentle. Despite these conditions, however, many of the fishes are capable of providing a uniquely dazzling display. Their bright, "electric" colours will shimmer through even the murkiest waters.

TWIG CATFISH
Farlowella acus
When resting on the tank floor, this fish looks like a stray twig.

THREE-LINE CATFISH
Corydoras trilineatus
Corydoras spp. use their pelvic fins to carry eggs to a suitable site for spawning.

DWARF SWORDPLANT
Echinodorus tenellus

FANWORT
Cabomba aquatica

LEMON TETRA
Hyphessobrycon pulchripinnis
A robust, slim tetra that is lively and sociable.

RED-EYE TETRA
Moenkhausia sanctaefilomenae
Keep a constant eye on the temperature of the aquarium, as tetras are sensitive to temperature changes.

BLACK WIDOW
Gymnocorymbus ternetzi
Note the well-developed adipose fin (*see* p. 31) of this fish.

ADOLF'S CORYDORAS
Corydoras adolfoi
This popular catfish is relatively new to the aquarium hobby.

WATER MILFOIL
Myriophyllum aquaticum

NEON TETRA
Paracheirodon innesi
The tiny teeth of the neon tetra are almost invisible to the human eye.

AMAZON SWORDPLANT
Echinodorus paniculatus

RAM (BUTTERFLY CICHLID)
Apistogramma ramirezi
Despite its spectacular livery, this fish is shy and will often hide among plants.

ZAIRE RIVER RAPIDS

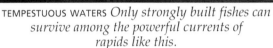

TEMPESTUOUS WATERS *Only strongly built fishes can survive among the powerful currents of rapids like this.*

THE ZAIRE RIVER (previously called the Congo River) in tropical west Africa is over 4,500 km (2,796 miles) long, and has a vast drainage area covering almost 4 million square kilometres (1½ million square miles) (*see* p. 16). The river is fed by an enormous central basin that was once a lake.

An astonishing variety of environments exists along the great, curved course of the river – permanent swamps, whitewater rapids, mangrove estuaries – each of which has its own unique collection of fishes. This tank is based on the longest section of whitewater rapids in the world, a stretch of the Zaire River downstream of Kinshasa that covers 350 km (217 miles). There are no less than 32 waterfalls along this stretch of river, and many of them are spectacular. Over 60 species of fish have become specially adapted to the chaotic, tumbling waters of the rapids. Cichlids like blockheads and *Nanochromis* spp. are powerful swimmers, and they move between rocks in short bursts to avoid being swept away. The streamlined bodies of other fishes, such as the glass catfish that appear in this tank, allow them to hold their own against the relentless flow.

Oxygen levels in these waters are particularly high, as the constant turbulence generally forces far greater contact between the water and the air than would happen in other parts of the river. Because eyesight is of little use in a world of bubbles, 25 species of fish that live in these waters have either very small, token eyes, or no eyes at all. Many species retreat to the stiller waters of caves for spawning. Any fry born there are unlikely to be caught in the stream. After spawning, the parent fishes may not emerge from the caves until the fry are strong enough to look after themselves.

Planning the tank

LYING LOW *Most of the fishes suitable for this tank populate the lower, less turbulent levels of the water.*

BECAUSE OF the number of sizeable rocks used here, a large tank is needed. It is particularly important in this case to make sure that both the tank and the floor on which the stand is resting are able to take the weight of the rocks. If you intend to vary the design of your aquarium however, for example by including smaller and lighter rocks, such precautions may not be necessary. As long as you follow the guidelines provided for water chemistry, heating, and lighting conditions, the contents of your aquarium can be organized in a variety of different ways.

The temperature of the aquarium should be carefully maintained at around 25 to 27°C (77 to 80°F). Ideally, you should aim for a pH of between 7 and 7.5, and a water hardness of 150 mg/litre $CaCO_3$. The aquarium should be provided with a good level of lighting.

A power filter is the best choice here – the significant amount of heavy rocks in the aquarium would make an undergravel filter unsuitable, as the rocks would impede the flow of water through the filter bed. A power filter also has the capacity to reproduce the heavy waterflow that the fishes chosen for this aquarium experience in the wild. Furthermore, it will ensure that the water receives the necessary high levels of aeration, and waste removal, that are so characteristic of the Zaire River rapids.

See also Heating, p.163; pH and alkalinity in fresh water, p. 156; Lighting, p.164; Power filters, p. 159.

Essential equipment

The dimensions of the tank used here are 91 × 46 × 38 cm (36 × 18 × 15 in). This tank will hold 159 litres (35 gallons) of water, and should not be stocked with more than 115 cm (45 in) of fishes. Tapwater is generally suitable for this type of environment. The tank should be heated by two 150-watt heater/thermostats, and can be lit by a fluorescent tube. A power filter that gives a very good flow should be chosen. Also used in this tank are pea gravel, fine gravel, silver sand, large, rounded rocks, a selection of smooth, rounded pebbles, and a variety of aquarium plants.

See also Stocking levels, p. 42; Preparing fresh water, p. 154; Heating, p. 163; Lighting, p. 164; Power filters, p. 159.

INGREDIENTS

PEA GRAVEL
Gravel provides a secure bed for the large rocks in the tank.

CONGO ANUBIAS
Anubias congensis
The thick stems of this broad-leaved anubias allow it to stand upright in strong currents.

Anubias lanceolata
The sword-like leaves of this plant stand straight and tall in the water.

DWARF ANUBIAS
Anubias nana
A small plant that grows from the crevices between rocks.

SILVER SAND This fine sand is easy to spread between the rocks.

ROCKS
These large, rounded rocks have been shaped by continual water erosion.

Bolbitis heudeloti
A plant that will readily attach itself to rocks.

PEBBLES
The pebbles scattered across the floor of this tank should be smooth and rounded.

FINE GRAVEL
This gravel adds to the desired appearance of the tank, and will not block the filtration system.

Building the tank

The sand that forms the base of this tank is laid over a layer of gravel to prevent it from shifting. The thrust of water in river rapids erodes rocks into large, rounded boulders and smaller pebbles, so be sure to choose smooth specimens for your tank. Arrange them towards the back, with the plants tucked in between. The plants that live in this environment must be hardy to withstand being battered by the heavy waterflow. The anubias are strong and upstanding, and can be planted before the water is added. This allows you to manipulate them more easily than when planting in water.

See also Aquascaping, p. 48; Adding the plants, p. 49; Introducing the fishes, p. 50; Completing the tank, p. 50.

1 In the base of the tank, lay a layer of gravel that rises gradually towards the back. Introduce the rocks and pebbles, then add the silver sand.

2 Add the plants, tucking them firmly into the gravel. When positioning the plants, make sure that they will not be crushed by any of the heavy rocks.

3 Pour in the water very gradually. Running it in carefully over a plastic sheet or bag helps to prevent the water from becoming clouded by the sand.

THE AQUASCAPED TANK

Vigorous flow
A good power filter can recreate in miniature the swirl of fast-flowing waters.

Distinctive flower
The dwarf anubias can be recognised by the unique shape of its flowers.

Standing guard
Tall, sturdy plants like the Congo anubias make excellent cornerpieces for the aquarium.

SUITABLE FISHES

Arnoldichthys spilopterus
AFRICAN RED-EYED TETRA
Description Iridescent pink and brown body.
Length 12 cm (5 in).
Ease of keeping Fairly easy; ideal in shoals.
Food Live foods, especially bloodworm; flake.
Breeding Egg-scatterer.
Swimming level Midwater to upper levels.

Chiloglanis cameroonensis
AFRICAN SUCKERMOUTH CATFISH
Description Dark, rather crudely defined bands on grey body; distinctively elongated, to suit fast-flowing water.
Length 5 cm (2 in).
Ease of keeping Fairly easy; requires flowing water.
Food Live foods, especially gnat-larvae and daphnia; flake.
Breeding Egg-depositor; hides eggs beneath boulders.
Swimming level Lower levels.

Chrysichthys ornatus
ORNATE CATFISH
Description Generally silver body; black stripes.
Length 20 cm (8 in).
Ease of keeping Fairly difficult; predator of most small fishes.
Food Live foods; flake.
Breeding Unknown in the aquarium.
Swimming level Lower levels.

Distichodus sexfasciatus
BANDED AFRICAN TETRA

Description Pale orange body; black bands.
Length 30 cm (12 in).
Ease of keeping Fairly easy; enjoys large aquaria.
Food Live foods, especially shrimp and earthworm. Also lettuce; pellet; flake.

Breeding Egg-scatterer; difficult.
Swimming level Midwater.

Euchilichthys guentheri
GUNTHER'S SUCKERMOUTH CATFISH
Description Similar to *Chiloglanis cameroonensis*, but body is plain in colour.
Length 10 cm (4 in).
Ease of keeping As *Chiloglanis cameroonensis*.
Food Live foods, especially daphnia and bloodworm; flake.
Breeding Egg-depositor; hides eggs beneath boulders.
Swimming level Lower levels.

Eutropiellus "debauwi"
AFRICAN GLASS CATFISH
Description Silver body; black lateral stripe.
Length 6 cm (2½ in).
Ease of keeping Fairly easy; should preferably be kept in medium-sized shoals.
Food Live foods, especially gnat-larvae, daphnia, and bloodworm; also flake.
Breeding Egg-scatterer; never breeds in the aquarium.
Swimming level Midwater to upper levels.

Hemichromis thomasi
BUTTERFLY CICHLID

Description Spangled, with four small, black blotches.
Length 8 cm (3 in).
Ease of keeping Easy; excellent community cichlid.
Food Live foods, especially bloodworm and daphnia; flake.
Breeding Egg-depositor; normally spawns in substrate.
Swimming level Midwater to lower levels.

Phenacogrammus interruptus
CONGO TETRA
Description Iridescent green and blue; male has long, fringed fins.

Length 12 cm (5 in).
Ease of keeping Fairly easy; ideal in shoals.
Food Live foods, especially bloodworm; flake.
Breeding Egg-scatterer.
Swimming level Midwater to upper levels.

Steatocranus casuarius
BLOCKHEAD (LUMP-HEAD CICHLID)
Description Grey-black body; male has distinctive frontal gibbosity (head-lump).
Length 14 cm (5½ in).
Ease of keeping Easy.
Food Live foods, especially bloodworm; flake.
Breeding Egg-depositor; in caves and pots; parental.
Swimming level Lower levels.

Synodontis angelicus
POLKA DOT CATFISH
Description Black, with white dots; black- and white-banded caudal fin.
Length 20 cm (8 in)
Ease of keeping Easy; can be rather territorial.
Food Live foods, especially shrimp and gnat-larvae; flake; chopped leaf spinach.
Breeding Egg-scatterer; fairly difficult in the aquarium.
Swimming level Lower levels.

Synodontis brichardi
BRICHARD'S CATFISH
Description Black and white bands on body; elongated to suit fast-flowing water.
Length 15 cm (6 in).
Ease of keeping Easy.
Food As *Synodontis angelicus*.
Breeding As *Synodontis angelicus*.
Swimming level As *Synodontis angelicus*.

Synodontis camelopardalis
GIRAFFE SYNODONTIS
Description Giraffe-like, silver-grey blotches; elongated to suit fast-flowing water.
Length 15 cm (6 in).
Ease of keeping Easy.
Food As *Synodontis angelicus*.
Breeding As *Synodontis angelicus*.
Swimming level As *Synodontis angelicus*.

Synodontis flavitaeniatus
PYJAMA CATFISH
Description Brown and beige stripes on body.
Length 15 cm (6 in).
Ease of keeping Easy.
Food Live foods, especially shrimp and gnat-larvae; flake; chopped leaf spinach.
Breeding Egg-scatterer; difficult in the aquarium.
Swimming level As *Synodontis angelicus*.

Synodontis nigriventris
UPSIDE-DOWN CATFISH
Description Grey body; black speckles and pale bands.
Length 8 cm (3 in).
Ease of keeping Fairly easy; thrives in small shoals.
Food As *Synodontis angelicus*.
Breeding As *Synodontis angelicus*.
Swimming level Midwater to upper levels.

Synodontis robertsi
ROBERT'S CATFISH

Description Silver, giraffe-like pattern; large eyes.
Length 10 cm (4 in).
Ease of keeping Easy.
Food As *Synodontis angelicus*.
Breeding As *Synodontis angelicus*.
Swimming level As *Synodontis angelicus*.

Teleogramma brichardi
BRICHARD'S CICHLID
Description Black; male has white edges.
Length 20 cm (8 in).
Ease of keeping Difficult; extremely aggressive.
Food Live foods, especially bloodworm; flake.
Breeding Egg-depositor; lays eggs in caves; bi-parental.
Swimming level Lower levels.

The finished tank

In the fast-flowing, turbulent waters of Africa's great Zaire River, sturdy plants root themselves among the sand and bare rock. Strong-bodied, bottom-dwelling fishes spend large parts of their lives swimming against the stream, taking occasional refuge in caves and crevices. The peculiar beauty of this aquarium is difficult to relate. Its apparent simplicity, combined with the crisp, fresh colours, suggests a wonderful sense of purity. The fishes suitable for this aquarium generally require extremely well-oxygenated water, so make sure that the tank is adequately aerated.

CONGO ANUBIAS
Anubias congensis

BLOCKHEAD
Steatocranus casuarius
The female blockhead (below) is smaller than the male. Both parents guard their fry, hiding them in gaps between the rocks.

DWARF ANUBIAS
Anubias nana

BLOCKHEAD
Steatocranus casuarius
The head of the male blockhead
(below) is cushioned by fat. This
species has a relatively small swim-
bladder (*see* p. 31), so it moves
around the bottom of the tank in
small jumps.

AFRICAN GLASS CATFISH
Eutropiellus "debauwi"
These fishes have a distinctive
spiny first ray on the
dorsal fin.

Bolbitis heudeloti

Anubias lanceolata

SOUTHEAST ASIA BACK-WATER

RED FLOOR *The red, iron-stained substrate and leafy debris of a stream in the Khao Yai National Park, Thailand, can clearly be seen in the shallow waters.*

SOUTHEAST ASIA is home to a large proportion of the species that dominate fishkeeping (*see* p. 46). Its waters are generally neither too hard nor soft, and the majority of fishes are tolerant and able to acclimatize well to aquarium conditions.

The back-waters of Southeast Asia are both slow-moving and thick with vegetation (*see* p. 16). Above and below the waterline are varieties of bamboo, moss, and fern. The streams are packed with organic matter, and are often stained brown by the iron-rich, red rocks that litter the floor. The waters are fairly soft, with few minerals other than iron, and often low in oxygen.

This tank incorporates fishes from the back-water streams of Malaya, Borneo, Sumatra, and Thailand, countries that have very similar fish fauna. These waters favour labyrinth fishes such as *Trichogaster trichopterus*, which have additional breathing organs to help

cope with the lack of oxygen. Labyrinth fishes are found widely across Southeast Asia and Southwest Africa, often in slow-flowing or still waters with heavy vegetation. The blackwaters of the irrigation streams associated with paddyfields in Southeast Asia (*see* p.16), have been particularly well colonized by labyrinth fishes. The bottoms of these slow-flowing waters are crammed with the rich foods that support the fishes. Dead insects floating on the water are particularly welcome, and some of the fishes included in this tank, such as *Trichogaster trichopterus*, have even been reliably recorded shooting down flies in the same spectacular way as the archer fish (*Toxotes jaculator*) (*see* p. 125).

Some of the fishes that are suitable for this tank can be fiercely territorial, hence the name Siamese fighting fish for one member of the group.

Planning the tank

HARDY INMATES *The fishes chosen for this tank can survive in some very inhospitable waters.*

THE SIZE of this tank is not crucial, although there should be enough room, and a sufficient number of plants, for shy fishes to hide from belligerent tankmates. The highly cantankerous nature of some of the fishes included in this tank means that it may ultimately be necessary to remove over-aggressive individuals. It is a good idea to check with the aquarium dealer before buying to ensure that your selection of fishes will consist of species that are compatible with one another.

Although some aquarists claim that a slight temperature rise – say to 28°C (82°F) – acts as a stimulus to breeding, the basic temperature for the tank is 24 to 26°C (75 to 79°C). pH in the tank should be low – between 6 and 6.5 – and hardness

should be below 100 mg/litre CaCO$_3$. Although most of the fishes in this tank are accustomed to coping with difficult conditions in the wild and are fairly tolerant of different water chemistries, the pH and hardness should not be allowed to rise too high. To soften the water, peat can be added to the filter, and a fair amount of wood in the tank will provide shelter and interest for the aquarium inhabitants. These slow streams are often very shallow, which means that the tank lighting should be reasonably strong. A power filter is especially suitable for this tank, as it encourages good plant growth.

See also Heating, p. 163; pH and alkalinity in fresh water, p. 156; Lighting, p. 164; Power filters, p. 159.

Essential equipment

The dimensions of the tank used here are 91 × 46 × 38 cm (36 × 18 × 15 in). This tank will hold 159 litres (35 gallons) of water, and should not be stocked with more than 115 cm (45 in) of fishes. Tapwater is generally suitable for the tank, but it should be mixed with demineralized water to keep its hardness down. The tank should be heated by one 250-watt heater/thermostat, and can be lit by two fluorescent tubes. A power filter that is not too strong should be chosen. Also used in the tank are aquatic soil, silver sand, red gravel, pebbles, and plants.

See also Stocking levels, p. 42; Preparing fresh water, p. 154; Heating, p. 163; Lighting, p. 164; Power filters, p. 159.

INGREDIENTS

STONES
Multicoloured stones give a welcome element of colour to the tank.

SILVER SAND
This sand helps to bind the aquatic soil base.

RED GRAVEL
The red gravel suggests the iron-rich gravels of a Malaysian stream.

BAMBOO PLANT *Blyxa japonica*
The long leaves of this plant flow elegantly in water.

GIANT HYGROPHILA
Nomaphila stricta
This plant grows very rapidly, often protruding right out of the water.

AQUATIC SOIL
Special soil sold for aquaria provides an excellent growing medium for the difficult bamboo plant.

PEBBLES
Carefully chosen pebbles and small rocks can also add red to the substrate.

Building the tank

A base of aquatic soil is an excellent complement to silver sand as it encourages plant growth. It is important that a good plant cover is able to develop in this tank, as many of the fishes that may be included are inclined to aggression, and the other fishes will need somewhere to hide. To reflect the iron-rich substrates of Southeast Asia, the pebbles and gravels used in the tank should be red, or contain an element of red. The long leaves and light roots of many of the plants give them a tendency to lift from the tank bed, so they may need to be anchored with lead weights.

See also Aquascaping, p. 48; Adding the plants, p. 49; Introducing the fishes, p. 50; Completing the tank, p. 50.

1 Cover the base of the tank with aquatic soil, and on top of this lay approximately 2 cm (¾ in) of silver sand. Pat this into the sand with your fingers.

2 Add the pebbles and a generous sprinkling of red gravel. Gaps between the pebbles may be used as hiding places by more reclusive fishes.

3 Run the water over a plastic sheet to avoid too much agitation of the soil. This can cause clouding of the water, and may coat the leaves with a fine tilth of soil.

THE AQUASCAPED TANK

Collapsed bank
You can place the pebbles so as to create the impression of a dilapidated bank.

Tall plants
Plants in the tank should be big enough to allow fishes to hide among them.

Sandy patch
Feed the fishes over areas of exposed sand, so that excess fallen food is not hidden.

SUITABLE FISHES

Barbus tetrazona tetrazona
TIGER BARB
Description Silver-gold body; four distinctive, vertical black bands; red tint to pectoral and pelvic fins.
Length 6 cm (2½ in).
Ease of keeping Fairly easy; sensitive to nitrites. Best as a shoal, otherwise may become awkward fin nippers.
Food Accepts most foods.
Breeding Egg-depositor; eggs left in fine plants, but are often eaten by parents.
Swimming level All levels.

Betta splendens
SIAMESE FIGHTING FISH
Description Various; generally red or purple body.
Length 6 cm (2½ in).
Ease of keeping Fairly easy; aquarium water must be stable and well-filtered.
Food Flake.
Breeding Bubble-nester; keep one male with two females.
Swimming level Upper levels.

Botia macracantha
CLOWN LOACH
(*see* p. 81)

Brachydanio rerio
ZEBRA DANIO

Description Blue-grey body; horizontal silver-gold lines.
Length 5 cm (2 in).
Ease of keeping Easy.
Food Accepts most foods.
Breeding Egg-scatterer; spawns in shoals.
Swimming level Upper levels.

Colisa chuna
HONEY GOURAMI
Description Generally orange-gold. "Throat" and "chest" become dark turquoise as male approaches breeding period.
Length 4 cm (1½ in).
Ease of keeping Easy; prefers peaceful aquarium.

Food Accepts most foods.
Breeding Bubble-nester.
Swimming level Midwater.

Colisa fasciata
BANDED GOURAMI
Description Various. Male usually has orange-red body with deep red and blue vertical bands. Female generally has grey body with dark bands.
Length Male 10 cm (4 in); female 8 cm (3 in).
Ease of keeping Easy.
Food Accepts most foods.
Breeding Bubble-nester; isolate species for best results.
Swimming level Midwater to upper levels.

Colisa lalia
DWARF GOURAMI

Description Male has light blue body; red-orange vertical lines across rear half.
Length 6 cm (2½ in).
Ease of keeping Easy.
Food Flake.
Breeding Bubble-nester; fry can be difficult to rear.
Swimming level Midwater.

Gyrinocheilus aymonieri
SUCKING LOACH
(*see* p. 81)

Kryptopterus bicirrhus
GLASS CATFISH
Description Transparent, iridescent body; abdomen contained by silver sac.
Length 10 cm (4 in).
Ease of keeping Easy, if water is stable and well-filtered.
Food Flake.
Breeding Egg-depositor; difficult in the aquarium.
Swimming level: Midwater to upper levels.

Labeo bicolor
RED-TAILED BLACK SHARK
(*see* p. 81)

Macropodus opercularis
PARADISE FISH

Description Various colours; generally metallic-blue and red vertical bands. Female is lighter; red bands.
Length Male 11 cm (4½ in); female 8 cm (3 in).
Ease of keeping Fairly easy; species prefers temperatures of 15 to 20°C (59 to 68°F). Temperature of this tank is at upper end of preferred range. Can be aggressive during breeding period.
Food Flake.
Breeding Bubble-nester.
Swimming level Midwater to upper levels.

Pangasius sutchi
ASIAN SHARK CATFISH
Description Silver-grey body; black colouration on upper half.
Length 46 cm (18 in).
Ease of keeping Fairly easy; best kept in shoals; prefers good water movement; grows quickly, needing large aquarium when over 15 cm (6 in) long.
Food Accepts most foods; adults of species will prey upon small fishes in the aquarium.
Breeding Egg-depositor; difficult in the aquarium.
Swimming level Lower levels.

Trichogaster leeri
PEARL GOURAMI
Description Light brown body, divided along middle by distinctive black line; fine pattern of light blue spots spreads backwards across body from eye; when breeding, chest becomes bright red.
Length 12 cm (5 in).
Ease of keeping Easy.
Food Accepts most foods.
Breeding Bubble-nester; breeds at surface; often incorporates sand and leaves in bubble mass.
Swimming level All levels.

Trichogaster trichopterus sumatranus
BLUE GOURAMI
Description Silver-blue body.
Length 12 cm (5 in).
Ease of keeping Easy.
Food Accepts most foods.
Breeding Bubble-nester; breeds at surface.
Swimming level All levels.

Trichogaster trichopterus sumatranus
GOLDEN GOURAMI
As **BLUE GOURAMI**. A different member of the same subspecies, which has a distinctive gold body-colouring.

Trichogaster trichopterus sumatranus
COSBY GOURAMI

As **BLUE GOURAMI**. This is a natural mutation of the same subspecies, cultivated in captivity, and with darker blue patches on its body.

Trichogaster trichopterus sumatranus
SILVER GOURAMI
As **BLUE GOURAMI**. This is a silver-bodied mutation of the same subspecies, again cultivated in captivity.

Trichogaster trichopterus trichopterus
THREE SPOT GOURAMI
As **BLUE GOURAMI**. This member of the subspecies is blue, with two black spots, one in the middle of its body and the other located on its tail (the eye forms the third spot referred to in its name). The three spot gourami has been seen, on occasion, to capture its prey in the same extraordinary manner as the archer fish (*see* p. 125), by spitting out a powerful jet of water.

The finished tank

This aquarium aims to capture the spirit of one of the slow-flowing streams, thick with strong and fast-growing vegetation, that predominate throughout Malaysia. These streams are generally shallow, allowing a relatively large amount of light to penetrate the water; the lighting level in the aquarium should be correspondingly high. The low pH that is required can be maintained by adding peat to the filter. This is an active aquarium – the tiger barbs, for example, will continually chase each other's tails; keeping them in a group may distract their attention from the fins of other species.

ASIAN SHARK CATFISH
Pangasius sutchi
This species likes to shoal.

PEARL GOURAMI
Trichogaster leeri
After laying her eggs, the female of this species should be separated from the male.

GLASS CATFISH
Kryptopterus bicirrhus

HONEY GOURAMI
Colisa chuna
Many colour variations of this fish are known to exist.

BLUE GOURAMI
Trichogaster trichopterus sumatranus
In many parts of the world, large gouramis are used as food fishes.

TIGER BARB
Barbus tetrazona tetrazona
This busy, active fish often
nips the fins of more passive
tankmates.

RED-TAILED BLACK SHARK
Labeo bicolor
These fishes are grey when young.
They mature to a superb, velvet-
black colour, with a scarlet tail.

GIANT HYGROPHILA
Nomaphila stricta

PARADISE FISH
Macropodus opercularis
The paradise fish can occasion-
ally be aggressive.

BAMBOO PLANT
Blyxa japonica

THREE SPOT GOURAMI
*Trichogaster trichopterus
trichopterus*
This gourami has splendid,
thread-like ventral fins.

SIAMESE FIGHTING FISH
Betta splendens
Before fighting to the death,
two males will spread their
fins and raise their gill covers.

SOUTHEAST ASIA RIVER

MUDDY WATERS *The Segama River runs down through the Danum Valley, Sabah, Malaysia. By this stage of its journey the river is packed with sediment.*

THE FRESHWATER fishes of mainland Asia, and the Asiatic islands such as Sumatra, Borneo, and Java, have many similarities. This is because these areas were once joined by land, and one river system flowed through the whole area (*see* p. 16). The busy tank featured here is based on the lower reaches of a river on one of these Asiatic islands, upriver from the true estuary. This part of the river shares many of the characteristics of the waters both upstream and downstream of it – but it has at the same time a character all of its own. Lowland sections of such a river may even contain salt, and you may wish to add a small amount to the tank.

Many of the rivers on which this tank is based are supplied by the reservoirs that are found in profusion throughout Southeast Asia. Building began on these reservoirs over 4,000 years ago, to take advantage of the high rainfall of the region for irrigation and for food-fish farming. The reservoirs have had a considerable impact on the fish fauna of rivers in the region, as many food fishes have now driven other species out of these waters.

The list of fishes suitable for this tank is dominated by members of the cyprinid family; the constantly moving, shoaling habit of many of these fishes – particularly when they are young – catches the eye in the aquarium. Even the slow, shy loach is gregarious, and several of the fishes may congregate at the bottom of the tank.

Most of the fishes suitable for this tank are extremely hardy. Their adaptability has helped carp and barbs to become established, in numerous different forms, in waters in most parts of the world, and many species are used extensively as food fishes.

Planning the tank

HUSTLE AND BUSTLE *Many of the fishes in this tank are small, but it is a tank that is full of life, with plenty of activity.*

ANY SIZE of tank can be used for this type of river habitat. The tank featured here is large because it is stocked heavily with juvenile fishes that will need additional room as they grow. A large tank such as this also provides the fishes with enough space to shoal. The temperature of the tank should be kept at around 24°C (75°F). The water should have a pH of 7 to 7.5 and a hardness of around 150 mg/litre $CaCO_3$.

The level of lighting in the tank should be standard. A power filter is used here because it provides the best form of filtration for the reasonably high level of plant growth that is wanted for this tank. Most of the fishes suggested for inclusion are quite capable of acclimatizing to different types of water. This tank is therefore ideal for beginners.

The fishes are generally gregarious, although some barbs have a tendency to become boisterous. This may result in them nipping the fins of slower-moving and long-finned tankmates. If this behaviour persists you should remove the troublemaker from the aquarium. Good plant growth in the aquarium will help shy or reserved fishes to hide from any aggressive tankmates; as many as eight different species of aquatic plant are included in this particular tank.

Many of the fishes will do better, and none will suffer, if a very small amount of aquarium salt, at up to 0.5 grams per litre (½ to 1 teaspoon per gallon), is added to the water.

See also Heating, p. 163; pH and alkalinity in fresh water, p. 156; Lighting, p. 164; Power filters, p. 159.

Essential equipment

The dimensions of the tank used here are 122 × 46 × 38 cm (48 × 18 × 15 in). This tank will hold 212 litres (47 gallons) of water, and should not be stocked with more than a maximum 152 cm (60 in) of fishes. Tapwater is suitable for the aquarium, but demineralized water may need to be added to it. This spacious tank needs to be heated by two 150-watt heater/thermostats, and can be lit by a fluorescent tube.

Choose a power filter that provides a good, steady flow, but one that is, at the same time, not too strong. Also used to conjure up an assortment of effects in the aquarium are pea gravel, fine silver sand, bogwood, pebbles, and a selection of different aquatic plants.

See also Stocking levels, p. 42; Preparing fresh water, p. 154; Heating, p. 163; Lighting, p. 164; Power filters, p. 159.

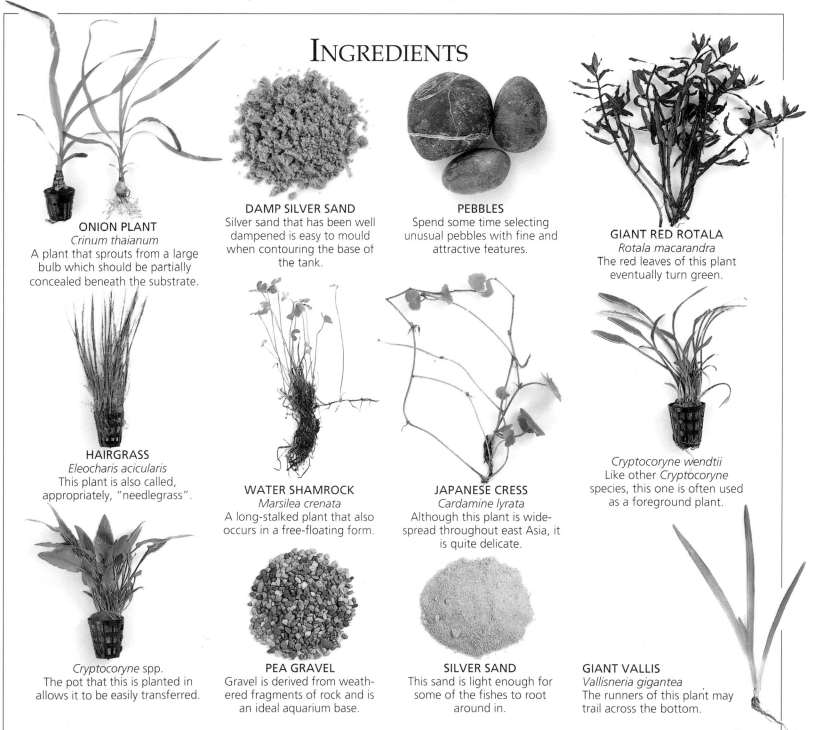

INGREDIENTS

ONION PLANT
Crinum thaianum
A plant that sprouts from a large bulb which should be partially concealed beneath the substrate.

DAMP SILVER SAND
Silver sand that has been well dampened is easy to mould when contouring the base of the tank.

PEBBLES
Spend some time selecting unusual pebbles with fine and attractive features.

GIANT RED ROTALA
Rotala macarandra
The red leaves of this plant eventually turn green.

HAIRGRASS
Eleocharis acicularis
This plant is also called, appropriately, "needlegrass".

WATER SHAMROCK
Marsilea crenata
A long-stalked plant that also occurs in a free-floating form.

JAPANESE CRESS
Cardamine lyrata
Although this plant is widespread throughout east Asia, it is quite delicate.

Cryptocoryne wendtii
Like other *Cryptocoryne* species, this one is often used as a foreground plant.

Cryptocoryne spp.
The pot that this is planted in allows it to be easily transferred.

PEA GRAVEL
Gravel is derived from weathered fragments of rock and is an ideal aquarium base.

SILVER SAND
This sand is light enough for some of the fishes to root around in.

GIANT VALLIS
Vallisneria gigantea
The runners of this plant may trail across the bottom.

Building the tank

This tank is designed to suggest an area around a large tree root. The base of the tank is liberally littered with pebbles, and a surprising number are needed to create a really good display. The traditional way of planting an aquarium is to line the taller specimens along the back of the tank, with smaller, bunchy items to the front. In this environment, however, tall plants are more likely to grow in the centre of the river (i.e. towards the centre of the tank) and smaller ones along the bank, and to reflect this the usual relationship is reversed here.

See also Aquascaping, p. 48; Adding the plants, p. 49; Introducing the fishes, p. 50; Completing the tank, p. 50.

1 Build up a shallow bank of pea gravel in one back corner of the tank. This can be shaped to suggest the gentle curve of a bend. Shore the bank up with pebbles to keep it stable. Place the most interesting rocks at the front of the tank.

2 Completely cover the gravel, pebbles, and the rest of the base of the tank with a layer of damp sand – as may, perhaps, have been deposited naturally, in the river. Brush off sand that has been disturbed and has collected on top of the rocks.

3 Position a large piece of bogwood so that it appears as a root that has been exposed by the movement of the water in the river, emerging from the shallow bank. Arrange more pebbles around the base of the wood and across the whole tank.

THE AQUASCAPED TANK

Colour change
As it matures, the giant red rotala will change in colour from red to green.

Open spaces
It is easy to reach all parts of this tank for cleaning and tidying.

White flowers
If it is allowed to grow out of the water, the onion plant may produce flowers.

SUITABLE FISHES

Acanthophthalmus kuhli
COOLIE LOACH
Description Dark brown or mauve body; yellow bands.
Length 11 cm (4½ in).
Ease of keeping Easy; best kept in shoals.
Food Flake.
Breeding Egg-scatterer.
Swimming level Lower levels.

Balantiocheilus melanopterus
BALA SHARK
(*see* p. 51)

Barbus conchonius
ROSY BARB
Description Silver-gold body; males have pink lower bodies, turning rust-red during the breeding period.
Length 8 cm (3 in).
Ease of keeping Easy.
Food Flake.
Breeding Egg-scatterer.
Swimming level Midwater.

Barbus fasciatus
STRIPED BARB (ZEBRA BARB)

Description Pale gold body; black spots on juveniles develop into horizontal black stripes.
Length 6 cm (2½ in).
Ease of keeping Easy.
Food Accepts most foods.
Breeding Egg-scatterer; difficult in the aquarium.
Swimming level All levels, but generally likes to rummage through substrate.

Barbus lateristriga
SPANNER BARB
Description Green-gold, deep body; two dark bands descend to point on belly.
Length 12 cm (5 in).
Ease of keeping Easy.
Food Accepts most foods.
Breeding Egg-scatterer.
Swimming level All levels.

Barbus pentazona pentazona
FIVE-BANDED BARB
Description Silver-yellow body; five vertical black bands.
Length 5 cm (12 in).
Ease of keeping Difficult; sensitive to water chemistry problems; less aggressive than its close relative *Barbus tetrazona tetrazona* (*see* p. 75)
Food Accepts most foods.
Breeding Egg-depositor; difficult in the aquarium.
Swimming level All levels.

Betta splendens
SIAMESE FIGHTING FISH
(*see* p. 75)

Botia macracantha
CLOWN LOACH
Description Yellow body; three vertical black bands
Length 30 cm (12 in).
Ease of keeping Easy; can grow slowly to a spectacular fish.
Food Dried foods; live foods; vegetable matter; pellet.
Breeding Egg-depositor; extremely difficult to breed in the aquarium.
Swimming level Lower levels.

Brachydanio albolineatus
PEARL DANIO
Description Pastel-blue tint to body; distinctive gold lines running along flanks.
Length 6 cm (2½ in).
Ease of keeping Easy.
Food Accepts most foods.
Breeding Egg-scatterer.
Swimming level Midwater to upper levels.

Brachygobius nunus
BUMBLEBEE GOBY

Description Black body; distinctive yellow bands.
Length 4 cm (1½ in).
Ease of keeping Easy, but

normally prefers brackish water.
Food Accepts most foods.
Breeding Egg-depositor; generally lays eggs under rocks; difficult in the aquarium.
Swimming level Lower levels.

Danio aequipinnatus
GIANT DANIO

Description Yellow-gold body; distinctive steel-blue horizontal bands.
Length 15 cm (6 in) in the wild, but much smaller in the aquarium.
Ease of keeping Easy.
Food Dried foods; live foods.
Breeding Egg-depositor; lays eggs among plants.
Swimming levels Midwater to upper levels.

Gyrinocheilus aymonieri
SUCKING LOACH
Description Dull, olive-brown body; dark band along flanks.
Length 15 cm (6 in).
Ease of keeping Easy; if keeping more than one, individuals may fight with one another.
Food Dried foods; fresh plants; will eat algae.
Breeding Egg-depositor; very difficult in the aquarium.
Swimming level Lower levels, but will occasionally rise towards surface of water.

Labeo bicolor
RED-TAILED BLACK SHARK
Description Black body, with a distinctive red tail.
Length 12 cm (5 in).
Ease of keeping Easy, but as it grows it can become territorial.
Breeding Egg-depositor; rare in the aquarium.
Food Accepts most foods.
Swimming level Lower levels.

Ophiocara apores
GOBY
Description Basic body colour

normally changes from silver to brown or olive-green as fish matures; dark lines and other markings are generally obvious near eye.
Length 30 cm (12 in).
Ease of keeping Easy.
Food Live foods.
Breeding Egg-depositor.
Swimming level Midwater to upper levels.

Pangasius sutchi
ASIAN SHARK CATFISH
(*see* p.75)

Rasbora heteromorpha
HARLEQUIN
Description Silver body; black triangle from mid-body to tail.
Length 15 cm (6 in).
Ease of keeping Easy.
Food Flake.
Breeding Egg-depositor; female lays eggs on undersides of leaves.
Swimming level Midwater.

Rasbora trilineata
SCISSORTAIL

Description Attractive, silver body; black tips to forks of caudal fin. Dark line, with yellow upper edge, runs along the flanks. Name derives from rather unusual twitching motion of forked caudal fin, whenever fish ceases to be in motion.
Length 6 in (15 cm).
Ease of keeping Easy. An active, shoaling fish that requires a fair amount of swimming space, and therefore, ideally, a spacious aquarium.
Food Accepts most foods.
Breeding Egg-scatterer; lays eggs among plants; prefers soft water for breeding.
Swimming level Midwater to upper levels.

The finished tank

Being both light and well oxygenated, this is a sound environment for many of the most popular aquarium species. In this tank, careful aquascaping has produced a convincing section of the riverbed, with some of the taller plants, which would normally grow in midstream in the wild, positioned towards the front of the aquarium. The waving green mass of onion plant and giant vallis provides a strong counterfoil to the solid, dark bogwood. There is activity at all levels in this aquarium: shoals of cyprinids enjoy darting in and out of the upper foliage, while the more sluggish loaches move over the sandy, pebble-scattered riverbed. As they grow, you can remove several of the larger aquarium inhabitants at some stage (*see* p. 43), and replace them with a further stock of juvenile fishes, therefore maintaining the aquarium's busy feel – a concentration of juveniles normally allows heavy stocking.

WATER SHAMROCK
Marsilea crenata

GIANT RED ROTALA
Rotala macarandra

BUMBLEBEE GOBY
Brachygobius nunus
The eggs of the bumble-bee goby are laid under pebbles, where they are guarded by the male.

RED-TAILED BLACK SHARK
Labeo bicolor
The inferior mouth (*see* p. 32) of this species has sucker-shaped organs for collecting food.

JAPANESE CRESS
Cardamine lyrata

Cryptocoryne spp.

HAIRGRASS
Eleocharis acicularis

HARLEQUIN
Rasbora heteromorpha
The distinctive "lamb-chop"
markings on the sides
of the harlequin make
it instantly recogniseable.

ROSY BARB
Barbus conchonius
The colour of the male rosy
barb changes to a deep red
in the breeding season.

GOBY
Ophiocara apores
The attractive goby like to
patrol areas of vegetation.

COOLIE LOACH
Acanthophthalmus kuhli
Loaches burrow under
rocks to establish hiding
places for themselves.

FIVE-BANDED BARB
*Barbus pentazona
pentazona*
A less aggressive fish than
the similar tiger barb.

GIANT VALLIS
Vallisneria gigantea

Cryptocoryne wendtii

BALA SHARK
Balantiocheilus melanopterus
Only small juveniles of this
species are suitable for
the aquarium.

ONION PLANT
Crinum thaianum

PAPUA NEW GUINEA SANDY RIVER

HIGH AND HANDSOME *Lofty plants, which grow both in and out of the water, line up along the banks of the Wahgi River of the highlands of Papua New Guinea.*

HUNDREDS OF MILLIONS of years ago, when the land-mass that gave rise to what is now Australasia broke away from the main block of Gond-wanaland (*see* p. 27), a large gulf developed between the Molucca Islands and Sulawesi. In the ages that followed this break, animals that were en-tirely different from each other developed on either side of the gulf. This disparity in fauna was noted in the nineteenth century by a contemporary of Charles Darwin, Alfred Russel Wallace, and the line drawn by biologists that marks the separation was named "Wallace's Line" after him.

Shallow, slow-moving, sandy rivers are a dominant feature of the region that developed to the south of this line. These rivers have a unique fish fauna (*see* p. 16), and it is a part of this fauna that forms the basis for this tank. The region has many small rivers, rather than one major watercourse, so there is not enough flow for rainfall to wash away the sand as happens in the Amazon.

Sediment may build up quite spectacularly, and this fosters a very good amount of vegeta-tion; both these features should be reflected in the tank.

The aquarium is designed to appear like one of the many shallow upland rivers or side-streams of the hills of Irian Jaya in Papua New Guinea. It is built around three species of rain-bowfish found only in New Guinea: the red New Guinea rainbowfish (*Glossolepis incisus*), which lives in the easy, slow-moving rivers that descend from Lake Sentani; Boesman's rainbowfish (*Melanotaenia boesmani*), which inhabits the Ajamaru Lakes; and the Goldie River rain-bowfish (*Melanotaenia goldiei*), which is widespread throughout the whole of the region.

Rainbowfish are actually related to the ocean mullet. They are splendidly coloured fishes and their tempera-ment makes them excellent aquarium species; other rainbowfish, perhaps from different parts of Australasia, should also be suitable for this tank.

Planning the tank

STEEP SLOPE *A high bank of gravel allows plants to stream out dramatically across the tank.*

THE SIZE of the tank is not of great importance, although it should not be smaller than about 91 cm (36 in) long, as the rainbow-fish like to shoal, and there should be enough room for them to do this. The temperature should be around 24°C (75°F). Most rainbow-fish prefer water of a pH between 6.5 and 7, and of low to medium hardness, in the region of 50 to 100 mg/litre $CaCO_3$. Because these sandy rivers are invariably shallow, the tank should be well lit. A power filter is suitable for this tank. It should keep the water agitated, but the flow should not be too fast. An undergravel filter is not suitable,

as the depth of the gravel would inhibit the flow of the filter. In addition, rainbowfish appreciate heavy vegetation; a power filter is ideal for a densely planted tank, and will also create the flow the fishes enjoy. Other fishes of Papua New Guinea – like the yellow winged popondetta (*Popondich-thys furcata*) – which prefer slightly brackish water (*see* p. 110), can be used instead of the fishes in this tank. Remember to add the appropriate amount of salt (*see* p. 85).

See also Heating, p. 163; pH and alkalinity in fresh water, p.156; Lighting, p. 164; Power filters, p.159.

Essential equipment

The dimensions of the tank used here are 91 × 46 × 38 cm (36 × 18 × 15 in). This tank will hold 159 litres (35 gallons) of water, and should not be stocked with more than 115 cm (45 in) of fishes. Tapwater can be used, but it will probably need to be mixed with demineralized water. Marine salt can be added at up to 5 grams per litre (1 oz per gallon). The tank should be heated by one 250-watt heater/thermostat, and lit by two fluorescent tubes. A power filter helps plant growth. Also used here are fine gravel, red gravel, silver sand, shale, curio wood, and two species of aquatic plant.

See also Stocking levels, p. 42; Preparing fresh water, p. 154; Heating, p. 163; Lighting, p. 164; Power filters, p. 159.

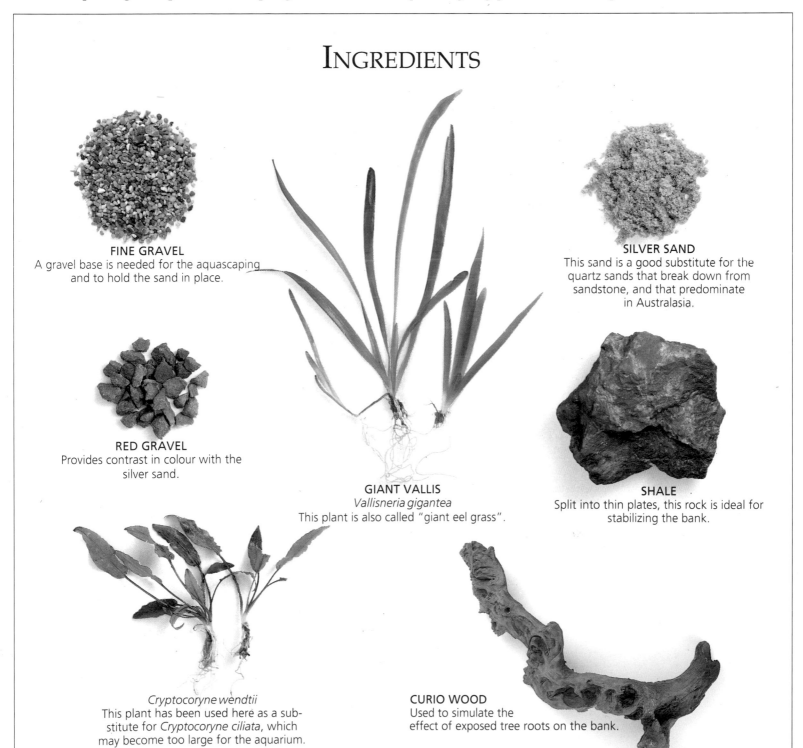

INGREDIENTS

FINE GRAVEL
A gravel base is needed for the aquascaping and to hold the sand in place.

SILVER SAND
This sand is a good substitute for the quartz sands that break down from sandstone, and that predominate in Australasia.

RED GRAVEL
Provides contrast in colour with the silver sand.

GIANT VALLIS
Vallisneria gigantea
This plant is also called "giant eel grass".

SHALE
Split into thin plates, this rock is ideal for stabilizing the bank.

Cryptocoryne wendtii
This plant has been used here as a substitute for *Cryptocoryne ciliata*, which may become too large for the aquarium.

CURIO WOOD
Used to simulate the effect of exposed tree roots on the bank.

Building the tank

To recreate a sandy river bank, you need to build a stable base in which to arrange plants and rockwork. Build the bank up with fine gravel, to which damp sand can be added. Once you have laid the basic profile of the bank, pull back the gravel close to the glass, and then use sand to mask it from the front. The bank can be anchored into position with shale.

Add the plants. Planting should not be so heavy as to prevent plenty of light illuminating the base of the tank. A light sprinkling of large, coarse, red gravel can be used to help create the right effect.

See also Aquascaping, p. 48; Adding the plants, p. 49; Introducing the fishes, p. 50; Completing the tank, p. 50.

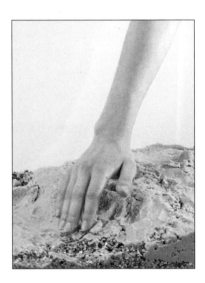

1 Wash the silver sand thoroughly, and pat the damp sand on to the surface of the gravel bed.

2 Add the shale and curio wood. Jagged, iron-rich shale simulates red, rocky outcrops from the bank.

3 Stands of plants may look best on the highest part of the bank. The giant vallis (Vallisneria gigantea) will soon trail across the aquarium.

THE AQUASCAPED TANK

Open space
A midwater area left free of plants will allow the gregarious rainbow-fish room to congregate.

Jagged rocks
A slow-flowing section of river does not have the tumbling activity that smooths rocks.

Vallis
The female reproductive organ of *Vallisneria gigantea* can be seen trailing up to the surface.

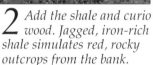

SUITABLE FISHES

Ambassias reticulata
RETICULATED PERCHLET
Description Metallic-pink body; dark tracery on fin edges.
Length 8 cm (3 in).
Ease of keeping Fairly easy; prefers plenty of plant cover.
Food Accepts most foods.
Breeding Egg-depositor; lays eggs among fine-leaved plants.
Swimming level Midwater.

Glossolepis incisus
RED NEW GUINEA RAINBOWFISH
Description Male has rust-red, or scarlet body when displaying; female has silver body.
Length Male 12 cm (5 in); female 10 cm (4 in).
Ease of keeping Fairly easy.
Food Accepts most foods.
Breeding Egg-depositor; fry should be removed to a rearing tank. Use Artemia as food.
Swimming level All levels, but generally midwater.

Glossolepis wanamensis
EMERALD RAINBOWFISH

Description Metallic-green body; red tint to elongated dorsal and anal fins.
Length 10 cm (4 in).
Ease of keeping Fairly easy; prefers medium-hard, slightly alkaline water.
Food Accepts most foods.
Breeding As *Glossolepis incisus*.
Swimming level All levels, but generally midwater.

Melanotaenia affinis
NORTH NEW GUINEA RAINBOWFISH
Description Silver body; blue and yellow tint towards rear.
Length 4 cm (1½ in).
Ease of keeping Easy; prefers slightly alkaline water.

Food Accepts most foods.
Breeding As *Glossolepis incisus*. Note that *Melanotaenia* spp. will interbreed.
Swimming level All levels, but generally midwater.

Melanotaenia boesmani
BOESMAN'S RAINBOWFISH
Description Front of fish generally coloured purple-blue; rear is yellow.
Length 9 cm (3½ in).
Ease of keeping Easy.
Food Accepts most foods.
Breeding As *Glossolepis incisus*.
Swimming level All levels, but generally midwater.

Melanotaenia goldiei
GOLDIE RIVER RAINBOWFISH

Description Silver body; broad, dark stripe along flanks; develops yellow-orange tracery along upper half of body, and yellow on anal fin.
Length Male 11 cm (4½ in); female 10 cm (4 in).
Ease of keeping Fairly easy; prefers medium-hard, slightly alkaline water.
Food Accepts most foods.
Breeding As *Glossolepis incisus*.
Swimming level All levels, but generally midwater.

Melanotaenia lacustris
TURQUOISE RAINBOWFISH
Description Blue-green body; red edge to dorsal and anal fins; dark bar runs from caudal peduncle, crossed by gold and green markings.
Length 10 cm (4 in).
Ease of keeping Fairly easy; should be kept in medium-hard,

slightly alkaline water.
Food Accepts most foods.
Breeding As *Glossolepis incisus*.
Swimming level All levels, but generally midwater.

Melanotaenia parkinsoni
PARKINSON'S RAINBOWFISH
Description Silver-blue body; base of fins normally develop orange hue; male develops orange horizontal lines, running from mid-body to tail.
Length Male 11 cm (4½ in); female 9 cm (3½ in).
Ease of keeping Easy.
Food Accepts most foods, especially live foods.
Breeding As *Glossolepis incisus*.
Swimming level Midwater.

Melanotaenia splendida rubrostriata
RED-STRIPED RAINBOWFISH
Description Distinctive red colouration to top of body and underside of male.
Length 10 cm (4 in).
Ease of keeping Easy.
Food Accepts most foods.
Breeding As *Glossolepis incisus*.
Swimming level Midwater.

Neosilurus novaeguinea
NEW GUINEA TANDAN
Description Brown body.
Length 8 cm (3 in).
Ease of keeping Very easy; should not be kept with rainbowfish.
Food Accepts most foods.
Breeding Egg-depositor; difficult in the aquarium.
Swimming level Lower levels.

Parambassis confinis
PAPUAN PERCHLET
Description Silver-yellow body.
Length 10 cm (4 in).
Ease of keeping Easy.
Food Accepts most foods.
Breeding Egg-depositor.
Swimming level Midwater.

Parambassis gulliveri
GIANT GLASSFISH
Description Attractive silver body, entirely covered by dark tracery; yellow edges to pelvic and anal fins.
Length 28 cm (11 in).
Ease of keeping Easy; this species generally prefers

turbulent water conditions.
Food Accepts most foods.
Breeding Egg-layer.
Swimming level Midwater.

Popondichthys connieae
POPONDETTA RAINBOWFISH

Description Silver body, normally with dark edges; yellow edges to fins.
Length 5 cm (2 in).
Ease of keeping Fairly difficult; prefers water that is slightly alkaline and brackish; sensitive to water changes.
Food Accepts most foods.
Breeding Egg-depositor, fry should be removed to rearing tank. Use Artemia as food.
Swimming level Midwater.

Popondichthys furcata
YELLOW-WINGED POPONDETTA
Description Silver body; black bars on tail.
Length 5 cm (2 in).
Ease of keeping Fairly difficult; prefers slightly alkaline, brackish water conditions; fairly sensitive to fluctuations in water chemistry.
Food Accepts most foods.
Breeding Egg-depositor; fry should be removed to breeding tank. Use Artemia as food.
Swimming level Midwater.

Toxotes chatareus
ARCHER FISH
Description Yellow-green body, with dark markings .
Length 20 cm (8 in).
Ease of keeping Difficult; prefers brackish-water conditions. Archer fish can be difficult to feed; introduce insects to the aquarium.
Food Accepts most foods.
Breeding Egg-layer.
Swimming level Midwater to upper levels.

The finished tank

This aquarium attempts to recreate the type of environment that characterises one of the slow-flowing, sandy streams from the uplands of Papua New Guinea. Among the most spectacular inhabitants of these streams are the delicately coloured rainbowfish. The sandy bank in the aquarium is covered with streaming leaves of vallis. Despite the high level of planting, however, there should also be a fair amount of space for the naturally gregarious and peaceful rainbowfish to shoal. Make sure that the floor of the tank is well lit. Once they become mature, there is a very strong possibility that different species of *Melanotaenia* will interbreed, producing hybrids. You may therefore wish to thin out the mature individuals at this stage, until there are only fishes of one *Melanotaenia* species present.

Cryptocoryne wendtii

GOLDIE RIVER RAINBOWFISH
Melanotaenia goldiei
This rainbowfish can be identified by a spot of red behind the gills.

RED NEW GUINEA RAINBOWFISH
Glossolepis incisus
The dark red colour of this rainbowfish often appears to be almost black.

BOESMAN'S RAINBOWFISH
Melanotaenia boesmani
Different species of *Melanotaenia* are likely to interbreed, so they need to be separated before they mature.

Giant vallis
Vallisneria gigantea

CENTRAL AMERICA ROCKY LAKE

STEEP WALLS *The rocky slopes of the imposing volcanoes Toliman and Atitlan run right down to the still waters of Lake Atitlan, Guatemala.*

AMONG the mountains of the countries that form the narrow bridge between North and South America are numerous volcanic crater lakes (*see* p. 18), and it is one of the lakes that is recreated here.

These lakes, which include Lakes Nicaragua, Managua, and Atitlan, are very deep indeed, and they are distinguished by their particularly steep, rocky sides and hard, alkaline water. The waters of the crater lakes are home to some extraordinary fishes, including, in Lake Nicaragua, the bull shark (*Carcharhinus leucas*) – a shark that has evolved to live in fresh water as well as in the sea – and a number of spectacular species of cichlid, such as Dow's cichlid (*Cichlasoma dovii*) from Nicaragua and Honduras, and Friedrichsthal's cichlid (*Cichlasoma friedrichsthalii*), which is found throughout most parts of Central America. Also prominent in the lakes of Central America are catfish of the Pimelodidae family, like *Rhamdia quelen*, the plecostomus (*Hypostomus plecostomus*), and the bumblebee catfish (*Microglanis iheringi*). In general, however, the lakes are not well populated, as many are at great altitude and this makes the water too cold for many species.

Civil unrest and the fact that human populations in the region are on the increase have created new demands that have resulted in two problems – an increasing amount of water being drawn off from the lakes and serious pollution in some areas.

Many cichlids that would be suitable for a Central American tank can also be found in the rivers of the region. The rivers are more acidic than the lakes and, as a rule, the fishes that live in them are less aggressive than the lake fishes. They include *Cichlasoma cyanoguttatum* and *Cichlasoma intermedium*.

Planning the tank

DEVILISH RIVALRY *The red devils in this tank will fight for the use of spaces between the rocks.*

BECAUSE OF the amount of sizeable rocks used, a large tank is needed to recreate a rocky lake. It is very important to make sure that the tank stand and the floor on which it is resting are both able to take the weight of the tank and the rocks in it. The temperature of this tank should be maintained at 27 to 29°C (77 to 81°F). The tank water should be kept alkaline – a pH of around 8 is ideal – with a hardness of 250 to 400 mg/litre $CaCO_3$.

A standard level of lighting should be used. The fishes in this tank live among rocks around the side of the lake and they do not like too much light. In addition, excessive lighting is likely to cause an undesirable amount of algal growth. A power filter is the most suitable form of filter for this tank. The flow of the water should be light.

Many Central American fishes can be hostile to fellow inhabitants. Therefore it is important to find out how sociable the fishes that you intend to keep are likely to be. In this tank, sailfin plecostomus are included to act as housemaids to juvenile red devils, eating their waste food and tidying up after them. Although plants are found in the lakes of Nicaragua, in the aquarium they are likely to be destroyed by the fishes (both of these species of fish enjoy vegetation and have particularly voracious appetites). If you really desire to add plants, try hardy species such as the Java fern (*Microsorium pteropus*). Alternatively, use plastic plants.

See also Heating, p. 163; pH and alkalinity in fresh water, p. 156; Lighting, p. 164; Power filters, p. 159.

Essential equipment

The dimensions of the tank used here are 122 × 46 × 38 cm (48 × 18 × 15 in). This tank will hold 212 litres (47 gallons) of water, and should not be stocked with more than 152 cm (60 in) of fishes. Tapwater can generally be used, but it may need hardening. The tank should be heated by two 150-watt heater/thermostats, and can be lit by a fluorescent tube.

Because of the large amount of rocks in the tank, a power filter, rather than an undergravel filter, is used here. Also used in the tank are coral sand, silver sand, pea gravel, and a large assortment of rocks. No plants are required.

See also Stocking levels, p. 42; Preparing fresh water, p. 154; Heating, p. 163; Lighting, p. 164; Power filters, p. 159.

INGREDIENTS

TWO-COLOURED ROCK
A boldly marked rock adds a visual accent when placed among the more monotone rocks.

FACETTED ROCK
An angular rock like this catches the light attractively in the tank.

FOSSIL ROCKS
Both the shapes and markings of these provide visual interest.

PEA GRAVEL
A very small amount of gravel is used here, thinly scattered on the sand.

FRAGMENTS OF ROCK
In combination with other rocks, small, jagged or angular fragments can be used to dramatic effect.

SILVER SAND
Mixed with coral sand in the proportion of four to one, silver sand forms the main tank bed.

REDDISH PEBBLES
Colour interest can be provided by small stones and pebbles.

MARBLE
Attractive, warm-toned marble rocks are a handsome addition to the tank.

LARGE IGNEOUS ROCK
A mottled, rounded rock provides a smooth contour for the back of the tank.

STRATIFIED ROCKS
Naturally banded rocks can be particularly attractive.

Building the tank

The effect to be created in this aquarium is of the steep, rocky underwater side of a lake. The shapes and textures of the rocks make this an exciting tank to design. When choosing rocks for the tank, try to make sure that what you intend to build is realistic. It may be useful to look at photographs of lakes before actually collecting or buying the rocks. Make sure that you can lift the rocks into the tank easily, and that there is no danger of them tumbling over once they have been built up. Glueing some of the rocks together with aquarium silicone sealant will help to avoid this.

See also Aquascaping, p. 48; Introducing the fishes, p. 50; Completing the tank, p. 50.

1 Mix coral sand with the silver sand in the proportion of about one to four to keep a high pH in the water and maintain a good level of buffering (see p. 157). Lay a base of silver and coral sand mix to about 5 cm (2 in). Shape the sand as a relief impression of the way that you would like the rock face to build up.

2 Build up a wall of rocks to appear like large boulders along the rear of the tank. These need not be visible when the tank is complete, so their shape is not important. Smaller rocks may be used to fill the gaps. The taller you are able to build this wall of rocks, the more impressive the finished aquarium will be.

3 Add the feature rocks, then cover the base of the tank with slab-like pebbles. The effect created here is of rocks that have tumbled down to the base of a bank. Take a good look at the tank at this stage. Now is the time to make adjustments. Moving large rocks once the fishes are introduced may result in injury or stress.

THE AQUASCAPED TANK

Private places
Gaps between the rocks may be used for spawning.

Resting places
Rocks with flat surfaces allow the catfish in this tank to rest.

Vein in the rocks
A scar of pinkish-yellow rocks suggests a geological seam.

SUITABLE FISHES

Cichlasoma aureum
GOLD CICHLID
Description Yellow-blue body; similar to *Cichlasoma meeki*.
Length 15 cm (6 in).
Ease of keeping Easy; excellent community cichlid.
Food Live foods, especially shrimp and bloodworm.
Breeding Egg-depositor; spawns on rocks or in substrate; parental.
Swimming level Midwater to lower levels.

Cichlasoma bifascatium
ROSE-BREASTED CICHLID
Description Red, yellow, or orange body.
Length 25 cm (10 in).
Ease of keeping Fairly easy.
Food Live foods, especially shrimp and chopped earthworm; chopped spinach.
Breeding As *Cichlasoma aureum*.
Swimming level Midwater to lower levels.

Cichlasoma citrinellum
RED DEVIL (LEMON CICHLID)
Description Red-lemon to corn-coloured body.
Length 25 cm (10 in).
Ease of keeping Difficult; aggressive, especially when this fish is mature.
Food Live foods, especially shrimp and chopped earthworm; chopped spinach.
Breeding As *Cichlasoma aureum*.
Swimming level Midwater to lower levels.

Cichlasoma intermedium
INTERMEDIUM CICHLID
Description Green-grey body; black, L-shaped blotch.
Length 15 cm (6 in).
Ease of keeping Easy; excellent community cichlid.
Food Live foods, especially shrimp and chopped earthworm; chopped spinach.
Breeding As *Cichlasoma aureum*.
Swimming level Midwater to lower levels.

Cichlasoma maculicauda
BLACK BELT CICHLID
Description Red, green, or blue body; mid-lateral blue blotch.

Length 30 cm (12 in).
Ease of keeping Fairly easy; can be aggressive towards other fishes when not breeding.
Food Live foods, especially shrimp; chopped spinach.
Breeding As *Cichlasoma aureum*.
Swimming level Midwater to lower levels.

Cichlasoma managuense
JAGUAR CICHLID

Description Elongated, silver body; black speckles.
Length 30 cm (12 in).
Ease of keeping Difficult; this fish is normally an aggressive predator in the aquarium.
Food Live foods; particularly partial to shrimp and earthworm; beef heart.
Breeding As *Cichlasoma aureum*.
Swimming level Midwater.

Cichlasoma meeki
FIREMOUTH CICHLID

Description Red-brown body. Red intensifies on breast and throat; male has extended fins.
Length 15 cm (6 in).
Ease of keeping Fairly easy to keep; territorial; excellent community cichlid.
Food Live foods, especially shrimp and chopped earthworm; chopped spinach.
Breeding As *Cichlasoma aureum*.
Swimming level Midwater to lower levels.

Cichlasoma nicaraguensis
NICARAGUA CICHLID
Description Yellow, orange, blue, or green body; juvenile has black lateral stripe.
Length Male 24 cm (10 in), female 20 cm (8 in).
Ease of keeping Fairly easy; aggressive when sexually mature.
Food Live foods, especially shrimp and chopped earthworm; chopped spinach.
Breeding As *Cichlasoma aureum*.
Swimming level Midwater to lower levels.

Cichlasoma salvini
TRICOLOUR CICHLID
Description Yellow-red body; black blotches.
Length 15 cm (6 in).
Ease of keeping Easy; compatible with other cichlids.
Food Live foods; particularly partial to shrimp, bloodworm, and gnat-larvae.
Breeding As *Cichlasoma aureum*.
Swimming level Midwater.

Cichlasoma spilurum
BLUE-EYED (JADE-EYED) CICHLID

Description Yellow-blue body.
Length 12 cm (5 in).
Ease of keeping Easy; compatible with other cichlids.
Food Live foods; particularly partial to shrimp, bloodworm, and gnat-larvae.
Breeding As *Cichlasoma aureum*.
Swimming level Midwater.

Cichlasoma synspilum
FIREHEAD CICHLID
Description Rose head; blue or orange body with black pigment.
Length 30 cm (12 in).
Ease of keeping Fairly easy; can be aggressive towards other

fishes when not breeding.
Food Live foods, especially shrimp and chopped earthworm; chopped spinach.
Breeding As *Cichlasoma aureum*.
Swimming level Midwater to lower levels.

Herotilapia multispinosa
RAINBOW CICHLID
Description Yellow-brown body; pale red, vertical stripes.
Length 12 cm (5 in).
Ease of keeping Easy; compatible with other cichlids.
Food Live foods; particularly partial to shrimp, bloodworm, and gnat-larvae.
Breeding As *Cichlasoma aureum*.
Swimming level Midwater.

Hypostomus plecostomus
SUCKERMOUTH PLECOSTOMUS
Description Brown body.
Length 20 to 30 cm (8 to 12 in).
Ease of keeping Easy.
Food Live foods; particularly partial to shrimp and earthworm; spinach; lettuce.
Breeding Unknown in the aquarium.
Swimming level Lower levels.

Pterygoplichthys multiradiatus
SAILFIN PLECOSTOMUS
Description Black and grey body; elongated, "suckermouth" catfish.
Length 40 to 50 cm (16 to 20 in).
Ease of keeping Fairly easy.
Food Live foods, especially shrimp and earthworm. Also green foods, such as spinach and lettuce.
Breeding Unknown in the aquarium.
Swimming level Lower levels.

Rhamdia quelen
RHAMDIA CATFISH
Description Brown-grey speckles when the fish is juvenile; grey body when mature.
Length 30 cm (12 in).
Ease of keeping Fairly easy; requires high oxygen levels.
Food Accepts most foods.
Breeding Egg-scatterer; non-parental.
Swimming level Midwater to lower levels.

The finished tank

This spectacular tank, when completed to its greatest effect, contains a dramatic, apparently haphazard, collection of rocks – imitating the result of a volcanic landslide. In reality, the rocks and pebbles should be carefully selected, to provide a variety of colours, shapes, and textures. As this tank contains just two large fish species, and no plants, not only the authenticity, but also much of the appeal of this aquarium depends upon an inspired rock composition. You can use a silicone sealant to assist in stabilizing particularly complex structures. Before finally assembling the rocks in the tank, you might find it useful to first build up the structure on a flat surface, and to experiment with various arrangements, until you achieve the effect you desire. When selecting inhabitants for this environment, always make sure that your chosen species are compatible; the two included here live in harmony, but other combinations may

RED DEVIL
Cichlasoma citrinellum
Parent fishes of this species spend a lot of time caring for their eggs.

not take so readily to each other, and South American lake dwellers are inclined to be especially belligerent. As the young red devils grow, and certain pairs become dominant, subordinate fishes, which have been unable to mark out their own territory, can be removed from the tank and either placed in another tank or returned to the dealer (*see* p. 43). It is interesting to note, and some aquarists may even be lucky enough to witness it occurring, that male and female red devils will often remain as a pair, faithful to each other for years. If the female eventually manages to spawn, however, you must ensure that any catfish present in the aquarium do not eat the eggs. Cichlids are often referred to as one of the most advanced groups of fish in the world. In general, they display a high standard of parental care, guarding their fry fiercely against other fishes, and keeping a watchful eye for predators.

SAILFIN PLECOSTOMUS
Pterygoplichthys multiradiatus
This wedge-shaped, sucking catfish gets its name from the shape of its majestic dorsal fin.

EAST AFRICA ROCKY LAKE

STERN BEAUTY *This uncompromising shoreline merely hints at the deep, rocky waters that are so characteristic of these lakes.*

THE GREAT rift valleys of Africa were formed in prehistoric times, as plate movement and volcanic activity tore apart the earth's crust. Two major series of rifts run south from the Red Sea and across Africa and each have a number of lakes along their length (*see* p. 18). It is one of these lakes that is the inspiration for this tank.

On the western rift lie Lake Albert to the north and Lake Tanganyika to the south, while lakes on the eastern rift include Lake Turkana to the north and Lake Nyasa to the south. All of these lakes are very deep, but Lake Tanganyika at 1,470 m (4,810 ft) and Lake Nyasa at 704 m (2,302 ft) are both substantially deeper than the larger Lake Victoria, which straddles the two rifts.

The great depths of these lakes means that they have an almost permanent thermocline (*see* p. 18), although in the case of Lake Tanganyika, it seems that somehow the waters do circulate. One theory for why this should be the case is that the lake is actually heated at its extreme depths by the Earth's core.

Rift valley lakes are generally steep-sided and rocky, both above and below the waterline. There are, however, sandy beaches on the shores and in the upper layers of the lakes. The fishes that live in the lakes inhabit mainly the upper 50 m (165 ft) of water. The fish fauna of the lakes is dominated by cichlids. These heavy-bodied fishes are most at home among the boulders of the shore, which contain the rocky retreats needed for spawning, so this aquarium should be designed to appear as rocky as possible. Predatory fishes such as *Lamprologus* spp. are particularly well adapted to the limited food sources that are to be found in the lakes, and some fishes, such as *Perissodus* spp., will even eat the scales of other fishes.

Planning the tank

A CONSIDERABLE TASK *Time and patience are needed to successfully recreate the uncanny beauty of a rocky lake.*

BECAUSE of the number of sizeable rocks used, a large tank is needed. Make sure that the tank and the floor on which the stand is resting are strong enough to support the weight of the rocks.

The temperature of the tank should be maintained at around 26°C (79°F). The rift valley lakes are characterized by hard, alkaline water. To reflect this in the tank, the pH of the water should be kept at between 8.6 and 9.2, with a hardness of 250 to 300 mg/litre $CaCO_3$. The level of lighting should be high, as East African lake fishes are used to water that is exposed all day long to the tropical sun.

Adding vegetation to this tank is not a good idea, as it is very likely to be either eaten or uprooted by fishes in search of places to spawn. Algae, however, will grow in the tank and will provide welcome food for the fishes. A power filter is the most suitable form of filter for the tank. Do not use an undergravel filter, as it may create dead areas beneath the rocks in which unwanted bacteria can develop. Furthermore, an undergravel filter base is unlikely to be able to take the weight of the rocks. The water should be calm, and the flow of the filter no more than is sufficient to filter the water satisfactorily. Remember that some rocky lake fishes can be territorially aggressive. This aquarium therefore requires a number of caves, in which the fishes can hide, and from where they can escape in several different directions.

See also Heating, p. 163; pH and alkalinity in fresh water, p. 156; Lighting, p. 164; Power filters, p. 159.

Essential equipment

The dimensions of the tank used here are 122 × 46 × 38 cm (48 × 18 × 15 in). This tank will hold 212 litres (47 gallons) of water, and should not be stocked with more than 152 cm (60 in) of fishes. Tapwater may be used, but it will need to be hardened using limestone in the filter. This tank should be heated by two 150-watt heater/thermostats, and can be lit by a fluorescent tube. A power filter that gives a good flow, but is not too strong, should be chosen. Also used are coral sand, rocks, and shells. The coral sand is mixed with the silver sand in the ratio of about one to four.

See also Stocking levels, p. 42; Preparing fresh water, p. 154; Heating, p. 163; Lighting, p. 164; Power filters, p. 159.

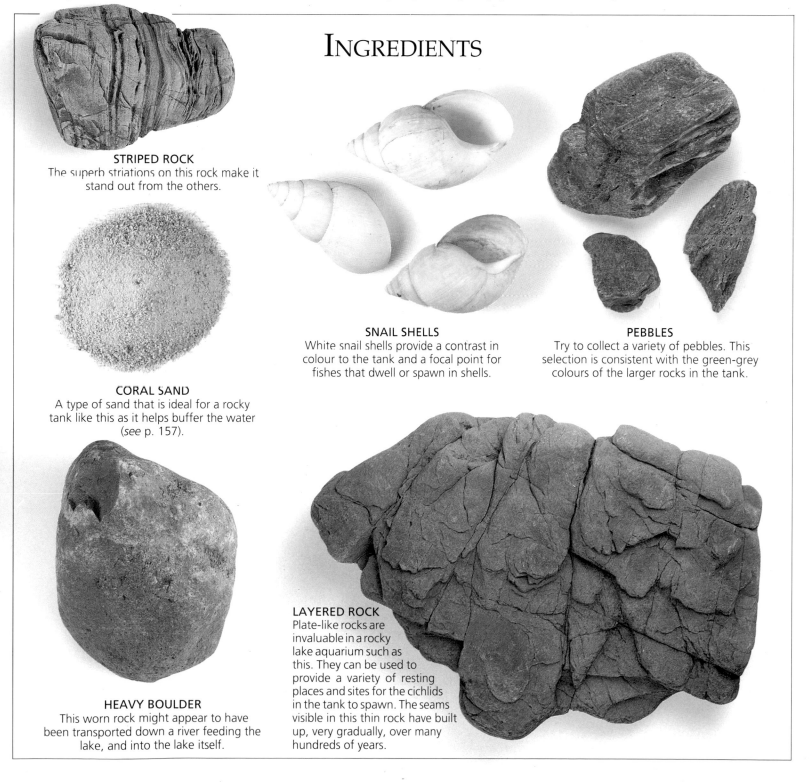

INGREDIENTS

STRIPED ROCK
The superb striations on this rock make it stand out from the others.

CORAL SAND
A type of sand that is ideal for a rocky tank like this as it helps buffer the water (*see* p. 157).

SNAIL SHELLS
White snail shells provide a contrast in colour to the tank and a focal point for fishes that dwell or spawn in shells.

PEBBLES
Try to collect a variety of pebbles. This selection is consistent with the green-grey colours of the larger rocks in the tank.

HEAVY BOULDER
This worn rock might appear to have been transported down a river feeding the lake, and into the lake itself.

LAYERED ROCK
Plate-like rocks are invaluable in a rocky lake aquarium such as this. They can be used to provide a variety of resting places and sites for the cichlids in the tank to spawn. The seams visible in this thin rock have built up, very gradually, over many hundreds of years.

Building the tank

This tank is designed to suggest rocks that have tumbled down the steep side of a lake, and the materials that you gather together should allow plenty of opportunity for creativity. Many of the rocks used here are stratified (composed of different coloured layers) and, although the aim is to simulate the appearance of rocks that have fallen from above in a rock-slide, it is important that any particularly prominent rocks rest on the floor in a realistic way, with the strata aligned consistently. The plate-like rocks used here are particularly good for creating dramatic, jagged outcrops.

See also Aquascaping, p. 48; Introducing the fishes, p. 50; Completing the tank, p. 50.

1 Carefully lay a base of silver sand to a depth of about 5 cm (2 in). Build up a wall of boulders along the rear of the tank, making sure that the entire structure is perfectly stable. Then position the final feature rocks to their best advantage.

2 The shells of the African giant land snail can be added to provide a home for Lamprologus brevis. *These nest-building fishes normally like to live and spawn in shells. Place the shells prominently, towards the front of the tank.*

THE AQUASCAPED TANK

Site for spawning
Many species of fish will spawn in the empty shells of invertebrates.

Rocky ledge
A thin piece of layered rock provides excellent shelter for resting fishes.

Dark tones
The dark, silhouetted look of these stones is typical of the rocks found in an African rocky lake.

SUITABLE FISHES

Chalinochromis brichardi
Description Gold or tan body; dark lines on head.
Length 11 cm (4½ in).
Ease of keeping Easy.
Food Most kinds of vegetable matter; flake.
Breeding Nest-builder.
Swimming level All levels.

Cyphotilapia frontosa
DEEP-WATER CICHLID
Description Blue and white vertical bands.
Length 30 to 40 cm (12 to 16 in).
Ease of keeping Fairly easy; requires large aquarium.
Food Live foods, especially prawns; pellet; large flake.
Breeding Mouth-brooder; parental.
Swimming level Midwater; around rocks.

Cyprichromis leptosoma
BLUE CYPRINID
Description Pale brown body, lined with blue speckles.
Length 8 cm (3 in).
Ease of keeping Fairly difficult; prefers shoals; delicate, and therefore difficult to import.
Food Live foods, especially gnat-larvae and bloodworm; flake.
Breeding Egg-scatterer.
Swimming level Midwater.

Julidochromis dickfeldi
DICKFELD'S CICHLID

Description Predominantly black and beige body.
Length 6 cm (2½ in).
Ease of keeping Difficult; pair-bonding; aggressive.
Food Live foods, especially shrimp and bloodworm; flake.
Breeding Egg-depositor; spawns in caves; parental.
Swimming level All levels, especially among rocks.

Julidochromis marlieri
MARLIER'S CICHLID
Description Black and white "chequer-board" body.
Length 8 cm (3 in).
Ease of keeping As *Julidochromis dickfeldi*.
Food Live foods, especially shrimp and bloodworm; flake.
Breeding As *Julidochromis dickfeldi*.
Swimming level As *Julidochromis dickfeldi*.

Julidochromis ornatus
ORNATE CICHLID
Description Yellow and black lateral stripe.
Length 8 cm (3 in).
Ease of keeping As *Julidochromis dickfeldi*.
Food Live foods, especially shrimp and bloodworm; flake.
Breeding As *Julidochromis dickfeldi*.
Swimming level As *Julidochromis dickfeldi*.

Julidochromis regani
REGAN'S CICHLID
Description Elongated body; black and yellow lateral stripes.
Length 10 cm (4 in).
Ease of keeping As *Julidochromis dickfeldi*.
Food Live foods, especially shrimp and bloodworm; flake.
Breeding As *Julidochromis dickfeldi*.
Swimming level As *Julidochromis dickfeldi*.

Labidochromis coeruleus
Description Silver-white body. This fish has dark bars along dorsal and anal fins.
Length 12 cm (5 in).
Ease of keeping Easy.
Food Vegetable matter; flake.
Breeding Nest-builder; non-parental.
Swimming level All levels.

Lamprologus brevis
Description Tan body; light vertical bands; distinctive blue colouration obvious under eye.
Length 5 cm (2 in).
Ease of keeping Easy.
Food Vegetable matter; flake.
Breeding Nest-builder.
Swimming level Midwater to lower levels.

Lamprologus mustax
Description White tint around mouth and chest; dark, narrow and wide, vertical bands alternate along grey body.
Length 6 cm (2½ in).
Ease of keeping Easy.
Food Vegetable matter; flake.
Breeding Nest-builder.
Swimming level All levels.

Neolamprologus elongatus
(*Lamprologus brichardi*)
BRICHARD'S CICHLID
Description Grey body; elongated fins.
Length 8 cm (3 in).
Ease of keeping Difficult; aggressively territorial near breeding site.
Food Live foods; flake.
Breeding Egg-scatterer; spawns in substrate; parental.
Swimming level All levels, especially among rocks.

Neolamprologus leleupi longior
YELLOW CICHLID
Description Bright yellow body.
Length 8 cm (3 in).
Ease of keeping As *Neolamprologus elongatus*.
Food As *Neolamprologus elongatus*.
Breeding As *Neolamprologus elongatus*.
Swimming level As *Neolamprologus elongatus*.

Neolamprologus tretocephalus
BLUE-BANDED CICHLID
Description Blue and white bands on body.
Length 12 cm (5 in).
Ease of keeping Difficult; extremely territorial.
Food Live foods; flake.
Breeding Egg-depositor; spawns in caves.
Swimming level Midwater, especially among rocks.

Synodontis multipunctatus
CUCKOO CATFISH

Description Beige and brown body; white fins.
Length 20 cm (8 in).
Ease of keeping Easy; excellent community catfish.
Food Live foods, especially shrimp, bloodworm, and any crustacean.
Breeding Egg-depositor; spawns beside mouth-brooding cichlids; replaces cichlid eggs with own, in unique, fish parasitical, "cuckoo" method.
Swimming level Lower levels; among rocks.

Tropheus duboisi
DUBOIS'S CICHLID
Description Juvenile has black body, with white spots; mature fish has grey-black body, with single white stripe.
Length 8 to 10 cm (3 to 4 in).
Ease of keeping Difficult; pair-bonding; extremely aggressive; territorial when mature.
Food Live foods, especially shrimp and bloodworm; lettuce.
Breeding Mouth-brooder; parental.
Swimming level All levels, especially among rocks.

Tropheus moorei
MOORE'S CICHLID

Description Variously coloured bodies; red, yellow, and multi-coloured bands.
Length 8 to 10 cm (3 to 4 in).
Ease of keeping Difficult; pair-bonding; extremely aggressive; territorial when mature.
Food Live foods, especially shrimp and bloodworm. Also partial to most green foods, especially lettuce.
Breeding Mouth-brooder; parental.
Swimming level All levels, especially among rocks.

The finished tank

A convincing rocky lake aquarium contains a sensitive arrangement of many diverse and intriguing rock-types. This is an excellent aquarium for the creative aquarist, as there must be plenty of crannies, caves, and ledges, over which the territorial cichlids can stake a claim, and where individuals will be able to hide. It may be that you will have to remove overtly aggressive specimens from the aquarium, and perhaps exchange them (*see* p. 43). Be careful that you do not create a rock structure that is too heavy for your aquarium. It is also important to provide a series of quite exposed, flat rock surfaces, along with the shells which some of the fishes that are suitable for this aquarium need for spawning.

Lamprologus brevis
Like most cichlids, this tan-coloured species prefers a tank furnished with caves and crevasses.

YELLOW CICHLID
Neolamprologus leleupi longior
This brilliant-yellow fish stands out superbly against the dark rocks.

BRICHARD'S CICHLID
Neolamprologus elongatus
A species that lives in water up to 10 m (30 ft) deep.

There is no point in introducing plants to this aquarium – the fishes will eat or uproot any vegetation. Of course the growth of algae should not be discouraged; apart from providing a useful source of green food, it will, as long as it is not excessive, add to the overall authenticity and visual appeal of the tank. The sight of tiny air-bubbles caught among the algae – they are actually created by the algae – can be extremely attractive. If algal growth becomes too rampant, remove it from the glass of the aquarium with a scraper (you will probably need to do this periodically). Ensure that the water is kept hard and alkaline, and that the flow of water through the tank is very gentle.

DEEP-WATER CICHLID
Cyphotilapia frontosa
A magnificent cichlid that can grow much larger than most other species suitable for this tank.

Chalinochromis brichardi
A herbivorous cichlid that needs a regular supply of vegetable matter.

ORNATE CICHLID
Julidochromis ornatus
This thin cichlid has a long snout and a particularly small mouth.

DUBOIS'S CICHLID
Tropheus duboisi
The distribution of Dubois's cichlid is limited to Lake Tanganyika.

WEST AFRICA FLOODPLAIN SWAMP

AFRICAN SWAMP WATERS *Shallow swamps, dense with waterlogged vegetation and debris from flooded forests, provide a temporary home for many fish species.*

T HE FLOODPLAINS of Zaire, Gabon, and Cameroon in West Africa are criss-crossed by a latticework of small streams. At certain times of the year, these streams flood spectacularly, but at other times they may dry up completely. Swamps – which may be either temporary or permanent – often develop on the African floodplain (*see* p. 18), and these swamps are the inspiration for this tank. Floodplain swamps have a number of important features that should be taken into account when designing the tank. The water is very high indeed in humic acids, and it is often shallow. Sometimes little more than 10 cm (4 in) of water lies over the bed of peat or mud and rotting leaves. Fishes in these unusual waters can tolerate a pH as low as 3.5 and a hardness of less than 10 mg/litre CaCO$_3$, and although this tank should also contain soft, acid water, it does not need to be quite so extreme. The richness of the substrate means that aquatic plant life in the swamp is plentiful, with many plants growing right out of the water. The density of vegetation, however, means that little sunlight will penetrate through to the water. Stands of papyrus dominate the edges of many of the swamps, with a variety of submerged plants in areas of open water.

Insects are the main food of the fishes, so they take particularly well to live foods in the aquarium. This tank is inhabited by two species of killifish – the lyretail (*Aphyosemion australe*) and the firemouth epiplatys (*Epiplatys dageti*). Although these fishes are small, they are brilliantly coloured, presumably so that they can see each other through the murkiest of waters. Both species are usually found in the forest, where the swamps are likely to be permanent, and so, unlike savannah killifish, they do not die during the dry season (*see* p. 38). The lyretail and the epiplatys are both known to take mosquitoes in the wild, and as a result of this they have been introduced into many pools to combat these insects.

Planning the tank

EGG CACHE *The fishes of the swamp pools use the soft peat substrate as a place to bury their eggs.*

T O CREATE an aquarium based on a freshwater foodplain swamp, the size of the tank that you choose is not critical.

The temperature of the water should be around 21 to 23°C (70 to 74°F). Soft, acid water is essential. A good pH to aim for is 6, with a hardness of no more than 50 mg/litre CaCO$_3$. To help soften the water, aquarium peat can be added to the filter, while blackwater extract can be included in the tank water. If soft, mature water from another tank can be used, so much the better. To suggest water that in nature is constantly in the shadow of trees and debris, the tank should have a shadowy effect, but the level of lighting should be substantial enough to allow light to penetrate the dark, murky water and reach the plants.

An internal power filter has been chosen for this aquarium, as these filters are not too strong and are unlikely to disturb the peat on the tank bottom. (The high level of landscaping included in the tank makes an undergravel filter unsuitable.)

See also Heating, p. 163; pH and alkalinity in fresh water, p. 156; Lighting, p. 164; Power filters, p. 159.

Essential equipment

The dimensions of the tank used here are 91 × 46 × 38 cm (36 × 18 × 15 in). This tank will hold 159 litres (35 gallons) of water, and should not be stocked with more than 115 cm (45 in) of fishes. Tapwater is suitable for the tank, but it will generally need to be demineralized to reduce its hardness. The tank should be heated by two 150-watt heater/thermostats, and can be lit by a fluorescent tube. A power filter that gives a good flow, but is not so powerful that it will disturb the peat at the bottom of the tank, should be chosen. Also used in the tank are aquarium peat, interestingly patterned cork bark, and a sizeable mass of the dramatic red myriophyllum plant.

See also Stocking levels, p. 42; Preparing fresh water, p. 154; Heating, p. 163; Lighting, p. 164; Power filters, p.159.

INGREDIENTS

RED MYRIOPHYLLUM
Myriophyllum matogrossense
A dramatic South American plant that
thrives in the conditions of this tank.

AQUARIUM PEAT
The fabulous colours
of the fishes stand
out against the deep
black peat.

CORK BARK The bark of the cork oak
has a beautiful surface pattern.

Building the tank

Using aquarium peat for the substrate is an excellent way of achieving the dark, shadowy look that is characteristic of a floodplain swamp. Peat is soft and highly organic, and the killifish love to root around in it, particularly when egg-laying. The main feature of this tank is a large piece of hollow cork bark for the fishes to explore. Cork is resistant to water but, since it will float if not held down, large stones should be hidden inside it to weigh it down. From behind the bark a dense forest of red myriophyllum can be allowed to flow out across the tank.

See also Aquascaping, p. 48; Adding the plants, p. 49; Introducing the fishes, p. 50; Completing the tank, p. 50.

1 Lay down a base of peat to at least 5 cm (2 in), then add the cork bark. Once the bark is in position, add stones to hold it in place. Build up the peat behind the bark to anchor the plants.

2 Add the plants. These plants have been planted in baskets which give them a secure base in the peat. Planting before the water is added prevents the peat from floating up and clouding the water.

THE AQUASCAPED TANK

Colours of the rainbow
The inky-black peat is a superb foil for the warm colours of the killifish.

Focal point
The textured cork bark provides an excellent centrepiece for the tank.

Fast-grower
The red myriophyllum is a very quick-growing plant that needs regular pruning.

SUITABLE FISHES

Aphyosemion australe
LYRETAIL KILLIFISH
Description Often gold body; red speckles; orange delta fins.
Length 6 cm (2½ in).
Ease of keeping Easy.
Food Live foods, especially bloodworm; flake.
Breeding Egg-depositor; lays eggs on most items floating just beneath water's surface.
Swimming level Midwater to upper levels.

Aphyosemion gardneri
GARDNER'S KILLIFISH
Description Sky-blue body; red spots; either yellow or orange edges to fins.
Length 6 cm (2½ in).
Ease of keeping Fairly easy; this fish can be aggressive towards smaller fishes.
Food As *Aphyosemion australe*.
Breeding As *Aphyosemion australe*.
Swimming level Midwater to upper levels.

Aplocheilichthys flavipinnis
YELLOW-FINNED PANCHAX KILLIFISH
Description Distinctive silver-yellow body.
Length 4 cm (1½ in).
Ease of keeping Fairly easy; requires heavily planted tank.
Food Live foods, especially bloodworm; flake.
Breeding Egg-depositor; lays eggs among plants, over a period of several days.
Swimming level Midwater to upper levels.

Barbus callipterus
CLIPPER BARB
Description Pale brown body; distinctive rose stripes.
Length 8 cm (3 in).
Ease of keeping Fairly easy; thrives in large shoals.
Food Live foods, especially gnat-larvae and daphnia; flake.
Breeding Egg-scatterer.
Swimming level Midwater.

Chromidotilapia guntheri
GUNTHER'S CICHLID
Description Red body.
Length 12 to 14 cm (5 to 5½ in).
Ease of keeping Fairly easy; territorial when spawning.

Food Live foods, especially shrimp and bloodworm; flake.
Breeding Bi-parental substrate mouth-brooders.
Swimming level Midwater to lower levels.

Ctenopoma acutirostre
SPOTTED CLIMBING PERCH

Description Brown, speckled body; oval-shaped.
Length 12 cm (5 in).
Ease of keeping Easy.
Food Live foods, especially bloodworm; foodstick.
Breeding Unknown in the aquarium
Swimming level Midwater to upper levels.

Flestes (Brycinus) longipinnis
LONG-FINNED TETRA
Description Silver body; black bar at base of body and tail.
Length 14 cm (5½ in).
Ease of keeping Easy.
Food Live foods, especially bloodworm and tubifex; flake.
Breeding Egg-scatterer.
Swimming level Midwater to upper levels.

Epiplatys dageti
FIREMOUTH EPIPLATYS
Description Bright yellow body; vertical, grey-black bands beneath dorsal fin.
Length 5 to 6 cm (2 to 2½ in).
Ease of keeping Fairly easy; requires heavily planted tank.
Food Live foods; flake.
Breeding Egg-scatterer; lays eggs among plants.
Swimming level Midwater to upper levels.

Hemichromis lifalli
(H. bimaculatus)
JEWEL CICHLID
Description Red body, with distinctive silver speckles when breeding.

Length Male 8 cm (3 in); female 6 cm (2½ in).
Ease of keeping Difficult; tends to become very aggressive when spawning.
Food Live foods, especially shrimp and tubifex; flake.
Breeding Egg-depositor; lays eggs in caves or substrate.
Swimming level Midwater to lower levels.

Gnathonemus petersi
ELEPHANT-NOSED FISH

Description Black; soft-skinned; distinctive, pointed mouth extension.
Length 20 cm (8 in).
Ease of keeping Fairly difficult; territorial; must be kept in small aquarium to prevent bullying; needs soft sand substrate.
Food Live foods, especially shrimp and tubifex; flake.
Breeding Unknown in the aquarium.
Swimming level Lower levels.

Nanochromis splendens
NUDICEPS CICHLID
Description Olive-green body; female has blue-pink underside; striped tip to caudal fin.
Length 8 cm (3 in).
Ease of keeping Fairly easy.
Food Live foods, especially gnat-larvae and tubifex; flake.
Breeding Egg-depositor; in caves or substrate.
Swimming level Midwater to lower levels.

Notopterus afer
AFRICAN KNIFE FISH
Description Reticulated, grey-black body; elongated anal fin.
Length 60 cm (23½ in).
Ease of keeping Difficult; territorial and aggressive.
Food Live foods, especially earthworms; pellets.
Breeding Egg-scatterer.
Swimming level Midwater to lower levels.

Pantodon buchholzi
BUTTERFLY FISH
Description Brown; wing-shaped pectoral fins.
Length 10 cm (4 in).
Ease of keeping Easy. Peaceful fish, but can eat other fishes; needs plants in which to hide.
Food Live foods, especially tubifex. Also freeze-dried bloodworm and flake.
Breeding Egg-depositor; female places eggs just beneath the water's surface.
Swimming level Midwater to upper levels.

Pelvicachromis pulcher
KRIBENSIS

Description Gold body; distinctive plum belly; dark, horizontal bands.
Length 10 cm (4 in).
Ease of keeping Easy.
Food Live foods; flake.
Breeding Egg-depositor; lays eggs in caves and substrate.
Swimming level Midwater to lower levels.

Pseudocrenilibus philander
KENYAN MOUTH-BREEDER

Description Yellow; dwarf cichlid.
Length 10 cm (4 in).
Ease of keeping Fairly easy.
Food Accepts most live foods, especially bloodworm and gnat-larvae; flake.
Breeding Mouthbrooding cave spawner.
Swimming level Midwater to lower levels.

The finished tank

The extremely soft, acidic waters in this aquarium are home to two eye-catching species of killifish. Often a very shallow habitat, the murkiness of the floodplain swamp is accentuated by the dense fronds of red myriophyllum, here seen hanging over the cork bark. The red myriophyllum does not actually originate in this environment, but it is used here because it is more readily available to the aquarist than the region's indigenous plants. The peat substrate helps to keep the water soft, while providing a burrowing medium for the killifish. These may well breed in the tank, mating and burying their eggs in the soft and spongy peat, which has been included to recreate their familiar substrate. The sight

LYRETAIL KILLIFISH
Aphyosemion australe
Among the most colourful of all aquarium fishes, lyretails are alert hunters and will snap up live food that is added to the tank.

presented by some of the possible inhabitants for this aquarium, of them actually diving into the peat in order to spawn, can be extremely interesting to watch. Many of the smaller cichlids from this region are perfectly suitable for this aquarium. The lyretail is particularly notable for the fact that the female can take weeks to complete spawning, with the result that fry of varying ages may grow up in the aquarium together. Different species of *Aphyosemion* are likely to interbreed, so it is wise to keep only one species in an aquarium. When breeding both *Aphyosemion* and *Epiplatys* species in the same tank, it is a good idea to remove fry before cannibalism occurs.

FIREMOUTH EPIPLATYS
Epiplatys dageti
Efficient predators, these fishes are capable of a powerful jump if in pursuit of hovering insects.

Red myriophyllum
Myriophyllum matogrossense

Guppy
Poecilia reticulata

THE BRACKISH-WATER AQUARIUM

To many people interested in fishkeeping, establishing a brackish-water environment in a tank must seem relatively difficult. Brackish water occurs where fresh water meets sea water in estuaries. So depending on the time of year and general climatic conditions, as well as on the day-to-day ebb and flow of the tide, water salinity can vary dramatically. As well, these waters tend to be rich in nutrients, with sediments and detritus washed down from the faster-flowing upstream phases of rivers or skimmed off the land surface during

Fiddler crab
Uca spp.

Scat
Scatophagus argus

Fingerfish
Monodactylus argentus

periods of heavy rain and flooding, to become trapped within the tangled roots and fallen branches of the often lush vegetation typical of these regions. Brackish waters support a fascinating variety of fishes and plants, and this chapter explains how, with a little patience, you can create a reasonably accurate facsimile in your own home. The three specialist aquaria looked at in detail here are a Central America coastal stream tank, an East Africa mangrove swamp tank, and a Southeast Asia estuary tank.

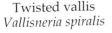

Twisted vallis
Vallisneria spiralis

Archer fish
Toxotes jaculator

CENTRAL AMERICA COASTAL STREAM

BLUE LAGOON *The calm waters of the Grey Whale Lagoon, Baja, Mexico, receive water from the coastal streams of the region.*

MUCH OF the coastal land of Central America is low-lying, with a multitude of rivers and streams. Some of these waters are fast-flowing, while others are slow-moving or static. Sea water mingles with the fresh waters of many of the coastal rivers and streams, making them brackish for a significant distance (*see* p. 19). This tank is based on a lazy, brackish, lowland stream.

The main rivers of the region are high in minerals, as much of the water runs down from the Sierra Madre Mountains, which are rich in limestone. Consequently, although many of the sidestreams are quite acidic due to decaying plant material, by the time the water reaches the estuary it is fairly hard and alkaline. Many of the lowland rivers contain very little vegetation, although a reasonable amount of plants has been included in this aquarium to act as shelter for the fishes.

Sadly, many of the rivers and lakes of the region have been severely polluted by sewage. The indigenous fish fauna has been further affected by the introduction of the food fish tilapia, and many waters have been choked by the introduction of the very invasive water hyacinth (*Eichornia crassipes*).

The region's fish fauna has a great deal in common with that of South America. Cichlids are common – although many of the Central American species are larger and more pugnacious than their South American relatives, and may therefore be difficult to keep in an aquarium.

In brackish waters, catfish and livebearers are the most common fishes. The latter group includes the green molly, which aquarists have bred into various forms of black molly, as well as the one-sided livebearer, the swordtail, and the sailfin molly.

Planning the tank

SOCIABLE CREATURES *The coastal stream aquarium is populated by peaceful, shoaling fishes.*

THE SIZE of the tank chosen for a Central American coastal stream habitat is not critical, as it does not rely on the inclusion of a wide range of fish species.

The temperature of the water should be around 23 to 25°C (72 to 77°F). Aim for a pH of 7 to 7.4, with a hardness of 200 mg/litre CaCO₃. As in marine tanks, you should keep a close eye on the quality of the water, making sure that the pH and hardness remain stable, and that the levels of ammonia, nitrites, and nitrates in the water do not become excessively high.

The level of lighting in the tank should be high, as much of the water in these shallow, slow-moving streams is naturally exposed to the sun. A power filter may be the best

choice here; it gives the best flexibility in landscaping, and the large amount of wood and pebbles in the aquarium make an undergravel filter unsuitable.

Marine salt should be added to the aquarium to maintain a salinity level less than a twentieth that of of sea water, at 1.5 grams per litre (¼ oz per gallon). This should provide a specific gravity in the region of 1.0002, and a salinity of between 7.6 and 14 ppt, suitably approximating the waters characteristic of this type of environment.

See also Heating, p. 163; pH and alkalinity in sea water, p. 157; Lighting, p. 164; Power filters, p. 159; Measuring salinity, p. 155; Specific gravity, p. 155.

Essential equipment

The dimensions of the tank used here are 91 × 46 × 38 cm (36 × 18 × 15 in). This tank will hold 159 litres (35 gallons) of water, and should not be stocked with more than 115 cm (45 in) of fishes. Tapwater is generally suitable for the tank; it should be combined with suitable synthetic mixes of minerals. The tank should be heated by two 150-watt heater/thermo-stats, and can be lit by a fluorescent tube. A power filter that gives a good flow should be chosen. Also used in this tank are pea gravel, silver sand, rocks, flat pebbles, treated drift-wood, and a selection of plants.

See also Stocking levels, p. 42; Preparing sea water, p. 155; Heating, p. 163; Lighting, p. 164; Power filters, p. 159.

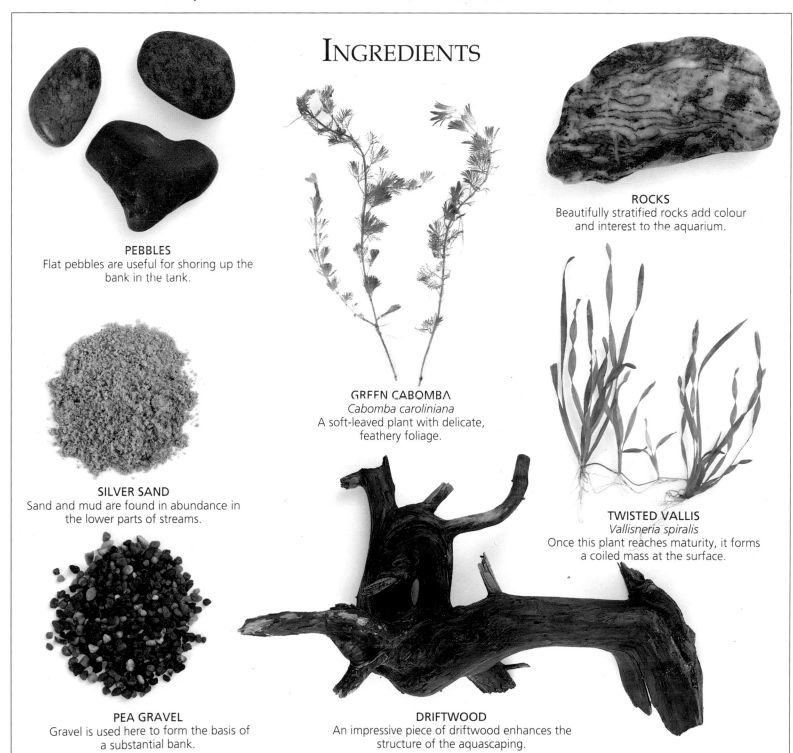

INGREDIENTS

PEBBLES
Flat pebbles are useful for shoring up the bank in the tank.

SILVER SAND
Sand and mud are found in abundance in the lower parts of streams.

PEA GRAVEL
Gravel is used here to form the basis of a substantial bank.

GREEN CABOMBA
Cabomba caroliniana
A soft-leaved plant with delicate, feathery foliage.

DRIFTWOOD
An impressive piece of driftwood enhances the structure of the aquascaping.

ROCKS
Beautifully stratified rocks add colour and interest to the aquarium.

TWISTED VALLIS
Vallisneria spiralis
Once this plant reaches maturity, it forms a coiled mass at the surface.

Building the tank

This tank depicts part of a low bank in an estuary stream. The large piece of driftwood that dominates the tank is heavy and unwieldy. If you plan to use a similar piece, take care not to damage the tank when moving and securing it into position. As a rule, the coastal streams of this region do not foster a great deal of vegetation. However the freely swim-ming young of the livebearer species need some form of cover when they are newly born. It is therefore advisable, if you wish to encourage breeding among your fishes, to stock this tank fairly heavily with plants.

See also Aquascaping, p. 48; Adding the plants, p. 49; Introducing the fishes, p. 50; Completing the tank, p. 50.

1 Build a bank of gravel, rising to halfway up the side of the tank. Then add the driftwood. A large and unusual piece like this provides an element of drama.

2 Cover the gravel bank with a layer of silver sand. The sand will stay in place more securely if a few handfuls of flat pebbles are scattered over it.

3 Add the water and plants to the bank. The green plants look particularly effective if they are positioned close to the reddish-brown driftwood.

THE AQUASCAPED TANK

Safe retreats
The arrangement of the ingredients ensures that there is shelter for fishes at all levels.

Intriguing shape
This impressive piece of wood gives the tank a stunning visual impact.

Firmly rooted
The vallis thrives in sand, reproducing itself by means of runners.

SUITABLE FISHES

Aequidens portalegrensis
BROWN ACARA

Description Brown body; black edges to scales.
Length 15 cm (6 in).
Ease of keeping Easy.
Food Live foods, especially shrimp and earthworm. Also pellet and flake.
Breeding Egg-depositor; parental.
Swimming level Midwater to lower levels.

Aequidens pulcher
BLUE ACARA
Description Grey body; blue speckles; eye stripe.
Length 15 cm (6 in).
Ease of keeping As *Aequidens portalegrensis*.
Food Live foods, especially shrimp and earthworm; flake.
Breeding As *Aequidens portalegrensis*.
Swimming level As *Aequidens portalegrensis*.

Aspredo cotylephorus
GUYANAN BANJO CATFISH

Description Black-and-white patterned body.
Length 30 cm (12 in).
Ease of keeping Newly imported specimens require time to adjust to variances in salt and pH levels. Live food and a darkened aquarium help.
Food Shrimp, tubifex, bloodworm; tablet food.
Breeding Female carries eggs until fry hatch.
Swimming level Midwater to lower levels.

Brachyraphis episcopi
THE BISHOP
Description Gold body; dark borders to scales; red and green lines along sides.
Length Male 4 cm (1⅓ in); female 5 cm (2 in).
Ease of keeping Easy.
Food Live foods; flake.
Breeding Livebearer.
Swimming level All levels.

Callichthys callichthys
CALLICHTHYS
Description Grey-brown.
Length 8 cm (3 in).
Ease of keeping Easy.
Food Live foods, especially shrimp and bloodworm; flake.
Breeding Bubble-nest breeder.
Swimming level Lower levels.

Cichlasoma severum
GREEN (GOLD) SEVERUM

Description Green-brown body; vertical stripes. Also yellow.
Length 18 cm (7 in).
Ease of keeping Easy.
Food Live foods; particularly partial to shrimp and earthworm; pellet; flake.
Breeding Egg-depositor; parental.
Swimming level Midwater.

Exodon paradoxus
TWO-SPOT TETRA
Description Yellow body with red ventral fins; large, black spot beneath dorsal fin and on base of caudal fin.
Length 12 cm (5 in).
Ease of keeping Active and aggressive. This fish is only suitable for large tanks.
Food Will eat both live and frozen foods; flake.
Breeding Egg-scatterer.
Swimming level Midwater.

Heterandria bimaculata
TWO-SPOTTED HETERANDRIA
Description Blue body with rose tint; black edges to scales; distinctive spots on gill cover and caudal peduncle.
Length Male 8 cm (3 in); female 15 cm (6 in).
Ease of keeping Easy.
Food Accepts most forms of vegetable matter; flake.
Breeding Livebearer.
Swimming level All levels.

Hypophthalmus edentatus
PLANKTON CATFISH
Description Dark-topped grey body; streamlined to suit fast-flowing water.
Length 30 cm (12 in).
Ease of keeping Fairly easy; requires high oxygen levels.
Food Accepts most live foods (microcrustaceans are essential to this species); flake.
Breeding Unknown in the aquarium.
Swimming level Upper levels.

Metynnis hypsauchen
FRUIT-EATING PIRAHNA (RED HOOK METYNNIS)
Description Silver body; bright-red anal fin.
Length Lengths vary from 12 to 15 cm (5 to 6 in).
Ease of keeping Thrives in medium-sized shoals; requires space provided by large aquarium.
Food Accepts most foods, especially live foods and fruit – hence its name.
Breeding Egg-scatterer.
Swimming level Midwater.

Metynnis schreitmuelleri
SCHREITNELLER'S METYNNIS
Description Silver body; spotted dorsal fin; red edge to anal fin.
Length 15 cm (6 in).
Ease of keeping Accepts most foods, especially live foods and most kinds of fruit.
Food As *Metynnis hypsauchen*.
Breeding As *Metynnis hypsauchen*.
Swimming level As *Metynnis hypsauchen*.

Parauchenoglanis geleatus
DRIFTWOOD CATFISH
Description Brown and beige mottled body.
Length 8 cm (3 in).
Ease of keeping Easy.
Food Live foods, especially shrimp and earthworm; flake.
Breeding Internal fertilization; egg-layer.
Swimming level Lower levels.

Poecilia latipinna
SAILFIN MOLLY

Description Olive-yellow body; blue, red, and green flecks. Male has gonopodium and large, impressive dorsal fin, which is erected in order to deter rival males, or to court females during breeding period.
Length Male 10 cm (4 in); female 12 cm (5 in).
Ease of keeping Easy.
Food Loves most forms of fresh, green food; flake.
Breeding Livebearer.
Swimming level All levels.

Poecilla reticulata
GUPPY
(see p. 51)

Poecilla sphenops
BLACK MOLLY
(see p. 51)

Xiphophorus helleri
GREEN SWORDTAIL
(see p. 51)

Xiphophorous hybrid
SWORDTAIL
Most common variety. Red body, sometimes with exaggerated finnage and double "swords". Otherwise as *Xiphophorus helleri*.
(see p. 51)

Xiphophorus variatus hybrid
VARIATUS PLATY
(see p. 51)

The finished tank

Water and wind erosion, together with the vast amounts of sediment that flow downstream, have sculpted the marshes and sandy banks of the coastline and estuaries of Central America. This peaceful tank, based around a bank of sand and a large piece of driftwood, represents a small cross-section of one of these brackish-water environments. Wild forms of livebearer, like the swordtail featured here, may be difficult to obtain, as many dealers prefer to stock the more colourful, artificially developed strains. Another livebearer, the guppy, is available in an enormous variety of colour strains. All of the species that can be kept in this aquarium are hardy, so this tank is relatively easy to run.

GREEN SWORDTAIL
Xiphophorus helleri
Swordtails are likely to eat their own young if the newborn fishes are not removed to a separate tank.

GUPPY
Poecilia reticulata
Originally discovered in
Venezuela, the guppy has
now been introduced to
waters all over the world.

DRIFTWOOD CATFISH
Parauchenoglanis geleatus
The peaceful driftwood
catfish can easily be
mistaken for a stone.

HORSE-FACE LOACH
Acanthopsis choirorhynchus
From a different environment to
that of the finished tank, but
useful while the aquarium matures.

GREEN CABOMBA
Cabomba caroliniana

TWISTED VALLIS
Vallisneria spiralis

EAST AFRICA MANGROVE SWAMP

AMID WOOD AND WATER *Characteristically contorted roots rise out of the still, muddy waters of this mangrove swamp.*

MANGROVE SWAMPS are common throughout the tropics, particularly around the estuaries of the major rivers (*see* p. 19), and it is on one of the thickly wooded coastal swamps that this tank is based.

The Rhizophoraceae family of plants is specifically classed as "mangroves", but the term is used more widely for any of the thicket-forming plants that may grow in these coastal swamps. Many mangroves have aerial roots hanging in tangles and covered in mosses. Mangroves also have strong buttress roots, that reach down into the ground at strange angles, guided by the effects of the tides and exposed by tidal erosion. Both of these kinds of root help the plants to breathe. The mangrove reproduces by allowing germinated seeds to fall into the sediment of the surrounding mud or sand, which is normally rich in organic material brought down by the river.

The sandy or muddy bed of the mangrove swamp constantly shifts with the tides, so plants that do not have roots that are as deep and substantial as those of mangroves have very little chance of becoming established. The swamp waters are often strongly brackish, with positive levels of oxygen.

Three genera of the mudskipper live in different parts of the swamp. *Periophthalmus* spp. spends some time on land, using its pectoral fins to "walk" down to the water for the occasional dip; *Boleophthalmus* spp. lives in the intertidal zone left dry at low tide; and *Scartelaos* spp. follows the tide and stays near the waterline. Many well-known species of crab, such as fiddler crabs (*Uca* spp.), land hermit crabs (*Coenobita* spp.), ghost crabs (*Ocypode* spp.), and the mangrove and waving crabs of the genera *Sarmatium, Dotilla, Sesarma,* and *Metoprograspus,* can also be included in this tank.

Planning the tank

BEST OF BOTH WORLDS *The inhabitants of this aquarium need to divide their time between land and water, so care should be taken to provide authentic examples of both habitats.*

THE SIZE of the aquarium needed to create a mangrove swamp environment depends largely upon the maturity and the natural demands of the specimens that you plan to keep. A number of the possible inhabitants for this aquarium will become quite big as they mature, and certain species will require a greater depth of water (*see* p. 119) to that shown in this aquarium. The possible ratios of land to water, the size of the inmates, and of course the demands created by your own aquascaping, or even landscaping, must all be taken into account when deciding upon the size of your tank.

The temperature of the water should be maintained at 24 to 29°C (75 to 85°F), with a pH of around 8. As in marine tanks, you should take care to keep a close eye on the water quality, making sure that the pH and hardness remain quite stable, and that the levels of ammonia, nitrites, and nitrates present in the water do not become too great. The level of lighting for this aquarium should be standard.

Marine salt should be added to the tank at 8 grams per litre (1¼ oz per gallon). This should provide a specific gravity of 1.005 to 1.01, and a salinity of between 7.6 and 14 ppt. A power filter is the most suitable form of filtration; if an undergravel filter is used, dead areas may be created where organic matter will decompose and release toxins.

See also Heating, p. 163; pH and alkalinity in sea water, p. 157; Lighting, p. 164; Power filters, p. 159; Measuring salinity, p. 155; Specific gravity, p. 155.

Essential equipment

The dimensions of the tank used here are 91 × 46 × 38 cm (36 × 18 × 15 in). To recreate a mangrove swamp in this style, the tank should not be filled with more than 45 litres (10 gallons) of water. Tapwater is generally suitable for this tank; it should be combined with suitable marine salt mixes. As there is relatively little water in the tank, it may be heated by one 150-watt heater/thermostat only, and lit by a fluorescent tube. The power filter should be a small model, as there is no need for a strong flow through this tank. Also used in this tank, to conjure up the singular combination of land and water, are silver sand, rocks, pebbles, curio wood, bogwood, twigs, mangrove plants, dead coral, and shells.

See also Stocking levels, p. 40; Preparing sea water, p. 155; Heating, p. 163; Lighting, p. 164; Power filters, p. 159.

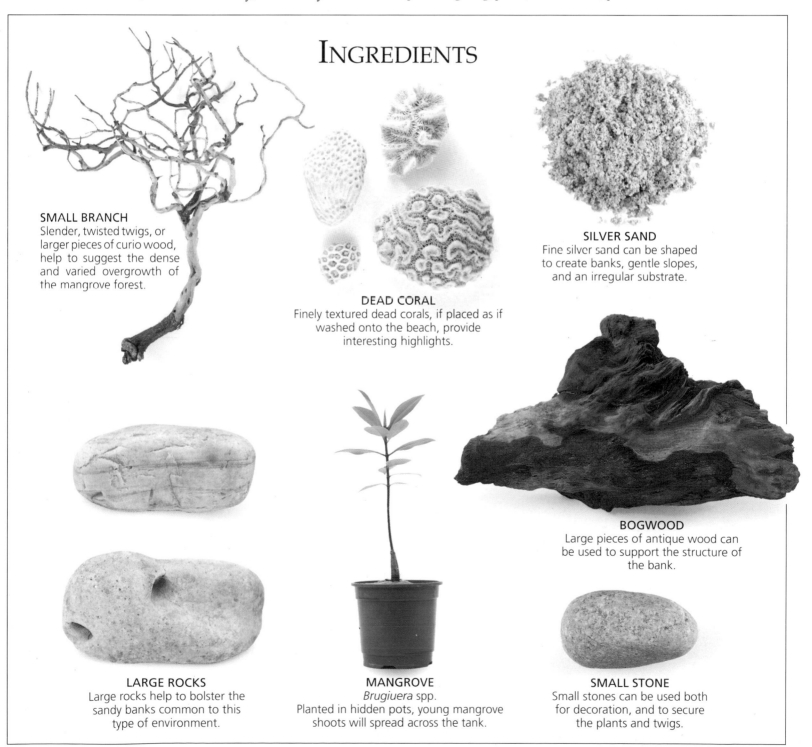

INGREDIENTS

SMALL BRANCH
Slender, twisted twigs, or larger pieces of curio wood, help to suggest the dense and varied overgrowth of the mangrove forest.

DEAD CORAL
Finely textured dead corals, if placed as if washed onto the beach, provide interesting highlights.

SILVER SAND
Fine silver sand can be shaped to create banks, gentle slopes, and an irregular substrate.

BOGWOOD
Large pieces of antique wood can be used to support the structure of the bank.

LARGE ROCKS
Large rocks help to bolster the sandy banks common to this type of environment.

MANGROVE
Brugiuera spp.
Planted in hidden pots, young mangrove shoots will spread across the tank.

SMALL STONE
Small stones can be used both for decoration, and to secure the plants and twigs.

Building the tank

A mangrove swamp presents a fascinating creative challenge for the aquarist. An interesting way to present this habitat is to build an aquarium in which a substantial part of the substrate is above the water level, with the tank no more than half full of water. Of course, you will have to make sure that any unsubmerged area is well supported. This tank is based on a bank of sand that rises gradually out of the shallow water, bearing a dense jungle of mangrove, wood, and twigs. The large amount of sand in the tank means that the substrate is liable to shift occasionally, and so the bank should be solidly bolstered by wood and rocks.

See also Introducing the fishes, p. 50; Completing the tank, p. 50.

1 Lay a base of sand at least 4 cm (1½ in) deep, then place the mangrove shoot pots and the feature rocks in position. When deciding upon the location of the mangrove pots, remember that you will have to provide suitable cover with which to hide them.

2 Build up the bank around blocks of bogwood and the mangrove pots. Fill the gaps between the pieces of wood with pebbles, all of the time checking that you are creating as stable a structure as possible. The pots should be thoroughly concealed.

3 Add the water, patting any sand that falls from the bank back into position. The pieces of curio wood and the twigs can now be added. Try not to use them solely as ornaments – you may be able to incorporate them within the structure of the bank.

THE AQUASCAPED TANK

Resting places
Flat-topped rocks at the waterline provide platforms for the mudskippers.

Woody maze
Interlacing the curio wood with thin, flexible twigs helps to evoke the atmosphere of a thick forest floor.

Mangrove fringe
A line of young mangrove shoots suggests the edge of a shoreline thicket.

SUITABLE INHABITANTS

The exceptional nature of this aquarium should not be considered restrictive. In some senses, the challenge of establishing an authentic habitat for mudskippers and fiddler crabs offers the aquarist far greater imaginative recourse than usual.

Mangroves in the aquarium

The mangrove swamp environment is distinguished more, perhaps, by its vegetation than by its animal inhabitants. Mangroves thrive when rooted in salt water. The salinity, however, and in some cases the humidity, that characterize the ideal conditions for maintaining them, directly affect the introduction of other plants to the aquarium. Black mangrove (*Avicennia marina*), the type shown in this aquarium – a member of the *Brugiuera* genus – is one of several forms available from specialist stockists. The following genera form the basis of a true mangrove swamp:

Brugiuera spp.
MANGROVE
Found nearest to dry land

Rhizophora spp.
RED MANGROVE
Occupy central region of mangrove swamp.

Sonneratia spp.
PIONEER MANGROVE
Occupy seaward border of mangrove swamp; breathe through aerial roots, from which spread lateral roots

Alternative vegetation

It is, of course, quite possible to also incorporate houseplants and a variety of palms, if they are carefully potted, so that their roots do not come into contact with the salt water.

— SUITABLE FISHES —

The incorporation of species other than those shown in this aquarium is likely to raise difficulties. A healthy environment for mudskippers and fiddler crabs demands almost equal proportions of land and water. To keep, for example, any of the bream listed below, and perhaps some anemones, the depth of water will have to be increased – usually this occurs at the expense of the land, as few aquarists will wish to actually invest in another, larger tank. It is therefore preferable to keep mudskippers and fiddler crabs separately from other types of fish. Most invertebrates present less of a problem, unless they are overtly aggressive.

Abudefduf annulatus
YELLOWTAIL SERGEANT MAJOR
Description Silver body; black vertical bands; yellow tail.
Length 8 cm (3 in).
Ease of keeping Fairly difficult; requires salinity approaching that of sea water; generally nervous, solitary fish; needs hiding places, such as rocks.
Food Live foods; flake.
Breeding Egg-depositor; guards eggs; unknown in the aquarium.
Swimming level Midwater.

Chelon labrosus
GREY MULLET
Description Silver-grey body.
Length Adults too large for the aquarium; fry of 8 to 10 cm (3 to 4 in) ideal.
Ease of keeping Easy; require plenty of swimming room; water temperature must be maintained above 10°C, (50°F).
Food Live foods, especially earthworm; pieces of fish; cooked mussel.
Breeding Egg-scatterer; unknown in the aquarium.
Swimming level All levels.

Rhabdosargus sarba
SILVER BREAM
Description Silver body; each scale has gold centre.
Length Mature fishes grow to 75 cm (30 in); only smaller specimens suitable for the aquarium.
Ease of keeping Easy; water temperature must be maintained below 10°C (50°F).
Food Accepts most live foods, especially snails.
Breeding Egg-scatterer; unknown in the aquarium.
Swimming level All levels.

Periophthalmus barbarus
MUDSKIPPER

Description Light brown body; prominent eyes (the name "*Periophthalminae*" means "able to turn eyes at will"), moistens eye by drawing eye-ball back inside socket. Very good eyesight. Stores water in gill cavities to keep gills moist when out of water; the water supply must be replenished after feeding, when the reserve is automatically discharged.
Length 15 cm (6 in).
Ease of keeping Easy; spends large proportion of time out of water, and therefore requires access to dry rocks, or similar land substitute.
Food Live foods, and small pieces of fish.
Breeding Unknown in the aquarium; presumed to spawn in holes, female guards nest.
Swimming level Lower levels; frequently climbs clear of water.

Spondyliosoma canthurus
BLACK BREAM (OLD WIFE)
Description Yellow-grey back; silvery sides; fins occasionally spotted white.
Length Only specimens smaller than 15 cm (6 in) suitable for the aquarium.
Ease of keeping Easy; water temperature must be maintained below 10°C (50°F).
Food Accepts most live foods, especially brine shrimp, and chopped fish or prawns.
Breeding Egg-scatterer; unknown in the aquarium.
Swimming level All levels.

Tetraodon fluviatilis
GREEN PUFFERFISH
Description Generally green back with black spots; white or grey underside. The body of this species is covered with many relatively small spines.
Length 18 cm (7 in).
Ease of keeping Fairly easy.
Food Chopped meat; flake.
Breeding Egg-depositor.
Swimming level Midwater.

— INVERTEBRATES —

Actinia equina
BEADLET ANEMONE
(*see* p. 149)

Anemonia viridis
SNAKELOCKS ANEMONE

(*see* p. 149)

Uca spp.
FIDDLER CRAB
Description Various; often brown or purple body; generally tan legs.
Length Fiddler crabs have a small carapace (bony shield covering back) normally approaching 5 cm (2 in) in diameter, and the male has an extremely large front claw. This overdeveloped front claw is actually of no use for feeding; it is instead waved at other males during territorial disputes.
Ease of keeping Easy. This species is often poorly treated – like *Periophthalmus barbarus*, it cannot survive in completely aquatic marine tanks, and requires some depth of sand for the construction of its burrows. In nature, these burrows retain a life-supporting bubble of air when they are covered by the tide. Fiddler crabs are ideal tankmates for *Periophthalmus barbarus*.
Food Normally sifts through sand for food, extracting organic matter, but will accept small pieces of fish, and similar scraps.
Breeding Unknown in the aquarium.
Swimming level Not applicable; the fiddler crab lives on sea-bottom and land.

The finished tank

This is a quiet, slow-moving, and in fact quite unique aquarium, that displays as much life out of the water as in it. All of the creatures pictured here divide their time between the water and the land. The mudskippers – which remain out of water for considerable periods – will happily climb up the branches of wood and across the mangrove shoots. They can sit up to survey the tank, or leap across the bank, using their well-developed pectoral fins. In the wild they can leap as far as 2 m (6 ft), so take great care when lifting up the lid of the tank. The crabs will spend most of their time moving between the water and the land – they need to dip themselves in the water regularly, in order to keep their bodies moist.

Be careful not to choose carnivorous crabs and, depending upon the size of your aquarium, do not allow any of them to grow too large. Male fiddler crabs are actually unable to use their overdeveloped front claws for feeding – they will chew the mud in the tank, in order to extract organic matter. The claw is used during territorial disputes, when its waved at other males of the species. The crabs will dig burrows both above and below the high-tide line, which you will be able to identify from the mounds of sand and mud that they remove during excavation. In nature, when these burrows are periodically covered by the tide, the crabs can remain "underwater" by virtue of the air that the burrows retain.

ROCK PLATFORMS
Use the rocks both structurally, and to provide isolated platforms for the mudskippers.

MUDSKIPPER
Periophthalmus barbarus
These intriguing fishes have excellent sight (*see* p. 119).

FIDDLER CRAB
Uca spp.
In the wild, this large-clawed crab scavenges for organic debris on the shore.

MANGROVE
Brugiuera spp.

SANDY BANK
To ensure that the sandy bank does not collapse, bolster it with other materials, such as the rocks and bogwood that are used in this aquarium.

ALTERNATIVE VEGETATION
As long as you follow the appropriate guidelines (*see* p. 119), a variety of other plants can be introduced to the aquarium.

SOUTHEAST ASIA ESTUARY

COASTAL JUNGLE *Heavy woods and flats of sand and mud are found at the mouth of the Cigenter River, Ujung Kulon, Java.*

THE WATERS of river mouths are generally rich in food that has been washed down-river, and therefore tend to be full of fish life. The estuaries of Southeast Asia (*see* p. 19) are no exception, and many of this region's estuarine fishes are caught in huge numbers by local people for food.

The sediment that pours down the muddy Asiatic rivers ensures that the shape of the estuary environment is constantly changing. Life there is tolerant enough to withstand the fluctuations in salinity that come with the tides. These fluctuations are particularly pronounced when heavy tropical rains flush flood waters down rivers and out into the estuary.

Versatile scavengers like the fingerfish and the scat do particularly well in these brackish waters. Indeed the latin name for the scat, *Scatophagus,* refers to the fish's habit of feeding on decomposing waste such us that pumped out of sewage outflows or trapped by the roots of mangrove trees.

The archer fish lurks beneath the plants that overhang the sand and mud of the estuary, and is renowned for its ability to "shoot down" insects, sometimes while they are actually in flight, with a powerful jet of water expelled from its mouth. The black- and orange-banded bumblebee goby, on the other hand, feeds on small animals that inhabit the bottom of the estuary. Many of the fishes that are suitable for this brackish-water aquarium are equally happy in sea water. A variety of species actually spend most of their lives in the sea, and only enter the estuary in order to feed. Other species are born, and then develop, entirely within the confines of an estuarine environment. Upon reaching maturity, they swim out to sea, where they spend the remainder of their lives.

Planning the tank

HIDING PLACES *The design of this tank provides plenty of places for these estuarine fish species to hide in.*

THE TANK that you choose to recreate a tropical estuary should be at least 90 cm (36 in) long, as the inhabitants need plenty of room to shoal, and some of them have the potential to reach a considerable size.

The temperature of the water should be maintained at 24 to 29°C (75 to 85°F), with a pH of around 8. As in marine tanks, you should keep a close eye on the water quality, making sure that the pH and salinity remain stable, and that the levels of ammonia, nitrites, and nitrates in the water do not become too high.

The level of lighting in the tank should be standard, and the most appropriate form of filtration is a power filter, bearing in mind the good level of plant growth here. The tank water will require regular partial water changes (*see* p. 45). Marine salt should be added to maintain a salinity level less than a tenth that of sea water, at 3 grams per litre (½ oz per gallon). This will give a specific gravity reading in the region of 1.0015. Some of the fishes, such as the scats, will need double this level as they grow, but be careful to make this adjustment gradually, as it will place a strain upon the aquarium vegetation. Given enough time, however, most of the plants should adapt successfully.

See also Heating, p. 163; pH and alkalinity in sea water, p. 157; Lighting, p. 164; Power filters, p. 159; Measuring salinity, p. 155; Specific gravity, p. 155.

Essential Equipment

The dimensions of the tank used here are 91 × 46 × 38 cm (36 × 18 × 15 in). This tank will hold 159 litres (35 gallons) of water, and should not be stocked with more than 115 cm (45 in) of fishes. Tapwater is generally suitable for the tank; it should be combined with suitable synthetic marine salt mixes. The tank should be heated by two 150-watt heater/thermostats, and can be lit by a fluorescent tube. A power filter with a standard flow should be chosen. Also used in this tank are pea gravel, silver sand, a selection of pebbles, curio wood, slate, and several plants.

See also Stocking levels, p. 42; Preparing sea water, p. 155; Heating, p. 163; Lighting, p. 164; Power filters, p. 159.

INGREDIENTS

PEA GRAVEL
This gravel is weighty enough to anchor the aquarium plants.

SILVER SAND
Mixed with the pea gravel, sand forms part of the substrate in the tank.

VALLIS *Vallisneria asiatica*
A fast-growing plant that is sometimes known as wild celery.

SLATE
Pieces of slate can be used to shore up the bank at the back of the tank.

PEBBLES
Attractive pebbles with a distinctive grain give character to the tank.

GIANT HYGROPHILA *Nomaphila stricta*
If it grows as high as the waterline, this woody plant may produce a purple flower.

CURIO WOOD
Gather together a good collection of wood to create the effect of a mass of roots.

JAVA FERN *Microsorium pteropus*
Young ferns will grow from the edges of the leaves of this plant.

Building the tank

In this tank, the aim is to recreate a corner of an Asian coastal estuary, where mangroves grow right up to the shoreline. Large amounts of curio wood are used to produce the effect of a mass of roots. Once the tank has become established, nooks and crannies will develop in the bank, allowing the fishes to weave their way under and over the roots. Planting should be fairly heavy. As the plants grow, the effect should be of a glorious confusion of life. The large amount of wood in the tank will give the water a yellow cast, which can be accentuated by the addition of blackwater extract.

See also Aquascaping, p. 48; Adding the plants, p. 49; Introducing the fishes, p. 50; Completing the tank, p. 50.

1 Mix the silver sand with the gravel and build it up to halfway up the back of the tank. Use pieces of slate inserted horizontally to shore up the bank.

2 Cover the sand and gravel with a layer of damp sand. Leave areas beneath the pieces of slate unfilled to create caves suitable for the fishes to hide in.

3 Embed the pieces of curio wood in the top of the bank, allowing them to run down towards the front of the tank. Scatter a few pebbles and more gravel over the tank floor.

THE AQUASCAPED TANK

New growth
Young plants of the Java fern will attach themselves to whatever they can in the tank.

Lofty bank
The tall bank of sand and gravel represents the side of the estuarine river.

Cloud of sand
The fine sand has made the tank cloudy, but this will clear once the tank has had time to settle.

SUITABLE FISHES

Arius seemani
SHARK CATFISH

Description Silver body; black-tipped fins before fully mature.
Size 30 cm (12 in).
Ease of keeping Fairly easy; generally happiest in shoals; requires large aquarium.
Food Live foods, especially crustaceans; flake.
Breeding Mouth-brooder.
Swimming level Midwater to lower levels.

Brachygobius doriae
BUMBLE BEE GOBY
Description Black and orange bands on body.
Length 3 cm (1 in).
Ease of keeping Fairly difficult; prefers to be kept separate from large fishes.
Food Live foods, especially microcrustaceans and bloodworm; flake.
Breeding Egg-depositor; spawns in caves or substrate.
Swimming level Lower levels.

Chanda ranga
GLASS FISH

Description Light amber to green, almost transparent body; black dorsal fin; artificially coloured specimens available.
Length 6 cm (2½ in).
Ease of keeping Fairly easy; prefers shoals.
Food Live foods, especially bloodworm and tubifex; flake.
Breeding Egg-scatterer; difficult

to breed in the aquarium.
Swimming level Midwater.

Datnoides microlepis
TIGER FISH
Description Beige body; broad, black, vertical stripes.
Size 30 cm (12 in).
Ease of keeping Fairly easy; although a predator, easy to keep with larger fishes.
Food Live foods, especially earthworm; prawn; small pieces of fish; pellet.
Breeding Unknown in the aquarium.
Swimming level Midwater; prefers plant thickets.

Etroplus maculatus
ORANGE (GREEN-GOLD) CHROMIDE

Description Green or orange body, lined with red spots; black blotch on anal fin.
Length 8 cm (3 in).
Ease of keeping Easy.
Food Live foods, especially bloodworm; spinach; flake.
Breeding Egg-depositor; spawns in substrate.
Swimming level Midwater.

Etroplus suratensis
SPECKLED CHROMIDE
Description Distinctive rows of silver spots on body.
Length 30 cm (12 in).
Ease of keeping Fairly difficult. Generally this fish is too robust to keep with smaller or nervous fishes; requires the space provided by a large aquarium.
Food Accepts most live foods, especially bloodworm and earthworm; flake.

Breeding Egg-depositor; spawns in substrate.
Swimming level Midwater.

Monodactylus argenteus
FINGERFISH (MONO ANGEL)
Description Silver body; yellow bands on ventral fins.
Length 15 to 20 cm (6 to 8 in).
Ease of keeping Fairly difficult; occasionally nervous when first inroduced to the aquarium; prefers shoals.
Food Live foods, especially shrimp and chopped earthworms; lettuce; spinach; peas; flake.
Breeding Egg-scatterer; difficult in the aquarium.
Swimming level Midwater.

Mugilogobius valigouva
COMMON GOBY
Description Olive-green body; lightly banded.
Length 3 cm (1 in).
Ease of keeping Easy; prefers small aquarium.
Food Live foods, especially shrimp and daphnia.
Breeding Egg-depositor; spawns in caves or substrate.
Swimming level Lower levels.

Scatophagus argus
SPOTTED SCAT
Description Large, black spots on body; laterally flat – almost box-shaped.
Length 15 to 20 cm (6 to 8 in).
Ease of keeping Fairly easy; needs varied diet.
Food Live foods, especially chopped earthworm; spinach; peas; lettuce; flake.
Breeding Egg-scatterer; difficult in the aquarium.
Swimming level Midwater.

Stigmatogobius sadanundio
LANCER (KNIGHT) GOBY
Description Cream-white body; black dots; distinctive extension to dorsal fin.
Length 8 cm (3 in).
Ease of keeping Fairly difficult.
Food Accepts most live foods, especially shrimp and tubifex; occasionally flake. Sometimes requires live shrimp when first introduced to the aquarium.
Breeding Egg-depositor; spawns in caves or substrate.
Swimming level Lower levels.

Toxotes jaculator
ARCHER FISH

Description Silver body; normally five triangular black saddle-marks along dorsal-lateral area; well-developed, mobile eyes; protruding lower jaw. In order to feed, the archer fish contracts its gill covers, forcing a powerful jet of water – the characteristic spitting – along a tube between its tongue and the roof of its mouth, and knocks down insects on to the surface of the water.
Length 14 cm (5½ in).
Ease of keeping Fairly difficult. This fish can occasionally be hard to feed, due to the unusual manner in which it catches its prey. Some aquarists prefer to keep archer fish in an environment similar to that required by mudskippers (Periophthalminae), and certain species of crab, in which land and water are combined in fairly equal proportions (*see* pp. 116 to 121). This makes it possible for suitable vegetation to be introduced to the aquarium (*see* p. 119), that can be cultivated to overhang the surface of the water. If insects, usually flies, are then also introduced to the aquarium, they will eventually settle on branches and leaves within the spitting range of the archer fish. Of course, in an aquarium with no land area, the archer fish will rely upon its extraordinary ability to shoot down insects while they are actually in flight.
Food Requires varied diet; live foods, especially insects – normally flies – and bloodworm; will also accept flake.
Breeding Unknown in the aquarium.
Swimming level Midwater to upper levels.

The finished tank

This lively tank is modelled on a world of continual change – the wooded estuarine shoreline of one of Asia's great rivers. Estuaries have few permanent inhabitants, and most of the fishes in this tank are periodic visitors, taking advantage of the food that becomes available in the estuary during times of flooding. Created on a substrate of mud and sand, the tank is heavily planted, and features a maze of curio wood representing the tortuous roots of mangroves. Both the wood in the tank and the added blackwater extract give the water a richly organic yellow tint.

ARCHER FISH
Toxotes jaculator
Aside from its spectacular spitting performances, the archer fish is a calm, generally peaceful species.

JAVA FERN
Microsorium pteropus

SCAT
Scatophagus argus
Like the fingerfish, the
juveniles live and grow in the
estuary.

FINGERFISH
Monodactylus argenteus
This large-eyed species has
extended dorsal and anal fin rays
that are covered with scales.

GLASS FISH
Chanda ranga
Beware of purchasing fishes
of this species that have been
coloured with artificial dyes.

VALLIS
Vallisneria asiatica

GIANT HYGROPHILA
Nomaphila stricta

Electric-blue damselfish
Pomacentrus coeruleus

THE MARINE AQUARIUM

Many aquarists are attracted to the idea of keeping temperate and tropical marine species. The bright, often iridescent, colours and bizarre shapes of many tropical marine fishes; the astonishing variety of marine invertebrates; and, of course, the wonder and beauty of what most people consider to be the hallmark of tropical marine environments – the majestic coral – have held many of us in thrall since our first visit to a public aquarium. This chapter commences with a general introduction to the various principles of setting up a marine

Clark's clown
Amphiprion percula

Grey mullet
Chelon labrosus

aquarium, using   as an example a
basic community   tank containing a variety of fishes
from different environments. Within this section, the chapter
then looks at such vital factors as suitable substrates, marine
aquascaping, and stocking and caring for appropriate
invertebrates and fishes. To give as broad a spread as possible
of different marine habitats, the tanks treated in this chapter
are a marine community tank, a Hawaii coral reef tank, and
a British temperate rock pool tank.

Coral beauty
Centropyge bispinosus

Featherduster worm
Eudistylia polymorpha

MARINE COMMUNITY AQUARIUM

FULL HOUSE *In the classic community aquarium, all of the swimming space in the tank should be used by the extraordinary variety of fishes.*

SETTING UP a marine community aquarium allows you to create an "aquatic tapestry" of colours and shapes. As well as being a rewarding aquarium in its own right, it is also the best way of learning the skills and discipline which are needed to maintain a successful coral reef tank (*see* p. 138). A marine community tank presents an opportunity to gather together a collection of spectacular fishes – not just from a single environment, but from all over the world. Fishes can be included in the aquarium because they are vividly coloured, vivacious, unusual in shape, or because they have particularly captivating looks or unusual habits.

Like the tank featured here, most marine community aquaria are based around the fishes in them, but living rock and invertebrates can play an equally important role. In fact, many successful marine aquaria have no fishes at all, relying instead on fantastically coloured, and diversely patterned, tubeworms and fanworms, sea slugs, sea urchins, starfish, clams, corals, and crabs.

Planning the tank

WHEN PLANNING a marine aquarium, try to obtain the largest tank possible – it should be at least 90 cm (36 in) long – since, as a general rule, the larger the tank, the more stable the water chemistry will be. You should bear in mind that marine tanks are in no sense of the word "instant", and that you will need to leave often considerable intervals between the various stages of setting up and populating the tank, while the filtration system matures and the fishes settle in. Any attempt to rush the process will almost certainly result in irreperable and quite unnecessary stress being caused to your fishes. Quite apart from the fact that this would obviously be extremely cruel, the losses of both fishes and invertebrates that would occur could prove to be prohibitively expensive.

The temperature of this tank should be maintained at 22 to 26°C (72 to 78°F). The pH should be between 8.1 and 8.3. The calcareous gravel and rock in a marine tank help to maintain this high pH. Plenty of light illuminates the shallow waters on which this tank is based, and the lighting level in the tank should be correspondingly high. Marine salt should be added to reach a specific gravity of 1.020 to 1.022 and a salinity of between 27.2 and 33.7 ppt.

Most of the fishes suitable for marine community tanks are relatively hardy, so the quality of the water is marginally less critical than in a coral reef tank. There is relatively little rock in this tank, so an undergravel filter is suitable in this instance. (Any significant quantity of rock would impede the flow.) To ensure that the flow of water through the filter is sufficiently strong to draw enough water through the filter bed, powerheads should be attached to the uplift tubes and a power filter used simultaneously as a back-up.

Because certain healthcare treatments that can be applied to tropical marine fishes will harm invertebrates, it is a good idea to set up a hospital tank (*see* p. 180) as a back-up to the main aquarium. This can also be used to quarantine fishes newly bought from a dealer, although you should bear in mind that the process of transferring fishes from a shop into a quarantine tank, and then into a display tank, may be stressful to certain species.

Algae form an important part of the diet of many of the fishes included here and, although they should not be allowed to overrun the tank, you should not be too vigorous in removing them. Until algae have had time to grow properly, you may need to provide a variety of green food supplements for some fishes.

Make sure that the fishes you choose for the marine community tank are not likely to be aggressive towards one another, or even eat each other. A number of species remain passive as individuals, but are likely to become anti-social in a shoal (*see* p. 43). Unfortunately, many suitable fishes will eat invertebrates if given the opportunity. Triggerfish are an excellent example of this, and should only be kept in tanks that contain no invertebrates.

See also Heating, p. 163; pH and alkalinity in sea water, p. 157; Lighting, p. 164; Undergravel filtration, p. 160; Power filters, p. 159; Measuring salinity, p. 155; Specific gravity, p. 155.

Essential equipment

The size of this tank is 122 × 61 × 38 cm (48 × 24 × 15 in). It will hold 283 litres (62 gallons) of water, and should initially include no more than 35 cm (15 in) of fishes. This level can be built up over six months, and then doubled over the next six months. Tapwater with nitrates removed (*see* p.161) is suitable; add the required amount of marine salt. The tank should be heated by two 200-watt heater/thermostats, and can be lit by a fluorescent tube. An undergravel filter with two filter plates of 61 × 38 cm (24 × 15 in) and powerheads on the uplift tubes is used here, with a power filter.

See also Stocking levels, p. 42; Preparing sea water, p. 155; Heating, p. 163; Lighting, p. 164; Undergravel filtration, p. 160; Power filters, p. 159.

INGREDIENTS

CORAL CHIPS
Like the coral sand, these smaller pieces of coral act as a buffer (*see* p. 157).

LIVING ROCK
This is rock that has been colonized by living organisms in the sea.

TUFA ROCK
In nature, this rock builds up from calcium carbonate deposits on the surface of objects that have been immersed in highly calcareous water.

GRAVEL TIDY
A piece of perforated sheeting prevents the undergravel filter from being disturbed by the fishes.

CORAL SAND
The composition of this unevenly grained sand helps to stabilize the pH of the tank.

Building the tank

The first stage in the creation of this aquarium involves building up, with rock, the basic shape of the aquascape that you have visualized. Plan the design of the tank well in advance, so that the final effect is a natural one. Take care not to damage the tank when lifting in the pieces of rock. Always choose the rocks for a marine aquarium with care. Sedimentary rocks can react with the water, although of these limestone is generally safe to use. Avoid any rocks that have metal ore in them, as this could well affect the quality of the water, and wash all the rocks thoroughly before using them in the tank. Tufa rock and living rock are both popular choices for the marine aquarium.

1 Lay the undergravel filter plate along the base of the aquarium. Add a layer of coral chips 2.5 cm (1 in) deep, then lay a plastic gravel tidy on top.

2 Lay an even bed of coral sand 5 cm (2 in) deep on top of the gravel tidy. This, if applied with due care and attention, will act as the necessary filter bed.

3 At the back, build up a wall of tufa rock, which includes crevices and terraces. Incorporate flat, appropriately lit surfaces where anemones can attach themselves.

STARTING THE AQUASCAPING

Solid structure
Use aquarium silicone sealant to glue some of the rocks together if they seem loose.

Building a cave
With careful construction, you can create caves for fishes to hide in.

Steady flow
For the benefit of filter-feeders, and to prevent dead areas, a degree of turbulence is vital.

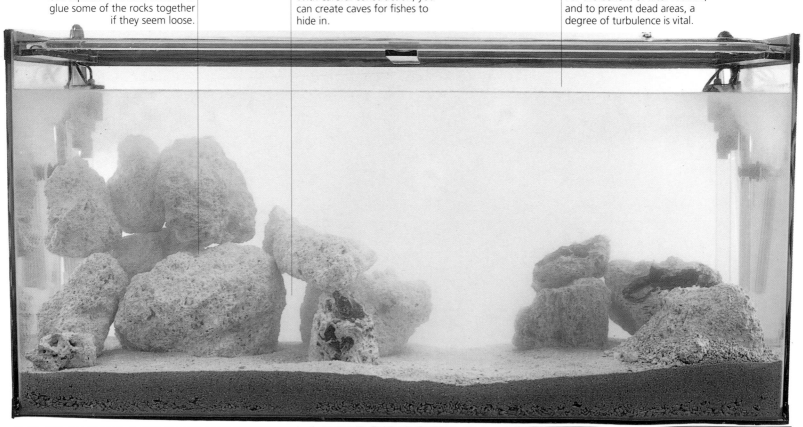

Adding live animals

Once the substrate and rocks are in place, you can prepare the tank for the fishes. Do not hurry this process, as the nitrifying bacteria that are necessary for the filtration of the tank need time to become established. Make sure that the salinity is correct before introducing any marine life. The first step in "maturing" the marine aquarium is to add living rock. The best rock for display is anemone rock, which is light and porous, and which is the home of anemones, tubeworms, fan worms, sponges, and soft corals. Once the tank is ready, the fishes should be added over a period of six months or more (*see* p. 131), at the rate of one or two every two weeks, monitoring water chemistry all the time.

1 Arrange the pieces of living rock so as to produce different levels on which to position the anemones and corals. As always when dealing with marine materials, handle the rock with care, as it may contain creatures that bite or sting.

2 A few anemones and some of the more robust fishes, such as clownfish and damselfish (Pomacentridae), can now be added to the tank. The introduction of these species will accelerate the rate at which the filtration system will mature.

THE AQUASCAPED TANK

Bolt-holes
Some fishes appreciate caves where they can take refuge from aggressive tankmates.

Hidden food
Fishes may dig in the coral sand in search of food.

Neighbours
A single piece of living rock can be home to lots of different invertebrates.

SUITABLE INHABITANTS

LIVING ROCK

The living rock used in this aquarium is simply normal rock that has been colonised by small invertebrates and algae. For prominent display, it is probably best to buy anemone rock, a porous rock, usually covered densely by anemones and sponges (see below), tube-worms, fanworms, and soft corals (see p.142 for all of these).

ANEMONES

General description Anemones consist of a polyp, with multiples of six tentacles emerging around the mouth. Generally, they fasten themselves to rocks by means of a suction-disc. However, some species of anemone have a modified base, which allows for burrowing and slow movement. Anemones are frequently brightly coloured – even a single species may have several very different colour variations.
Ease of keeping Generally, as corals (see p. 142).
Anemones must be removed from the aquarium if they show signs of decomposition (pale areas on the body). Failure to do this will result in the water becoming polluted. Many species of anemone have a rather low tolerance to nitrite.
Food Various foods are sold specifically for filter-feeders such as anemones and corals. However, although these are extremely useful, they should not be used exclusively. It is worth using vitamin supplements, and an amount of fresh foods, to enhance any invertebrate's diet. Liquidized fish or shellfish meat can easily be blended with salt water, and added on a daily basis. Some species of anemone, however, benefit a great deal from being fed small pieces of fish, or alternatively shrimp, once or twice a week. This is best achieved by carefully sprinkling crumbs of the food over the anemone, or by actually placing tiny scraps on to the fully extended tentacles.
(see also Zooxanthellae, p. 143).

Aiptasia spp.
ROCK ANEMONE

Virtually transparent; often found on good-quality living rock; can become too large, endangering fishes and crustaceans.

Condylactis gigantea
CARIBBEAN ANEMONE

White or pink tentacles; grows to diameter of 15 cm (6 in).

Gyrostoma helianthus
ATLANTIC ANEMONE
Numerous tentacles; grows to 50 cm (20 in).

Heteractis aurora
SAND ANEMONE
Grey-white; ringed tentacles; this specimen grows to diameter of 15 cm (6 in).

Heteractis magnifica
RADIANTHUS ANEMONE
Brown, with purple base; smaller specimens ideal for the aquarium – fully mature *Heteractis magnifica* grows to diameter of 70 cm (28 in).

Heteractis malu
MALU ANEMONE
White, cream, or tan; grows to diameter of 40 cm (16 in).

Pachycerianthus mana
FIREWORKS ANEMONE
Various colours; long, attractive tentacles. At diameter of 40 cm (16 in) may endanger fishes and crustaceans.

Stoichactis kenti
CARPET ANEMONE
May grow to an overall diameter of 50 cm (20 in).

ANNELIDS

General description
Annelids are segmented worms, with long, soft bodies, and an oval cross-section. They have no skeleton, but maintain their shape through the pressure of a fluid-filled body cavity.
Ease of keeping Unlike most invertebrates, annelids do not require a high level of lighting. However, they do prefer a reasonably strong flow of water.
Food As anemones.

Sabellastarte spp.
FANWORM
(see p. 142)

Serpulid spp.
CALCAREOUS TUBEWORM
(see p. 142)

FISHES

Amphiprion ocellaris
COMMON CLOWN
Description Deep orange, with white bands.
Length 10 cm (4 in).
Ease of keeping Fairly easy; susceptible to disease on import.
Food Live foods, especially shrimp and bloodworm; flake.
Breeding Egg-depositor; unlikely in the aquarium.
Swimming level Midwater to lower levels.

Amphiprion percula
FALSE COMMON CLOWN
Description Yellow-orange body; white bands.
Length 8 cm (3 in).
Ease of keeping Fairly easy; aggressive when spawning.
Food Live foods; flake.
Breeding As *Amphiprion ocellaris*.
Swimming level Midwater to lower levels; around rocks.

Amphiprion percula
CLARK'S CLOWN
(see p. 142)

Bodianus pulchellus
CUBAN HOGFISH

Description Red front; yellow rear; white horizontal stripe below eye.
Length 20 cm (8 in).
Ease of keeping Fairly easy.
Food Live foods; flake.
Breeding Unknown in the aquarium.
Swimming level All levels, especially around rocks.

Bolbometapon bicolor
TWO-COLOURED PARROTFISH

Description Cream-white body; brown band running through eye.
Length 10 cm (4 in).
Ease of keeping Fairly easy; do not keep with soft corals.
Food Live foods, especially shrimp; fish; flake.
Breeding Unknown in the aquarium.
Swimming level All levels, especially around rocks.

Canthigaster valentini
VALENTIN'S SHARP-NOSED PUFFERFISH
Description White body; brown bands.
Length 10 cm (4 in).
Ease of keeping Fairly easy.
Food Live foods, especially shrimp; fish; flake.
Breeding Unknown in the aquarium.
Swimming level All levels, especially around rocks.

Centropyge bicolor
TWO-COLOURED ANGELFISH
(*see* p. 142)

Centropyge bispinosus
DUSKY ANGELFISH

Description Orange-red, rippled body pattern.
Length 8 cm (3 in).
Ease of Keeping Fairly easy.
Food Live foods; flake.
Breeding As *Amphiprion ocellaris*.
Swimming level Midwater to lower levels.

Chaetodon auriga
THREADFIN BUTTERFLYFISH
Description White front; yellow rear; black mask.
Length 10 cm (4 in).
Ease of keeping Fairly difficult; nervous fish.
Food Live foods; small pieces of fish; flake.
Breeding Egg-scatterer; unknown in the aquarium.
Swimming level Midwater.

Chaetodon vagabundus
VAGABOND BUTTERFLYFISH
Description White body; diagonal lines crossing body in two different directions; distinctive black bar across eye; tail yellow and black.
Length 20 cm (8 in).
Ease of keeping Fairly difficult; nervous fish.
Food Live foods; small pieces of fish; flake.
Breeding Egg-scatterer; unknown in the aquarium.
Swimming level Midwater.

Coris gaimardi "formosa"
BANDED WRASSE
Description Red and white body colour; half-banded.
Length 10 cm (4 in).
Ease of keeping Fairly difficult; frequently burrows down under the sand, therefore this fish is commonly prone to receiving inadequate amounts of food.

Food Shrimp; fish; flake.
Breeding Unknown in the aquarium.
Swimming level Midwater to lower levels.

Cryptocentrus leptocephalus
WATCHMAN GOBY
Description Striped pink and green body; pastel colours.
Length 14 to 15 cm (5½ to 6 in).
Ease of keeping Easy; requires high-quality water.
Feeding Accepts most foods.
Breeding Unknown in the aquarium.
Swimming level Lower levels, especially around rocks.

Dascyllus aruanus
HUMBUG DAMSELFISH
Description White body; three broad, black bars.
Length 8 cm (3 in).
Ease of keeping Fairly easy.
Food Shrimp; bloodworm; flake.
Breeding As *Amphiprion ocellaris*.
Swimming level Around rocks and corals.

Dascyllus trimaculatus
DOMINO DAMSELFISH
Description Black, with several white spots.
Length 11 cm (4½ in).
Ease of keeping Fairly easy, but any dominant individuals may behave aggressively towards other fishes. Spawning pairs are also likely to act antisocially towards their tankmates.
Food Live foods; flake.
Breeding As *Amphiprion ocellaris*.
Swimming level All levels.

Eupomacentrus (Stegastes) leucostictus
BEAU GREGORY
Description Yellow body; golden-brown top with blue dots.
Length 15 cm (6 in).
Ease of keeping Easy.
Food Live foods; flake.
Breeding Egg-depositor; spawns on rocks.
Swimming level All levels.

Holocanthus tricolor
ROCK BEAUTY
Description Yellow body; distinctive black blotch.
Length 30 cm (12 in).
Ease of keeping Fairly easy.
Food Shrimp; small pieces of fish;

prawn; will also eat sponges in the aquarium.
Breeding As *Amphiprion ocellaris*.
Swimming level All levels, particularly around rocks.

Holocentrus (Adioryx) diadema
SQUIRRELFISH
Description Red body; white, horizontal stripes.
Length 30 cm (12 in).
Ease of keeping Fairly easy; requires a large aquarium.
Food Accepts most foods.
Breeding Unknown in the aquarium.
Swimming level Midwater to upper levels.

Labroides dimidiatus
CLEANER WRASSE
(*see* p. 143)

Parablennius tentacularis
SCOOTER BLENNY
Description Mottled brown or cream body.
Length 8 cm (3 in).
Ease of keeping Easy; sensitive to changes in water chemistry; requires high-quality water.
Feeding Accepts most foods; scavenger.
Breeding Unknown in the aquarium.
Swimming level Lower levels, especially around rocks.

Paracanthurus hepatus
REGAL TANG (SURGEONFISH)

Description Blue body; distinctive black swirl.
Length 12 cm (5 in).
Ease of keeping Fairly easy.
Food Shrimp; spinach; flake; needs regular supply of lettuce.
Breeding Egg-scatterer.
Swimming level Midwater, especially around rocks.

Pomacentrus coeruleus
ELECTRIC-BLUE DAMSELFISH
(*see* p. 143)

Synchiropus splendidus
MANDARIN GOBY
Description Olive to dark-green body; multicoloured swirls.
Length 8 cm (3 in).
Ease of keeping Fairly difficult; distinctly territorial.
Food Live foods; requires live brine shrimp when first introduced; will eat flake when established.
Breeding Egg-scatterer; unlikely in the aquarium.
Swimming level Lower levels.

Zebrasoma flavescens
YELLOW TANG (SURGEONFISH)
(*see* p. 143)

─────── **SPONGES** ───────

General description Sponges, which are irregular in shape and size, have no true tissues or organs, and are incapable of movement. They are an association of similar individuals, rather than a single creature. Until it was possible to observe sponges under a microscope, naturalists assumed them to be plants. Unfortunately, most specimens are difficult to import – if, after removal from the water, an air bubble becomes trapped within a sponge, the specimen is certain to die. Therefore the majority of sponges which are on sale normally come from "living reef" aquaria. Stockists generally identify sponges by their colour. Those that derive originally from shallow tropical waters are available in greens, yellows, oranges, reds, and purples.
Ease of keeping Sponges should be introduced on to rocks, rather than directly into the substrate, therefore ensuring that there will be a steady flow of water around them. This reduces the risk of waste-poisoning and, along with carefully controlled lighting, stops them from developing an often fatal coating of algae.
Food As anemones.

Suitable sponges include blue tubular sponge (*Adocia* spp.), and red tubular sponge (*Verongia* spp.). Due to the common difficulty in identifying sponges, they are normally sold by colour.

The finished tank

Most fishes and invertebrates suitable for this aquarium can be found in the coastal waters and around the coral reefs of the Indo-Pacific, the Caribbean, and the Red Sea. This tank contains a wide range of personalities that will emerge as the habitat becomes established. Follow the correct procedures for adding the fishes and completing the tank (*see* p. 50).

ELECTRIC-BLUE DAMSELFISH
Pomacentrus coeruleus

RADIANTHUS ANEMONE
Heteractis magnifica

COMMON CLOWN
Amphiprion ocellaris

HUMBUG DAMSELFISH
Dascyllus aruanus

VAGABOND BUTTERFLYFISH
Chaetodon vagabundus

WATCHMAN GOBY
Cryptocentrus leptocephalus

MALU ANEMONE
Heteractis malu
The malu anemone is slightly
more nitrite-tolerant than
many other species.

ATLANTIC ANEMONE
Gyrostoma helianthus
A crevice-loving anemone
that retracts into an oval disc.

YELLOW TANG
Zebrasoma flavescens
Make sure that there is a reasonable
amount of algae in the tank before
introducing the yellow tang.

BEAU GREGORY
*Eupomacentrus (Stegastes)
leucostictus*
This fish will establish itself in
and around coral branches.

SCOOTER BLENNY
Parablennius tentacularis
These blunt-headed fishes are
relentless in their pursuit of
food scraps.

SQUIRRELFISH
Holocentrus (Adioryx) diadema
This is a very active, nocturnal fish.
It will have to be removed if it
begins to attack smaller tankmates.

CARPET ANEMONE
Stoichactis kenti
When its tentacles are retracted,
the carpet anemone has
a disc-shaped appearance.

HAWAII CORAL REEF

NEW LIFE *Year after year, the complex structures of the coral reef multiply, providing an essential habitat for some of the most diverse species in the world.*

WARMED by currents from the equator, the coral reefs of the Hawaiian islands are home to many beautiful marine fishes (*see* p. 21). The main islands of Hawaii, Maui, and Oahu are almost completely surrounded by coral reefs and there are well-managed marine parks off most of the islands. There are, however, two major threats to the coral reef habitats of Hawaii. The first of these is connected to the fact that some of the volcanoes responsible for creating the islands are still active. Occasionally, new flows of lava from these volcanoes smother large areas of reef. The second threat is from human interference – in particular by the thousands of sub-aqua divers who holiday on the islands.

This tank aims to recreate a very small part of one of the many fantastic reefs of this region. Geographically, Hawaii is rather isolated from the rest of the Indo-Pacific region. As a result, the fish fauna of the islands features both species from the major Indo-Pacific families and species that are considered to be unique to Hawaii, such as the lemon butterflyfish.

The waters around a coral reef are clean, well aerated, stable, and warm, while the shallowness of the water means that there is a lot of light, which encourages algae. Try to recreate all of these elements when building a coral reef tank. Of course, the task of reproducing a coral reef environment is never easy, and you should never let your imagination alone dictate your plans – the creation and maintenance of a stable environment demand a disciplined approach. Because the keeping of a coral reef aquarium requires some expertise, before setting up such a tank it is a good idea for beginners to first develop their skills with a marine community tank (*see* p. 130).

Planning the tank

PERSEVERANCE PAYS *It can take a long time for a coral reef tank to mature properly, but the result is always well worth the wait.*

A LARGE TANK – at least 122 cm (48 in) long – is essential for a serious attempt at recreating a portion of reef life; the water chemistry in smaller tanks is almost certain to be highly unstable.

The temperature of the tank should be maintained at 23 to 25°C (72 to 78°F). The pH should be between 8.1 and 8.3. Marine salt should be added to the tank to reach a specific gravity of 1.022 to 1.024, and a salinity of between 27.2 and 33.7 ppt. Tapwater can be used for this tank, but the level of nitrates may be too high for invertebrates, which are highly sensitive. Removal of these is important and can be achieved by using exchange resins or reverse osmosis (*see* p. 161).

Good lighting is vital for the health and well-being of live corals. A high lighting level is essential to support the Zooxanthellae (*see* p. 143) that live within the invertebrates. To help keep the microalgae in control, nitrates should be kept at below 5 mg/litre.

Without doubt, the most efficient type of filtration system to use for a coral reef aquarium is a relatively sophisticated total filtration system. The system should filter the water efficiently enough to provide a redox potential of over 30 pε (*see* p. 157).

See also Heating, p. 163; pH and alkalinity in sea water, p. 157; Lighting, p. 164; Integrated total filtration, p. 162; Measuring salinity, p. 155; Specific gravity, p. 155.

Essential equipment

The dimensions of this tank are 122 × 61 × 38 cm (48 × 24 × 15 in). This tank will hold 283 litres (62 gallons) of water, and should initially be stocked with no more than a total 35 cm (15 in) of fishes. This stocking level should ideally be built up gradually over a six month period; after this it may be possible to reach double this figure during the course of the next year. The tank should be heated by two 200-watt heater/thermostats, and lit by metal halide lamps. You may wish to set up an additional hospital/quarantine tank (*see* p. 180), as many invertebrates and fishes are prone to injury – very often from fighting among themselves – or disease in this type of environment.

See also Stocking levels, p. 42; Preparing sea water, p. 155; Heating, p. 163; Lighting, p. 164.

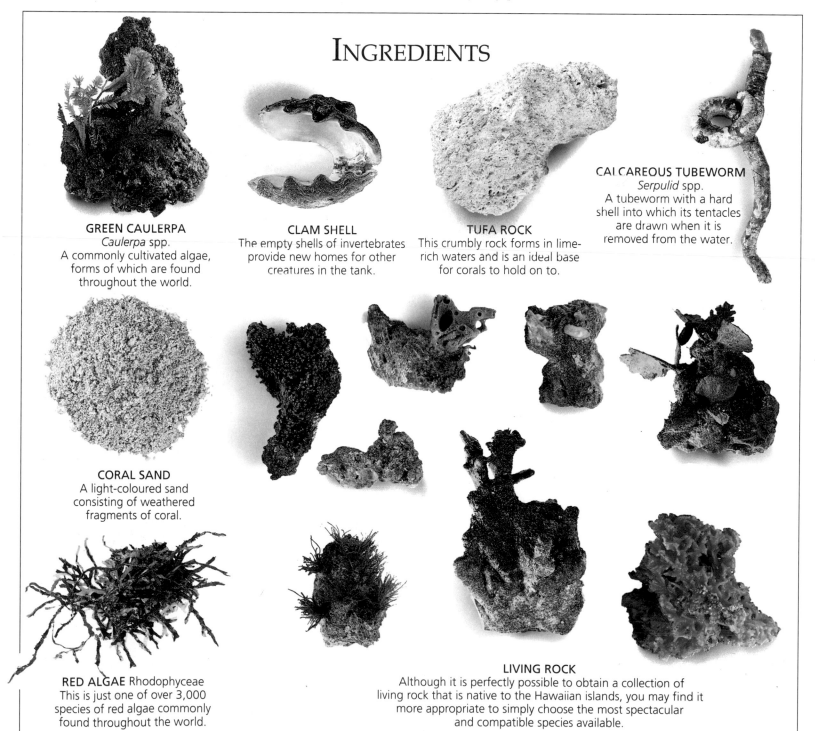

INGREDIENTS

GREEN CAULERPA
Caulerpa spp.
A commonly cultivated algae, forms of which are found throughout the world.

CLAM SHELL
The empty shells of invertebrates provide new homes for other creatures in the tank.

TUFA ROCK
This crumbly rock forms in lime-rich waters and is an ideal base for corals to hold on to.

CALCAREOUS TUBEWORM
Serpulid spp.
A tubeworm with a hard shell into which its tentacles are drawn when it is removed from the water.

CORAL SAND
A light-coloured sand consisting of weathered fragments of coral.

RED ALGAE Rhodophyceae
This is just one of over 3,000 species of red algae commonly found throughout the world.

LIVING ROCK
Although it is perfectly possible to obtain a collection of living rock that is native to the Hawaiian islands, you may find it more appropriate to simply choose the most spectacular and compatible species available.

Adding the rocks

The aim of the first stage of building this tank is to establish a healthy community of living rock and algae. To create a truly authentic Hawaiian coral reef, you may need to search many aquarium shops; alternatively, try to create the most attractive set-up possible with the best pieces that you can find. The more living rock there is in a coral reef tank, the sooner the tank will settle. Up to 1 kg (2.2 lb) of living rock can be used for each 4.5 litres (1 gallon) of water. You should handle living rock with gloves as hidden creatures such as fire coral (*Millepora* spp.) or bristle worms (*Hermodice carunculata*) can sting. Remove any normally aggressive small, striped mantis shrimps (*Pseudosquilla bigelowi*).

1 As part of a thoughtfully constructed wall, tufa rock provides a good base for pieces of colourful living rock.

2 Gently add the salt water to the tank, taking great care not to disturb the fine layer of coral sand.

3 Do not fill in the wall completely with living rock, as any remaining holes will gradually be taken up by the various invertebrates and algae as they grow.

THE AQUASCAPED TANK

Integrated system
This system should carry out all of the essential aspects of filtration.

Facing forward
Rocks are colonized only on their exposed surfaces.

Adding invertebrates

Once living rock has been added to the tank, the levels of nitrites and nitrates in the water should be measured to ensure that they are not too high. Run the tank for at least a week, testing the water daily. Providing that all is well, the tank is now ready for the invertebrates. Corals, crabs, tubeworms, fanworms, and sea urchins may be added to suit your preference over a period of several weeks. To reflect a real coral reef habitat, try to use only live material. Dead corals can be used as a base for the growth of new coral, but they should not dominate the tank – their prominence would be unnatural. In general, dead creatures should be removed without delay, before they pollute the tank.

1 Sea urchins should be handled with great care, as the spines are often venomous. A healthy sea urchin has erect spines and thousands of constantly moving feet between them. A few missing spines are not a problem, because, providing the animal is healthy, they will regrow. Once settled, sea urchins will make their slow way across the aquarium – they move mainly at night.

2 Calcareous tubeworms (Serpulidae) have delicate "feathers" – tentacles that actually filter the water, trapping fine particles of food. These emerge from a membranous tube. Take great care not to crush these as you lay the tubeworm in the tank. Some species have a calcareous plug that blocks the entrance to the tubes when the feathers have been withdrawn.

3 Related to the tubeworm, the fanworm (Sabellidae) has feathers too. Although these unusual invertebrates are tolerant of changing water conditions, they are highly sensitive to abrupt changes in light. From time to time they shed their feathers, but this does not mean that they are dead – simply remove the shed portion from the tank and the feathers will regrow.

4 When selecting corals remember that different types have different preferences for the amount of light that should reach them (see p. 142). Place them carefully and check with the dealer that they are compatible. When adding living rock to the water, turn it on its sides several times to loosen bubbles in the rock. This prevents invertebrates from being trapped in the bubbles. Failure to do this might result in the death of a mollusc, which could rot and cause water quality problems.

5 Tropical crabs are small, mobile, and more colourful than crabs from temperate waters, making them an excellent addition to the reef aquarium. Once established, the crabs may establish their own territories by burrowing or colonizing shells. Some crabs use the tentacles of anemones for protection. If including a hermit crab such as Dardanus spp., leave a selection of various-sized shells around the tank for the crab to use as its home.

SUITABLE INHABITANTS

ANEMONES

Radianthus koseirensis
Prefers sand-covered rocks; feeds during daytime.

Zoanthus spp.
POLYP ROCK
Mimics corals; prefers lower light levels, beneath overhangs.

(see also p. 134)

ANNELIDS

Sabellastarte spp.
FANWORM
Species grow to between 10 and 15 cm (4 and 6 in); tentacles occasionally banded red, brown, or white.

Serpulid spp.
CALCAREOUS TUBEWORM
Produces distinctive, stony tube; species grow to 5 cm (2 in).

(see also p. 134)

CORALS

General Description Corals, like jellyfish and anemones, belong to the vast group of animals known as Coelenterata. The polyps develop in soft or hard forms. Hard coral polyps form in three layers – a solid inner and outer wall enclosing a jelly-like mass. The outer wall emits skeletal limestone, which forms a tough, intricate structure over the creature. Generally, hard corals exist in colonies. Soft corals possess a similar basic structure, but have no solid limestone skeleton. However, like hard corals, they often form colonies.
Ease of keeping Corals require a steady flow of water in the aquarium. This ensures both that food is constantly brought within their reach, and that any discharged waste is safely drawn away. Hard corals, in particular, will tolerate neither poor water quality nor insufficient lighting. Leave a space between specimens in the aquarium; this should be equivalent to whichever new corals are being introduced.

Sufficient distancing will prevent fighting – a common problem when keeping corals – and will allow for the often considerable expansion of some species. Some corals do not fully expand until after dark.
Food (see p. 134)

Acropora spp.
Acropora corals constitute actual reef structure; vital for natural regeneration of reef. Species include staghorn coral (*Acropora cervicornis*), elkhorn coral (*Acropora palmata*), and plate coral (*Acropora pulchra*).

Goniopora
DAISY CORAL

Light-loving hard coral; lobed polyps often expand in daytime.

Gorgonia spp.
SEA FAN (GORGONIAN)
Soft coral; grows in flat, fan-like shapes; has appearance of dark lace; prefers to be sited away from direct light.

Heliopora coerulea
BLUE CORAL
Sole member of Helioporidae family; blue tint to skeleton caused by iron salts.

Lobophyllia spp.
Soft coral; grows in roughly circular mounds; fleshy polyps. Prefers to be sited out of direct light, beneath overhangs.

Pterogyra spp.
BUBBLE CORAL
Light-loving hard coral; may damage other corals in vicinity, so place carefully; species include *Pterogyra sinuosa*.

Sarcophyton spp.
LEATHER CORAL
Soft coral; convoluted, distinctively

mushroom-shaped form generally best for the aquarium; requires good lighting; needs regular supply of liquid feed.

Xenia spp.
XENIA ROCK
Soft coral; stout trunk; tentacles open and close regularly; generally easy to keep.

Zoanthus spp.
POLYP ROCK
(see anemones)

CRUSTACEANS

General Description
Crustaceans have segmented bodies, the number of segments and of limbs varying between species. In all cases there are, however, two distinctive pairs of antennae, emerging from the head, and at least three pairs of mouthparts. They possess often extremely tough skins of chitin – the carapace – which act as both a skeleton and an excellent form of protection.
Ease of keeping Like some molluscs, many crustaceans benefit from relatively high pH and calcium levels. This is particularly important when trying to heal injured specimens. Poor quality water will result in a slow, and often imperfect, recovery. Shrimps and crabs are not only attractive, but can be useful – as scavengers they help to keep the aquarium clean. They can, however, cause problems when kept with certain fishes and corals. Avoid the larger crabs, such as *Pagarus* spp., as they often prey upon smaller fishes, and tend to damage corals and anemones.
Food As molluscs (see opposite).

Dardanus spp.
PACIFIC HERMIT CRAB
Fairly small coral reef hermit crab; useful scavenger.

Lysmata amboinensis
CLEANER SHRIMP
Active shrimp; grows to 8 cm (3 in); will scavenge thoroughly in most parts of the aquarium; can sometimes become rather lethargic in captivity.

Rhynchocinetes spp.
PEPPERMINT (or DANCING) SHRIMP

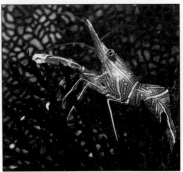

Attractive, commonly available shrimp; grows to 4 cm (1½ in); may damage living coral.

FISHES

Amphiprion percula
CLARK'S CLOWN
Description Various; including black with white stripes, and orange with white stripes.
Length 10 cm (4 in).
Ease of keeping Easy; aggressive when spawning.
Food Live foods, especially shrimp; fish; flake.
Breeding Unknown in the aquarium.
Swimming level Midwater to lower levels..

Centropyge bicolor
TWO-COLOURED ANGELFISH
Description Body yellow at front; blue at rear.
Length 10 cm (4 in).
Ease of keeping Fairly easy; difficult to establish.
Food Live foods, especially shrimp and bloodworm; flake.
Breeding Egg-depositor.
Swimming level Midwater to lower levels.

Centropyge bispinosus
CORAL BEAUTY ANGELFISH
Description Deep purple outline to body; orange sides; dark, vertical stripes.
Length 12 cm (5 in).
Ease of keeping Fairly easy.
Food Live foods, especially shrimp.
Breeding Unknown in the aquarium.
Swimming level All levels.

Centropyge loriculus
FLAME ANGEL

Description Brilliant red-orange body; black stripes.
Length 8 cm (3 in).
Ease of keeping Fairly difficult; highly territorial, but will pair up for breeding.
Food Live foods, especially shrimp and bloodworm; flake.
Breeding Egg-depositor.
Swimming level Around rocks and corals.

Chaetodon miliaris
LEMON BUTTERFLYFISH

Description Yellow; black eye stripe and spot on caudal peduncle.
Length 15 cm (6 in).
Ease of keeping Fairly easy; will thrive in most well-maintained systems.
Food Microcrustaceans; bloodworm; flake.
Breeding Egg-scatterer.
Swimming level All levels.

Chromis viridis
GREEN CHROMIS DAMSELFISH

Description Light metallic-green body; young fish very pale – almost white.
Length 10 cm (4 in).
Ease of keeping Easy. This is a placid fish, and should be kept separate from more aggressive fish species.
Feeding Accepts most foods.
Breeding Egg-depositor.
Swimming level All levels.

Labroides dimidiatus
CLEANER WRASSE

Description Blue body; lateral black stripe.
Length 10 cm (4 in).
Ease of keeping Fairly difficult; will normally feed off parasites on other fishes.
Food Shrimp; flake; needs copious amounts of microcrustacea.
Breeding Egg-scatterer.
Swimming level All levels.

Pomacentrus coeruleus
ELECTRIC-BLUE DAMSELFISH

Description Bright blue; occasional black markings on facial area.
Length 8 cm (3 in).
Ease of keeping Fairly difficult; often aggressive.
Food Dried foods; chopped meat; bloodworm; shrimp.
Breeding Egg-depositor.
Swimming level All levels, especially around rocks.

Pterosynchiropus splendidus
MANDARIN BLENNY

Description Various forms exist, but all extremely colourful; for example, green or turquoise body, with yellow dots around gills; vivid bright green lines covering back of fish; metallic-blue dots on dorsal fin; bright red lines radiating out across caudal fin.
Length 6 cm (2½ in).
Ease of keeping Fairly easy. This is a nervous fish that must be be isolated from aggressive species.
Food Live foods; a useful scavenging fish.
Breeding Unknown in the aquarium.
Swimming level Lower levels.

Zebrasoma flavescens
YELLOW TANG (SURGEONFISH)

Description Brilliant yellow.
Length 15 cm (6 in).
Ease of keeping Fairly easy; thrives in small shoals.
Food Live foods, especially shrimp; spinach; flake; must have regular supply of lettuce.
Breeding Egg-scatterer.
Swimming level All levels.

MARINE ALGAE

General description Forms of algae play a vital role in the maintenance of a healthy aquarium, often providing a vital source of aquarium food. Zooxanthellae is a particularly interesting form of algae, that actually exits within the body tissues of corals and anemones, and assists in the removal of waste products.
Ease of keeping It can at first be hard to establish the ideal balance of algal growth in the aquarium. Eventually though, after a variety of corals and similar invertebrates have become established in the aquarium, excessive amounts of algae will be consumed, and the correct balance will generally follow. It is always essential to find the appropriate levels of lighting, feeding, and water movement for the particular inhabitants of an aquarium.
Food In the correct conditions, algae will not need feeding.

Caulerpa spp.
CAULERPA

Most commonly kept form of algae; easy to grow; approaches 50 cm (20 in) high, or forms in low mats.

Rhodophyceae
RED ALGAE

Maroon-red algae, available in several species; normally fairly difficult to grow.

MOLLUSCS

General Description Molluscs have a main body mass, containing the vital organs; a muscular foot, with which they appear to glide over rocks and vegetation, and an occasionally underdeveloped head. Marine molluscs have gills, which in some cases have become adapted for feeding. These creatures are soft-bodied, but possess an external skeleton – the shell – which offers protection as well as bodily support. Mollusc shells develop into numerous highly patterned and coloured shapes.
Ease of keeping Unfortunately, most molluscs are an easy form of prey. It is this vulnerability, and their sensitivity to changing water conditions – particularly calcium levels – that often complicates their keeping. Some sea slugs graze on corals, and are therefore unsuitable for most aquaria.
Food Large molluscs will accept many different kinds of small fishes, shrimp, and flake when mixed thoroughly with fish meat. Smaller species, and sea slugs, will also accept these foods if they are offered in chopped pieces. Clams, scallops and oysters are filter-feeders, like corals and anemones. Feeding should take place not more than once each day, and if any material remains uneaten after an hour, it should then be removed from the aquarium.

Glossodoris spp.
Slow-moving sea slug; characterized by brilliant colours; feeds on sponge, and therefore unsuitable for some aquaria.

Hexabranchus imperialis
SPANISH DANCER

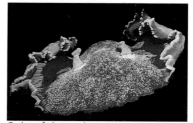

Colourful sea slug; grows to 15 cm (6 in); name derives from undulating movement when swimming.

Tridacna spp.
GIANT CLAM

Clams with ridged shells and attractively fluted edges; smaller members of species are suitable for the aquarium; must be kept within sight of aquarist – dead specimens emit poisons that will pollute the tank.

SEA URCHINS

General description Sea urchins are Echinoderms, like starfish. They have globular or flat bodies, and an internal shell, comprising of fused, skeletal plates. Normally they will burrow into sand, mud, or rock, digging with their spines.
Ease of keeping Sea urchins should never be removed from the water, since any air that becomes trapped within their bodies normally results in death.
Feeding As small molluscs.

SPONGES

For information on suitable sponges, *see* p. 135.

The finished tank

Living rock and invertebrates can be added to this tank at any stage. Fishes should be introduced gradually, to a maximum level of 1 cm per 8 litres (1 in per 4 gallons) of fish after six months (*see* p. 42). This level can, if you wish, be doubled over a year. The water needs to be as clear as that around a true Hawaiian reef. Sophisticated filtration systems can be called upon to maintain this high water quality, ensuring that the often sensitive invertebrates and fishes remain healthy. Follow the correct procedures for adding the fishes and completing your tank (*see* p. 50).

SEAGRASS
Najadaceae

ELECTRIC-BLUE DAMSELFISH
Pomacentrus coeruleus

CALCAREOUS TUBEWORM
Serpulid spp.

GREEN CHROMIS DAMSELFISH
Chromis viridis
This species takes on a brilliant green colour when it matures.

Radianthus koseirensis
Prefers sand-covered rocks.

LEATHER CORAL
Sarcophyton spp
The smooth surface of the leather coral is soft and fleshy.

BLUE CORAL
Heliopora coerulea

CORAL BEAUTY ANGELFISH
Centropyge bispinosus
There are numerous colour variations of this fish.

LEMON BUTTERFLYFISH
Chaetodon miliaris
As it matures this young butterflyfish will take on a rich yellow colour.

SEA URCHIN
Echinoidea

STAGHORN CORAL
Acropora cervicornis

FANWORM
Sabellastarte spp.

POLYP ROCK
Zoanthus spp.

BUBBLE CORAL
Pterogyra spp.

GREEN CAULERPA
Caulerpa spp.

CLAM SHELL

COLOURED SPONGE
Porifera
Sponges that are brightly coloured generally come from shallow waters.

BRITISH ROCK POOL

EXTREMITIES *Because of the constantly changing conditions in a rock pool, the creatures that live there must be both hardy and resourceful.*

ROCK POOLS are found on coasts all over the world, and they invariably contain many small creatures that are ideal for the aquarium (*see* p. 21). Although they are not as brightly coloured as tropical species, the intriguing behaviour of fishes and invertebrates in temperate pools is every bit as interesting to observe.

The rock pool is a specialized ecosystem, with inhabitants ranging from microscopic algae to seaweeds, and from tiny planktonic animals to fishes. Tides have a profound effect on the rock pool, as different portions of the pool are exposed to the various properties of, in turn, air and water throughout the day. The smaller the size of a pool, and the higher up on the shore that it lies, the more variable are the conditions for life within it. Each new tide brings in new life, while those creatures that have made a permanent home in the pool hide in nooks and crannies until the tide gradually recedes, and their familiar environment returns.

Each creature in the rock pool has a quite specific niche. Particular anemones, for example, are found at various levels. Plumous anemones (*Metridium senile*) are only found in areas exposed by the lowest summer tides, daisy anemones (*Cereus pedunculatus*) are found in the area close to the low-tide mark, and beadlet anemones (*Actinia equina*) live midway between the high- and low-water marks. Fishes such as gobies, cottids, wrasses, and blennies all like sheltered waters where seaweeds flourish. They move around the bottom of the pool, where they are hidden from the attention of gulls and the warmth of the sun. Sandy areas are inhabited by shrimps, crabs, cuttlefish, and flatfish. Areas of shingle are less well populated, due to the constant movement of the small stones.

Planning the tank

EQUILIBRIUM *A well-planned rock pool tank should provide space for shoaling fishes as well as crawling invertebrates.*

FOR THE MOST impressive display, a rock pool aquarium should ideally be stocked with fishes that will eventually grow to a considerable size. A relatively large tank will therefore be needed.

Many species of fish and invertebrate from the temperate rock pool are likely to suffer if the temperature in the aquarium rises to more than 15°C (59°F). To keep the water cool, cubes of frozen sea water can be placed in the tank. If you are unable to obtain sea water, freeze an amount of tapwater instead, and float it in the top of the tank, in a watertight container, until the water returns to the required temperature. The pH of the water should be maintained at between 8.1 and 8.5, and the lighting level should be high. Marine salt should be added to the tank to reach a specific gravity of 1.025 to 1.026 and a salinity of 34 to 35 ppt. Temperate marine tanks need regular water changes – 25 per cent every four to eight weeks should be sufficient. Monitor the levels of pH and nitrogen compounds regularly.

Do not allow any of the inhabitants to grow so large that they begin eating their smaller tankmates. If the rock pool tank is to include anemones, then ideally sea slugs should be avoided, as the latter may well eat the former.

See also pH and alkalinity in sea water, p. 157; Lighting p. 164; Power filters p. 159; Measuring salinity p. 155; Specific gravity, p. 155.

Essential equipment

The dimensions of the tank used here are 122 × 46 × 38 cm (48 × 18 × 15 in). It will hold 212 litres (47 gallons) of water. Because a temperate marine tank features a greater variety of creatures than most other tanks, it is difficult to give hard and fast rules on acceptable stocking levels. A good guide, however, is to gradually work up to 1 in of fishes per 2 gallons (1 cm per 3½ litres), so this tank will take up to 58 cm (23 in) of fishes. A power filter that gives a good flow should be chosen. Powerheads can be employed simultaneously to maintain good circulation. Fluorescent lighting can be used.

See also Stocking levels, p. 42; Preparing sea water, p. 155; Lighting, p. 164; Power filters, p. 159.

INGREDIENTS

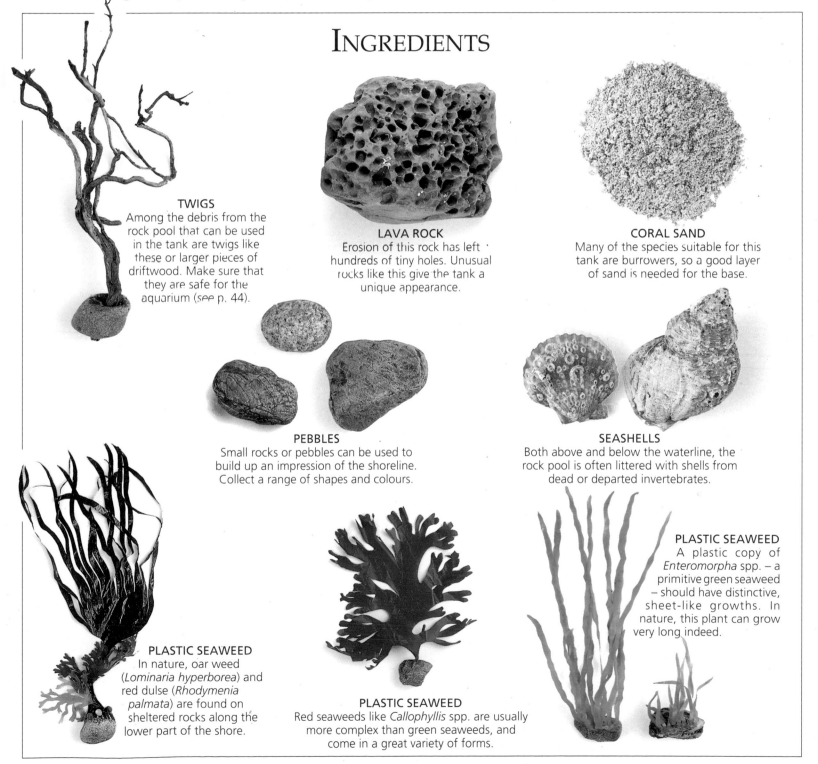

TWIGS
Among the debris from the rock pool that can be used in the tank are twigs like these or larger pieces of driftwood. Make sure that they are safe for the aquarium (*see* p. 44).

LAVA ROCK
Erosion of this rock has left hundreds of tiny holes. Unusual rocks like this give the tank a unique appearance.

CORAL SAND
Many of the species suitable for this tank are burrowers, so a good layer of sand is needed for the base.

PEBBLES
Small rocks or pebbles can be used to build up an impression of the shoreline. Collect a range of shapes and colours.

SEASHELLS
Both above and below the waterline, the rock pool is often littered with shells from dead or departed invertebrates.

PLASTIC SEAWEED
In nature, oar weed (*Lominaria hyperborea*) and red dulse (*Rhodymenia palmata*) are found on sheltered rocks along the lower part of the shore.

PLASTIC SEAWEED
Red seaweeds like *Callophyllis* spp. are usually more complex than green seaweeds, and come in a great variety of forms.

PLASTIC SEAWEED
A plastic copy of *Enteromorpha* spp. – a primitive green seaweed – should have distinctive, sheet-like growths. In nature, this plant can grow very long indeed.

Building the tank

The first step in creating a rock pool tank should be to build up an impressive bank, on a base of coral sand, with rocks and pebbles. Once this base is ready, the water can be added and the fishes and invertebrates introduced. One of the most spectacular features of this tank should be flowing bunches of seaweed. This, however, creates a problem. Seaweed is notoriously difficult to keep fresh in an aquarium, as it needs constant water movement. A perfectly acceptable alternative is artificial seaweed, cut out from sheets of coloured plastic. Try to imitate specific species by cutting the fronds to particular shapes. To secure the seaweed, attach it with aquarium sealant to a pebble or a lead weight.

1 Lay down a bed of coral sand 5 cm (2 in) deep and build up a bank of pebbles. Once the water is added, the tank is ready for invertebrates, like these mussels.

2 When adding anemones, as with all forms of marine life, handle them with care. Many species have powerful stinging cells contained in their tentacles.

3 Seaweeds do not have roots. Instead they anchor themselves on rocks. Place the plastic seaweed so that it can stream away from the rocky bank.

THE AQUASCAPED TANK

Stately seaweed
Tall stands of plastic seaweed provide an interesting corner-piece to the tank.

Varied textures
Select a variety of different species of anemone for the tank.

Ample room
Leave a reasonably sized sandy area for the prawns to colonize.

SUITABLE INHABITANTS

FISHES

Chelon labrosus
GREY MULLET
(see p. 119)

Ciliata mustela
FIVE-BEARED ROCKLING

Description Brown body.
Length Usually no bigger than 25 cm (10 in).
Ease of keeping Fairly difficult; sensitive to temperature and water changes.
Food Live foods, especially crustaceans, fishes, and molluscs.
Breeding Unknown in the aquarium.
Swimming level Midwater.

Crenilabrus melops
CORKWING WRASSE
Description Green to red or brown body.
Length 15 to 18 cm (6 to 7 in).
Ease of keeping Fairly easy; can sometimes become aggressive, especially towards members of own species.
Food Live foods, especially brine shrimp; finely chopped crab.
Breeding Unknown in the aquarium.
Swimming level All levels.

Gobius paganellus
ROCK GOBY
Description Dark brown or purple body; orange-yellow band on dorsal fin.
Length 12 cm (5 in).
Ease of keeping Easy; aggressive when mature.
Food Live foods, especially earthworm; pieces of fish.
Breeding Nest-builder; fairly easy, given space and privacy.
Swimming level Lower levels.

Lipophrys (blennius) pholis
SHANNY
Description Green or grey body; black blotches.

Length 15 cm (6 in).
Ease of keeping Easy; enjoys opportunity to leave water, to sit on a rock; large specimens may eat smaller fishes; water temperature must be maintained below 19°C (66°F).
Food Most foods accepted, especially prawn, fish, and vegetable matter.
Breeding Nest-builder; fairly easy, given space and privacy.
Swimming level Lower levels.

Platichthys flesus
FLOUNDER
Description Green-brown body; occasionally orange spots; white underside.
Length Only specimens smaller than 5 to 20 cm (6 to 8 in) suitable for the aquarium.
Ease of keeping Easy.
Food Live foods, especially shrimp, earthworm, and pieces of fish or ragworm.
Breeding Deep, offshore egg-scatterer; unknown in the aquarium.
Swimming level Lower levels.

Pomatoschistus minutus
SAND GOBY
Description Sand-coloured body; dark lines and speckles; red-brown bands on dorsal fin; males have dark, vertical bars on body and spot on dorsal fin.
Length 10 cm (4 in).
Ease of keeping Easy.
Food Live foods, especially mussel; finely chopped prawn.
Breeding Egg-depositor; unknown in the aquarium.
Swimming level Lower levels.

Spondyliosoma canthurus
BLACK BREAM (OLD WIFE)
(see p. 119)

INVERTEBRATES

Actinia equina
BEADLET ANEMONE
Description Red, green, or brown colour.
Length 6 cm (2½ in).
Ease of keeping Easy.
Food Live foods, especially shrimp, mussel, and small pieces of fish.
Breeding This anemone normally

divides readily if well fed.
Swimming level Not applicable.

Anemonia viridis
SNAKELOCKS ANEMONE
Description Green.
Length 25 to 30 cm (10 to 12 in) in diameter.
Ease of keeping Fairly easy; requires plenty of light; water temperature must be maintained above 10°C (50°F).
Food As *Actinia equina*.
Breeding Divides fairly easily; not as common as *Actinia equina*.
Swimming level Not applicable.

Crepidula fornicata
SLIPPER LIMPET
Description Red-brown shell.
Length 5 cm (2 in).
Ease of keeping Easy.
Food Algae.
Breeding Unknown in the aquarium.
Swimming level Not applicable.

Galathea squamifera
SQUAT LOBSTER

Description Green tint to red-coloured shell.
Length 10 cm (4 in).
Ease of keeping Fairly difficult; sensitive to changes in water chemistry, particularly ammonia and nitrite levels.
Food Live foods; also small pieces of fish.
Breeding Difficult.
Swimming level Bottom.

Mytilus edulis
EDIBLE MUSSEL
Description Dark blue or brown-coloured shell.
Length 9 cm (3½ in).
Ease of keeping Difficult.
Food Filter-feeder on particulate matter.
Breeding Unknown in the aquarium.
Swimming level Not applicable.

Ostrea edulis
EUROPEAN OYSTER
Description Grey shell.
Length 10 cm (4 in).
Ease of keeping Difficult.
Food Filter-feeder on particulate matter.
Breeding Unknown in the aquarium; carried out on farms.
Swimming level Lower levels.

Pagurus bernhardus
COMMON HERMIT CRAB

Description Red body. Small specimens commonly inhabit snail shells, while larger specimens live in the shells of whelks.
Length 10 cm (4 in).
Ease of keeping Fairly easy; relatively short life-span, generally less than one year.
Food Scraps of fish.
Breeding As *Galathea squamifera*.
Swimming level Bottom.

Palaemon serratus
COMMON PRAWN
Description Body almost entirely transparent; coloured by distinctive red-brown bands.
Length 10 cm (4 in).
Ease of keeping Easy.
Food Scraps; this prawn is ideal for tidying up aquarium.
Breeding Unknown in the aquarium; carried out commercially on farms.
Swimming level Lower levels.

(For general information on inhabitants that are suitable for this type of environment, *see also* Anemones, p. 134; Crustaceans, p. 142 ; Molluscs, p. 143.)

The finished tank

Add the fishes and complete the tank according to the instructions on p. 50. This fascinating temperate rock pool tank will need to be adapted and upgraded as new fishes and invertebrates are found, as fishes grow too large, and as the seasons change. In nature this is an environment that changes continually, and the aquarium inhabitants will each establish their own special niche, designed to cope with these changes. Some fishes will eat or bully smaller fishes as they themselves grow, and they may need to be removed from the aquarium (*see* p. 43).

SNAKELOCKS ANEMONE
Anemonia viridis
This anemone prefers strong light, so it is often found close to the water's surface.

EDIBLE MUSSEL
Mytilus edulis
This common and edible species is often found in dense groups.

GREY MULLET
Chelon labrosus
This fish will outgrow the tank before long and should be returned to the sea.

SHANNY
Lipophrys (Blennius) pholis
The male shanny, once mature, is a threat to most other species of fish.

BEADLET ANEMONE
Actinia equina
These restless invertebrates are always on the move.

EUROPEAN OYSTER
Ostrea edulis
This bivalve inhabits the lower levels of the sea.

SLIPPER LIMPET
Crepidula fornicata
These oval-shaped gastropods gather in chains, with the elder animals at the bottom of the pile.

SAND GOBY
Pomatoschistus minutus
Gobies like to adopt a position on a rock or other suitable territory.

Water milfoil
Myrophyllum aquaticum

TANK AND WATER MANAGEMENT

Fishes live in a very wide range of natural habitats. Over literally hundreds of millions of years, they have evolved and specialized in order to exploit particular environmental niches. They have adapted not only their body shapes to cope with different depths and flows of water, but also their major organs to accommodate wide-ranging temperatures and massively divergent water chemistries. For fishes to flourish in an aquarium, you need to monitor and control such factors as water acidity, alkalinity, and

External power filter

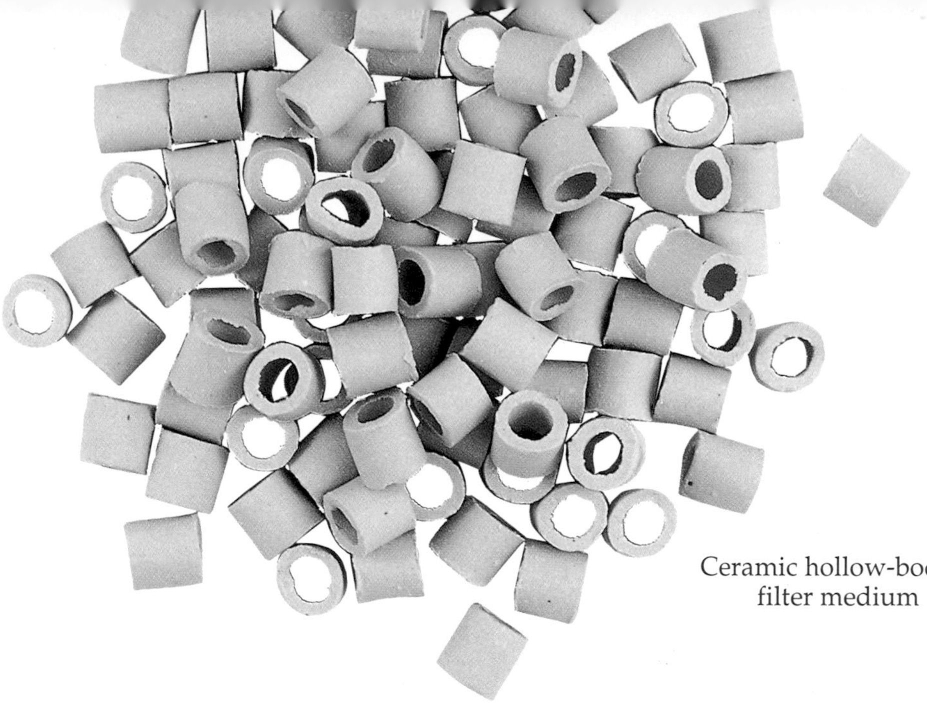

Ceramic hollow-bodied
filter medium

Peat fibre matting

mineral content, ammonia, nitrate, and nitrite levels, as well as water temperature, lighting type and intensity, and plant growth. Keeping fishes entails responsibility for their wellbeing, which means an expenditure not only of money, but also of time. In order to ensure a thriving environment in your tank, you should follow the advice given in this chapter on maintaining tank and water conditions correctly. In return, your aquarium will flourish and more than repay the hour or so a week it takes to manage it.

Bamboo plant
Blyxa japonica

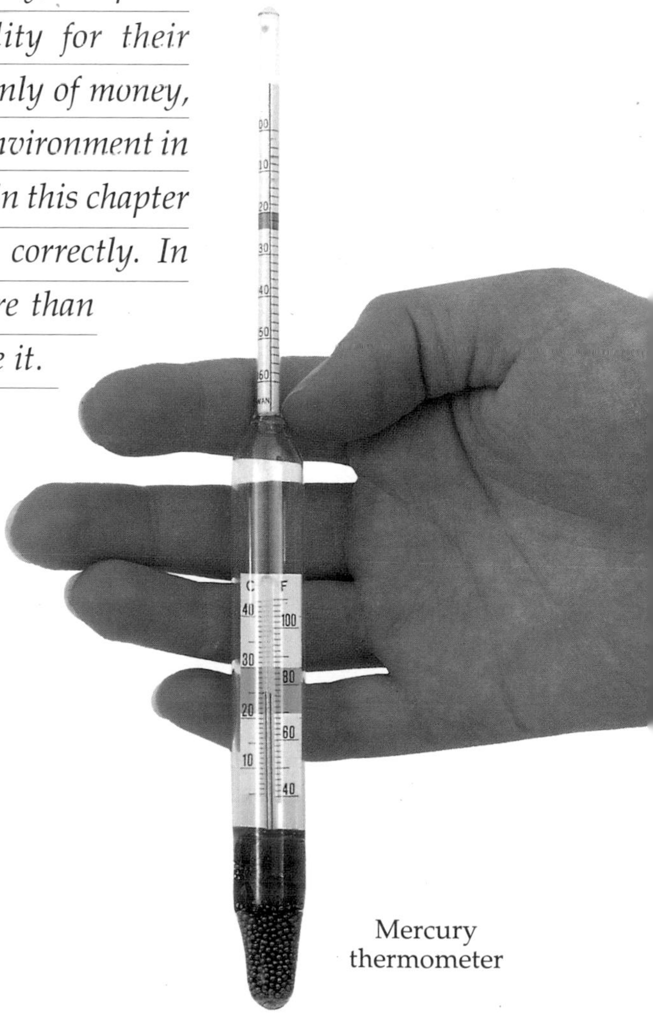

Mercury
thermometer

MANAGING WATER CHEMISTRY

Water suitable for fishkeeping is a complex "soup" consisting of gases, solids, and many different organisms. The combination and proportions of these components, and the resulting levels of, for example, acidity, hardness, salinity, and nitrogen for the types of fish that you want to keep, are vital for the long-term health of your aquarium.

So, managing the chemistry of your aquarium involves firstly designing your tank from the outset with the correct basic materials (*see* p. 42), and then monitoring water quality regularly so that you can spot and correct problems very early on. In this way, fishes or other tank inhabitants will not be subjected to any significant levels of stress.

PREPARING FRESH WATER

For the aquarist, the two commonest sources of fresh water are rainwater and tapwater (*see* p. 184). Tapwater, because of its convenience, is the one most people opt for. And although rainwater sounds like a good, natural alternative, atmospheric pollution, and acid rain in particular (*see* opposite), can make its use a risk in some areas.

However, you should not think that you are necessarily free from problems with tapwater, since it too may contain dissolved chemicals harmful to fishes. If you are in any doubt, check with you local water company. If your water is not safe, then there are other ways of obtaining suitable supplies.

Demineralized water is one such option. This water has had all minerals removed and so is free from substances that may be dangerous. Demineralized water is often available from fish dealers and chemists, but for the enthusiast it may be cheaper to invest in equipment to produce it at home from ordinary tapwater. There are two systems readily available for demineralizing water: "selective ion exchange resins" and "reverse osmosis".

Exchange-resin units These are used in homes for water softening, but the principle has a more general application in modifying water chemistry. In practice, water passes through a unit containing certain resins designed to draw out specific chemicals from the water. To leave only demineralized water, hydrogen (H^+) and hydroxyl (OH^-) ions (constituents of pure water) need to be added at different stages of the process. This type of unit is easy to use; simply attach it to a tap and follow the manufacturer's instructions.

Many synthetic resins have been developed for use in these units. Commercially available "mixed-bed" resins are preferred for producing aquarium water because they do not leave a chemical imbalance that would make the water unsuitable for fishes. In fact, they produce pure, demineralized water and pH, the measure of water's acidity or alkalinity (*see* p. 184), ends up at neutral (pH7), because the minerals that contribute to a higher or lower pH are no longer present. Once the resin is exhausted, however, it cannot be recharged, and so can work out expensive to produce large volumes of water.

One drawback with exchange-resin units is that they cannot distinguish between wanted and unwanted minerals in the water. They will, therefore, remove such beneficial trace elements as iron. To overcome this problem, it is advisable to add commercial packs of trace elements (*see* p. 180), suitable for your type of aquarium habitat, to the treated water.

In domestic water softeners, calcium and magnesium are removed by the exchange resin and are replaced with sodium. The result is not, therefore, pure water, and the high levels of sodium remaining make the water unsuitable for regular aquarium use.

Reverse-osmosis units A good alternative to resins is a reverse-osmosis system. Here, water is forced through a semipermeable membrane that holds back approximately 95 per cent of its mineral content. These units are not too expensive and some models will produce up to 160 litres (about 35 gallons) a day. Store any excess water in chemically inert containers, such as those made from glass or polythene, since these will not contaminate the water.

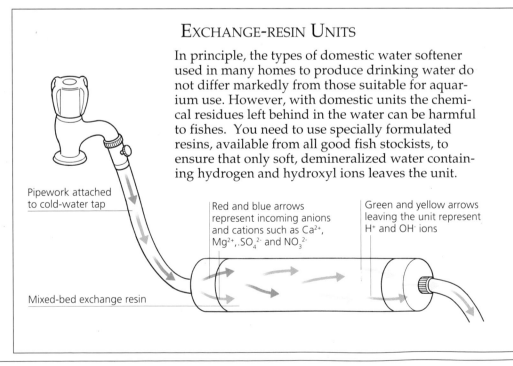

EXCHANGE-RESIN UNITS

In principle, the types of domestic water softener used in many homes to produce drinking water do not differ markedly from those suitable for aquarium use. However, with domestic units the chemical residues left behind in the water can be harmful to fishes. You need to use specially formulated resins, available from all good fish stockists, to ensure that only soft, demineralized water containing hydrogen and hydroxyl ions leaves the unit.

Pipework attached to cold-water tap

Mixed-bed exchange resin

Red and blue arrows represent incoming anions and cations such as Ca^{2+}, Mg^{2+}, SO_4^{2-} and NO_3^{2-}

Green and yellow arrows leaving the unit represent H^+ and OH^- ions

PREPARING SEA WATER

Using naturally brackish water and sea water in the aquarium is an attractive proposition, but there are safeguards you should be aware of. Do not, for example, take water from an area close to a source of pollution, such as a sewage outlet or a factory discharging effluent, or from an area receiving run-off of fresh water from the land.

Instead of collecting naturally brackish water and sea water, you should consider using synthetic mixes of minerals (marine salt). These come with instructions that allow you to produce a concentration of minerals similar to that found in sea water. Before introducing fishes to your tank, aerate the water thoroughly for several hours before testing for salinity and conductivity.

Measuring salinity The number of different minerals in sea water is much higher than in fresh water. While the measure of dissolved minerals in fresh water is termed its "hardness" (*see* p. 184), the measure of dissolved minerals in sea water is its "salinity", which is normally expressed as a number of parts per thousand (ppt).

Measuring salinity is quite straightforward, and the most common method is to use a hydrometer (*see* right), which compares the relative density, or specific gravity, of your water sample with that of pure water. Hydrometers are available, calibrated in salinity and with a gauge of ppt. The accuracy of a hydrometer as an indicator of salinity is, however, dependent on the temperature of the water, although in an aquarium with a fairly constant temperature, the readings for salinity should be relatively accurate.

A hydrometer is usually considered accurate enough to use for all seawater tanks except for a delicate reef system (*see* p. 138), in which the stability of the water salinity is particularly critical. Many of the more successful coral-reef systems are therefore monitored by measuring water conductivity.

Measuring conductivity A conductivity meter (*see* p. 156) can also be used to give an an indication of the level of minerals present in water. Conductivity is, in fact, a measure of water's ability to conduct an electrical current, which is dependent on the concentration of minerals in the water. Values are given on a conductivity meter in "microSiemens" ($\mu S/cm^{-1}$). The benefits of this system are accuracy and speed.

A conductivity meter is able to detect changes that are too small to register on a hydrometer, but changes that are, nevertheless, important in an aquarium that requires very stable conditions, such as a marine coral reef tank.

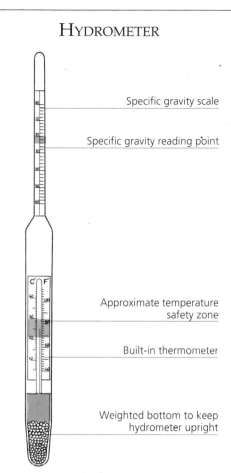

HYDROMETER

Specific gravity scale

Specific gravity reading point

Approximate temperature safety zone

Built-in thermometer

Weighted bottom to keep hydrometer upright

A hydrometer is the instrument used to check salinity in a marine aquarium. For accuracy, always attempt to take your readings at the same water temperature.

DECHLORINATION

Chlorination of tapwater is a problem for the aquarist. In areas where simple chlorine has been added, you can remove it by aerating the water which you want to use in your aquarium for 12 hours, or by using a commercial dechlorinator or activated carbon filter (*see* p. 161).

In some regions, however, chloramine is used in tapwater. Often this is added in greater concentrations than chlorine because it has less ability to disinfect. Unfortunately, chloramine is more difficult to remove, with activated carbon being the most effective at this.

If you are in any real doubt concerning the suitability of your tap supplies, you may need to obtain demineralized water (*see* opposite).

SOURCES OF POLLUTION *Industrial sources in particular generate extremely complex and often dangerous compounds which in many cases are not biodegradeable. In some instances, strange chemical reactions may continue to occur between these chemicals. Some interfere with the uptake of oxygen by the water by creating an impenetrable film; others may clog fishes' gills; and a great many are directly toxic in one way or another.*

CONDUCTIVITY METER

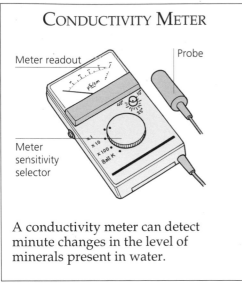

Meter readout

Probe

Meter sensitivity selector

A conductivity meter can detect minute changes in the level of minerals present in water.

pH TESTING

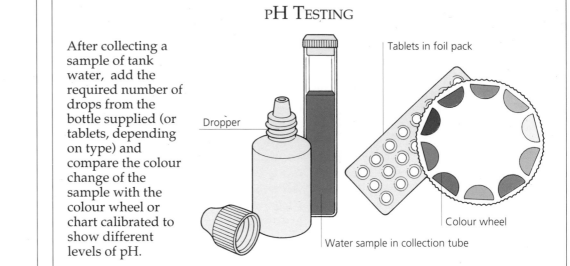

After collecting a sample of tank water, add the required number of drops from the bottle supplied (or tablets, depending on type) and compare the colour change of the sample with the colour wheel or chart calibrated to show different levels of pH.

Tablets in foil pack

Dropper

Colour wheel

Water sample in collection tube

Modifying salinity and conductivity
Electronic meters make possible the continuous monitoring of salinity and conductivity, and you can correct any irregularities by adding water. Tapwater may be suitable for this purpose. Because of the number of minerals already present in sea water, additional tapwater minerals, which might be unwanted in freshwater tanks, are not likely to have any significant impact. Some newer marine aquaria use "constant water dosing". With this system, a conductivity meter monitors the water and, as water evaporates – thus concentrating the minerals and increasing conductivity – additional water is pumped from a reservoir to correct the change.

pH AND ALKALINITY IN FRESH WATER
There are numerous tests you can perform while the tank is running, as well as when initially setting it up, to tell you if you need to take any action to correct water chemistry. Bear in mind, though, that you should not make major changes in the aquarium itself. Instead, carry out modifications on a bulk of water and then use that for gradual, frequent water changes.

Maintaining pH and hardness You need to monitor pH (the level of acidity or alkalinity) and hardness (*see* p. 184) regularly, especially in soft-water tanks. These have a more limited buffering capacity than seawater or hard-water tanks, and therefore may change pH more rapidly (*see* box, opposite).

pH and hardness will remain stable if there is sufficient buffering in the tank. Commercial adjusters, or buffers, which are based on sodium acid phosphate (to increase acidity) and sodium bicarbonate (to increase alkalinity), can be useful. Simply drip these into the water in the aquarium for minor, in-situ modification of fresh water. If you use amounts that are too large, however, you may overload the system with sodium and cause stress to the fishes.

Measuring pH Various methods of testing for pH are available, including meters. With a manual system such as that shown above, all you need do is to collect a sample of aquarium water, and then add the required number of drops of reagent (or tablets, depending on the type of system you are using), and compare the colour change of the sample with a colour wheel or chart callibrated to show different levels of pH.

The pH of aquarium water will fluctuate, and it is therefore important that all tests should be conducted at the same water temperature and at the same time of day. With similar systems, you can also test for nitrite, carbonate, and general hardness.

Altering pH and hardness According to the pH of your source water, and the way the tank has matured, you may need to make alterations in pH and hardness to suit the requirements of the fishes you want to keep. Corrective measures that you can take will be to

USING SAFE GRAVEL

The composition of the gravel, or substrate, can influence pH and hardness. Calcareous gravel (containing water-hardening materials such as limestone) should not be used in a soft-water aquarium. To produce gravel that is safe for use in soft, freshwater tanks and that will not affect hardness, you need to soak it in acid. A five-per-cent solution of nitric acid will react with any carbonates present, enabling them to be removed when you rinse the gravel.

When using nitric acid, even a weak solution, always wear rubber gloves and eye protection. You can also buy safe gravel – that is, lime- (calcium carbonate) free – from a good fish dealer.

BUFFERING

Buffering is the process that allows water to resist changes in its pH: the higher the mineral content of the water, the greater its buffering capacity will be. Compared with fresh water, sea water has a massive mineral content, and therefore undergoes only minor fluctuations in pH. In freshwater aquaria, however, pH fluctuations can be extreme enough to severely stress fishes, making them highly susceptible to all manner of stress-related disorders, ranging from organ failure to parasitic infestation.

INCREASING ACIDITY

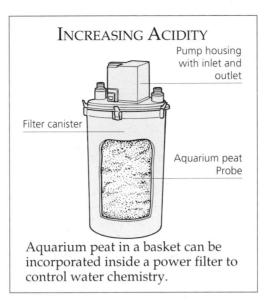

Aquarium peat in a basket can be incorporated inside a power filter to control water chemistry.

APPLYING ACIDS AND SALTS

Serious aquarists may want to control the pH and alkalinity of the fresh water in the aquarium using acids, such as hydrochloric or phosphoric acids, or salts, such as sodium hydrogen phosphate, sodium hydroxide, and sodium bicarbonate. The first three of these make the water more acidic, the last two increase its alkalinity.

The effects of these acids and salts are immediate and you should therefore make sure that you add them carefully in a separate container of water that you can then mix gradually with the tank water. Some aquarists prefer to apply these compounds via dosing equipment, which is capable of identifying even minor fluctuations in pH through constant electronic monitoring.

It is in the nature of pH pulses (*see* p. 184) that levels of pH in the tank can fall significantly during the night and yet return to normal by mid-morning. You should therefore not be deceived into believing that the pH level of your water is constant, and test for pH at different times of the day and night.

To sustain a very heavily planted tank you may need a dosing system for carbon dioxide. Such a system adds carbon dioxide to fuel the process of photosynthesis (*see* p. 165) necessary for plant growth. It will also reduce pH pulses.

reduce the alkalinity of the water, or to increase its acidity or its alkalinity (*see also* p. 184). Reducing the alkalinity of the aquarium water will not necessarily make it acidic: it may only reduce it to a neutral pH. In contrast, increasing the alkalinity will make the water less acidic, and it will always increase the water's buffering capacity.

Reducing alkalinity You can make water less alkaline by mixing in demineralized water. The calculations for mixing are straightforward, with hardness being reduced in proportion to the amount of demineralized water you add. For example, if a tested sample of water contains 250 mg/litre $CaCO_3$, combining it with 1 litre of demineralized water will produce 2 litres of water at 125 mg/litre $CaCO_3$.

Another simple method of reducing the alkalinity of tapwater is to bring it to the boil. This precipitates out the carbonates and bicarbonates that create "temporary hardness", but not those minerals responsible for "permanent hardness" (*see* p. 184).

Increasing acidity An excellent way of making water acidic is to add one handful of peat for every 5 litres (1 gallon) of water, and leave it to stand for up to a couple of weeks before use.

Peat is formed by the decay of swamp plants and contains such compounds as acids, resins, and even hormones. In hard water, peat releases humic acids, which attach to and bind with calcium,

thus softening the water. You should only use aquarium peat in your tank, however, since the garden variety may contain unwanted and potentially lethal fertilizers.

Before adding any water treated with peat to the tank, filter it through muslin or a section of old nylon tights.

A quick variation on this method involves packing the peat into a mechanical filter (*see* above) attached to the tank's water supply. You need to take care though, since pH changes resulting from this practice are likely to occur quickly. Hold back some untreated water that you can introduce if the water changes too radically. You should also note that if the water is initially too alkaline the aquarium treatment may not be effective.

Increasing alkalinity A useful way of making water more alkaline, and of increasing its buffering capacity, is to leave it in contact with crushed limestone or shells. When in contact with the water, the calcium carbonates in these materials form carbonic acid and then produce calcium bicarbonates and the hydrogen ions that are needed for buffering. Bear in mind, though, that if the tank bed is being used as an undergravel biological filter (*see* p. 160) the calcareous material is likely to become coated with bacterial slime and will soon contribute little to buffering.

You can also add limestone to a mechanical filter as for peat, and then cycle water through it to increase alkalinity.

—pH AND ALKALINITY IN SEA WATER—
To maintain the high alkalinity and excellent buffering capacity of brackish water and sea water, it is important to top up the tank's carbonate reserve regularly. The use of calcium carbonate gravels in the filter bed will prevent falls to below 50 mg/litre $CaCO_3$. However, without taking any extra measures, the carbonate and bicarbonate (which constitute the carbonate reserve) in these gravels will eventually be reduced by the removal of carbon dioxide and its continual replenishment from the reserve, as well as by the bacteria and algae that grow on the gravel. This will significantly reduce the water's buffering capacity. Freshening the gravel occasionally, by replacing a

quarter to a third, is a useful way of "de-coking" the filter bed. In many heavily aquascaped marine tanks, however, such as coral reef tanks, the gravel will be inaccessible, and you may therefore need to consider introducing soluble carbonate via a trickle filter (*see* below).

In general, sodium bicarbonate is the best buffer to use. Relying on the addition of crushed limestone or shells to marine systems in an attempt to maintain pH is not a good idea. It causes the calcium levels in the aquarium to rise abnormally and changes the chemical balance of the water.

Using trickle filters Calcium carbonate present in the tank involved in the processes of buffering eventually becomes coated with newer precipitates of calcium and magnesium carbonate. These inhibit the solubility of the calcium carbonate and hence its ability to contribute to buffering.

To overcome this problem, some marine filtration systems apply potentially soluble calcium carbonate, in the form of calcite, via trickle filters. These work by filtering water rapidly and constantly through trays containing calcite, thus ensuring that the calcium carbonate in the aquarium is replenished on a constant and regular basis. Because of the rapid throughput of water in trickle filters, there is less opportunity for precipitation to occur.

REDOX POTENTIAL

In addition to pH, you need to take another scale into account – the measure pε, termed the "redox potential" because it is a measure of potential for "**red**uction" or "**ox**idation". It is used to represent the balance of electrons in a body of water. Water with a high redox potential is of high quality, containing much surplus oxygen and complete mineralization of all waste organic material. It is, in other words, like the "gin-clear" mountain stream. Water with a low redox potential would, in contrast, be slow-moving and cloudy, and would contain waste material that was incompletely broken down.

In both nature and the aquarium, oxygen levels have the most potent effect on redox potential: waste products accumulate unless oxidized and mineralized. Plants have varying requirements: for example, while most algae (particularly in marine systems) prefer clear water with a high redox potential, others (such as *Cryptocoryne* spp.) tend to prefer lower values.

Levels of redox potential The pε scale on a redox meter is designed to run from 0 to 42, with 0 as the point representing the lowest oxidizing (strongest "reducing") powers, and 42 as the point representing the greatest oxidizing power. If the redox potential is too low, there is a chance that mineralization may not occur at all, and the process of bacterial nitrification (*see* p. 185) will be slowed because the bacteria cannot obtain sufficient oxygen. The pε of water in an aquarium should usually be in the region of 27 to 32.

AERATION

While very little of the air pumped into a tank by a filter (*see* p. 159) actually contributes oxygen directly to the water, the bubbles do have a vital role to play. By moving water around the tank and up to the surface, they expose more water to the air. This permits oxygen to diffuse into the water.

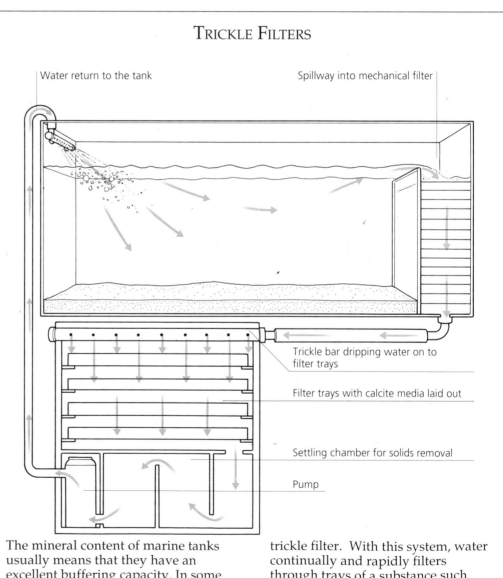

TRICKLE FILTERS

Water return to the tank / Spillway into mechanical filter / Trickle bar dripping water on to filter trays / Filter trays with calcite media laid out / Settling chamber for solids removal / Pump

The mineral content of marine tanks usually means that they have an excellent buffering capacity. In some cases, however, it may be beneficial to increase the amount of calcium carbonate in the water by using a trickle filter. With this system, water continually and rapidly filters through trays of a substance such as calcite, ensuring that the tank's carbonate reserve is always topped up sufficiently.

FILTRATION IN THE AQUARIUM

To keep aquarium water clean and well balanced demands an effective filtration system – one that not only removes waste materials from the water, but also mirrors the processes of biological filtration that occur in nature (*see* p. 185).

Stemming from this basic requirement, three different methods of filtration have been developed: mechanical filtration, undergravel filtration, and chemical filtration. Each of these is discussed below.

MECHANICAL FILTRATION

Early fishkeepers developed mechanical filtration to deal with what they identified as the main danger to the tank: faeces. Mechanical filtration began with internal ("corner-box") filters. These are driven by an airstone, using the principle that when air bubbles rise in water they "pull" water with them. The water is passed through one or more media (*see* p. 160) in a box or cylinder in the tank. This system is fairly inefficient, with a poor "draw", and is now less widely used. It is, however, useful in fry tanks, where the gentle action means that small fry are not pulled into the filter and killed.

Further developments of mechanical filters using the air-driven uplift principle include external box filters and internal sponge filters. However, all these systems of filtration have now been largely superseded by newer, power-driven filters.

Power filters Power filters have been developed that are quiet and much more efficient than the older air-driven filters. They are available in various forms, from powerheads used to improve undergravel filtration (*see* p. 161), internal or external cannister filters, to various units used to supply flow-through box filters. A variety of specifications can be found to suit all manner of tanks and different rates of flow.

Maintaining a mechanical filter Because of the accumulation of bacteria, most mechanical filters also develop a very good biological action as a bonus. In light of this, do not be too vigorous when cleaning out the sponges that are used in these systems. A quick rinse to wash out the solids should be sufficient and will leave the bacteria working away. Note also that if mechanical filtration is too powerful it will remove

FILTERS FOR A NEW TANK

Although bacteria will develop of their own accord in a new aquarium, adding "mature" gravel from an existing aquarium or commercially available bacterial cultures will give the filter a head start. Similarly, it is important to add fishes in stages in order to allow the system to get going. Introduce the most tolerant fishes initially.

FILTER TECHNOLOGY

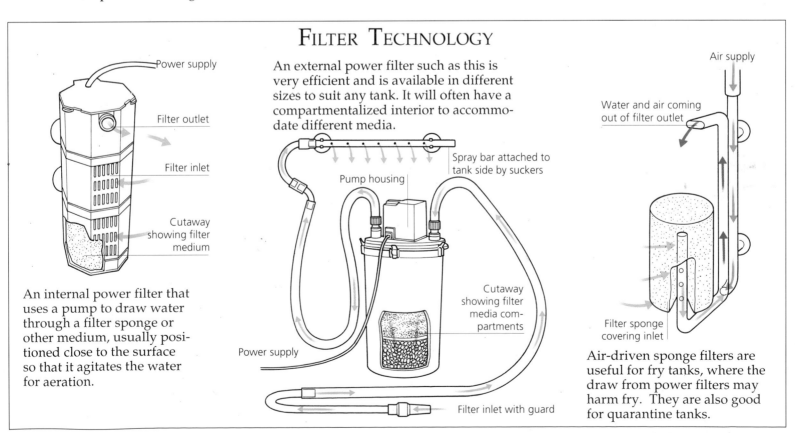

An external power filter such as this is very efficient and is available in different sizes to suit any tank. It will often have a compartmentalized interior to accommodate different media.

Power supply

Filter outlet

Filter inlet

Cutaway showing filter medium

An internal power filter that uses a pump to draw water through a filter sponge or other medium, usually positioned close to the surface so that it agitates the water for aeration.

Spray bar attached to tank side by suckers

Pump housing

Cutaway showing filter media compartments

Power supply

Filter inlet with guard

Air supply

Water and air coming out of filter outlet

Filter sponge covering inlet

Air-driven sponge filters are useful for fry tanks, where the draw from power filters may harm fry. They are also good for quarantine tanks.

any fine, suspended food particles, such as daphnia and algae, and fry and invertebrates in the tank may be starved.

UNDERGRAVEL FILTRATION

Undergravel filters have been by far the most popular way of creating the right circumstances in the aquarium for biological filtration (see p. 185). In undergravel filters, the gravel itself is the filter medium. The hardware consists of a simple perforated plate on which the gravel forms a base that can be colonized by the heterotrophic and autotrophic bacteria. These oxidize ammonia into relatively harmless nitrates. Since the gravel and any rock must sit on this plate, the stronger it is the better. Both *Nitrosomonas* and *Nitrobacter* – the bacteria responsible for nitrification – like to attach themselves to a surface rather than floating free in the water, and they find this system ideal.

Undergravel filtration systems The gravel should be laid on the filter plate. You can obtain suitable gravel for freshwater systems from most dealers. This gravel is a dark, yellow-brown mottled colour, slightly rough, and about 3 to 5 mm (¼ in) in diameter.

Water is drawn up from underneath the filter plate by air bubbles from a pump entering an uplift tube. In tanks with a plate of 90 x 30 cm (36 x 12 in) an uplift in each corner is normally adequate; but for tanks larger than this, you may need to place uplifts at intervals along the back of the tank. Newer systems may have powerheads on the uplifts to improve the draw on the water. Make sure that the powerhead you choose is suited to the size of your tank. A head that is too powerful will increase the turnover and thus reduce the time on each pass that the bacteria have available to work on the waste.

Reverse-flow undergravel filters Solid waste will inevitably be drawn into the undergravel filter, and if allowed to block the system the bacteria may die and the water become toxic. You can help prevent this possibility by using a reverse-flow system with a prefilter.

In this system, water is drawn off to be prefiltered mechanically (see p. 159) and/or chemically (see opposite) in a

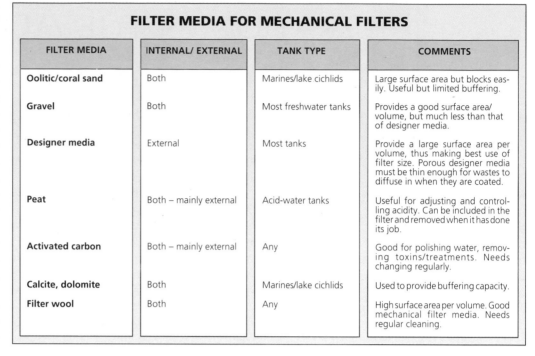

FILTER MEDIA FOR MECHANICAL FILTERS

FILTER MEDIA	INTERNAL/ EXTERNAL	TANK TYPE	COMMENTS
Oolitic/coral sand	Both	Marines/lake cichlids	Large surface area but blocks easily. Useful but limited buffering.
Gravel	Both	Most freshwater tanks	Provides a good surface area/volume, but much less than that of designer media.
Designer media	External	Most tanks	Provide a large surface area per volume, thus making best use of filter size. Porous designer media must be thin enough for wastes to diffuse in when they are coated.
Peat	Both – mainly external	Acid-water tanks	Useful for adjusting and controlling acidity. Can be included in the filter and removed when it has done its job.
Activated carbon	Both – mainly external	Any	Good for polishing water, removing toxins/treatments. Needs changing regularly.
Calcite, dolomite	Both	Marines/lake cichlids	Used to provide buffering capacity.
Filter wool	Both	Any	High surface area per volume. Good mechanical filter media. Needs regular cleaning.

UNDERGRAVEL FILTRATION

To install an undergravel filter system, first set up the uplift tube(s) and air stone(s) and then lay the gravel on the filter plate at the bottom of the tank. Make sure that the filter plate fits the bottom of the aquarium as closely as possible, so that the greatest possible filtration area can be covered. If the gravel is too fine, it will pack down and become ineffective. Most dealers supply suitable gravel, which should be rough-surfaced and about 3 to 5 mm (¼ in) in diameter.

Once the system has been set up, water is drawn up from underneath the filter plate by air bubbles from a pump entering the uplift tube. In tanks with a plate size of 90 x 30 cm (36 x 12 in) an uplift in each corner is usually sufficient; but for tanks larger than this you may need to place uplifts at intervals along the back of the tank.

New undergravel filtration systems may incorporate powerheads (see opposite) to improve the draw on the water. You must make sure that the powerhead that you choose is suited to the size of your aquarium. A head that is too powerful will increase the turnover of water and therefore reduce the time on each pass that the bacteria have available to work on the waste material that they are trying to break down.

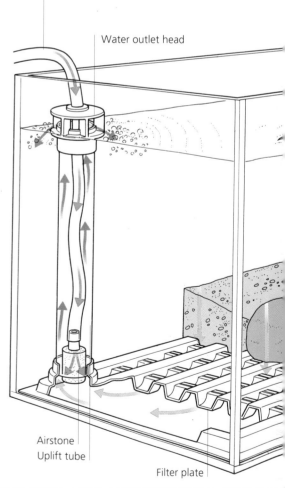

Air inlet

Water outlet head

Airstone

Uplift tube

Filter plate

power filter, and then returned to the tank down the uplift tube. It is then distributed to the body of the tank through the filter bed. This means that unmanageable solids are continually washed out of the filter bed into the water, and from there drawn into the power filter. This considerably extends the life of the filter bed and increases its efficiency.

Maintaining undergravel filters Using a mechanical filter in conjunction with an undergravel filter may prove useful in removing suspended material, such as faeces or undigested food. In addition, you should regularly remove mulm (organic waste) from nooks or crannies and the upper layers of the gravel with a gentle-action aquarium "vacuum cleaner" or syphon system, available from all good stockists. As well, you will periodically have to strip down the undergravel filter to clean out accumulated debris. How often you need to do this depends on the amount of work the filter has been doing – but every three to five years is a reasonable estimate. Syphoning out deposits from under the filter plate via the uplift tube helps extend filter life.

Pros and cons Plants tend not to thrive in tanks with undergravel filters unless they are planted in baskets or in areas where no filter bed has been laid down. Meanwhile, heavy planting, aquascaping, or the use of rockwork can sometimes create dead areas, and also other areas that, due to an abnormally high flow, are exposed to clogging. These latter problem areas can be responsible for the harmful release of toxins into the water in the aquarium, as the organic matter decomposes.

There is nevertheless one major advantage in using an undergravel filter – you can leave it to run successfully for long periods with little maintenance other than a periodic overhaul.

Chemical filtration

Ammonia, nitrites, nitrates, and any other undesireable elements in the aquarium can be kept under control by using efficient mechanical or undergravel filtration, or by regular, partial water changes. If, however, on testing the water (see p. 156) you find that the levels of the substances continue to rise (perhaps due to over-stocking or inefficient filtration), you may need to resort to additional action, which can take the form of chemical filtration. This includes ion exchange, activated carbon, ozone, and protein skimming. Remember that these procedures should only be used in conjunction with existing systems.

Ion exchange As well as being used in the preparation of water (see p. 154), you can also apply the principle of exchange resins to filtration. You can, for example, use the natural compound zeolite to remove ammonia, or artificial resins to remove nitrate. Removal of nitrates from tapwater before it is used in the aquarium is especially important for marine aquaria. You can buy these resins from your stockist for inclusion in a power filter, or buy a purpose-built exchange-resin unit. As with most other exchangers, it is recharged with saline water and so cannot be used in marine systems, which would continuously reverse any exchange.

Activated carbon Activated carbon is widely used for filtration. This material is fine carbon derived from wood charcoal, which attracts gases and complex compounds. You place the activated carbon in the power or internal filter to remove the metabolites that give the yellow colour cast to old aquarium water, to remove chlorine and chloramine from tapwater, or simply to "freshen" tank water and prevent the possibility of toxic build-ups.

Ozone There are a number of units available that produce small amounts of ozone (O_3) by generating an electric

Gravel bed

Rock creating a dead zone in the filter

POWERHEAD

Air bleed

Power supply

Pump housing

Outlet for aerated water

Top of the uplift tube
Waterflow

Powerheads are simply electrically driven pumps that you can mount on an uplift tube to increase the efficiency of the undergravel filter. They are particularly useful in marine systems, where the fine coral sand used as the filter bed creates resistance to the flow. An air bleed permits air to be drawn into the powerhead and be taken up by the water. These are often available with adjustable outlets to optimize the flow to the tank size, and to direct the waterflow.

arc. The ozone then oxidizes the "dead-end" compounds (from food and other organic wastes) that produce the yellow colour cast in tank water. Ozone is also used in protein skimmers to produce a more active foam. When using ozone, however, there is always some leakage into the atmosphere, so you should bear in mind that ozone is a potent greenhouse gas, some 2,000 times more efficient (molecule for molecule) than carbon dioxide in retaining atmospheric heat.

Protein skimmers Protein skimmers, also known as electrostatic filters, rely on charged molecules of unwanted substances in the tank becoming attracted to the surface of foam generated by air or ozone diffused into the water (*see* right). The foam then spills over and is collected in a container, where you can scoop it away.

The bubble size in this system is very important, and it only really operates efficiently in salt water. Skimmers actually remove much waste before it even breaks down into ammonia, and so generally help to stabilize the pH. However, filtration can sometimes be so thoroughly efficient that many valuable trace elements are also removed. To counteract this it may be necessary for you to add trace-element mixes to the water (*see* p. 180).

Denitrifying filters If nitrates build up to unacceptable levels in the tank, it may be a good idea to consider using a denitrifying filter. This type of system uses bacteria that obtain oxygen from dissolved nitrate. In order to grow, they may use waste carbon in the water or you may need to add a carbon source, such as methanol. You should follow the manufacturer's instructions precisely if this is necessary.

Algal filters, or algal scrubbers, promote the growth of nitrate-consuming algae. In this system, water is pumped out of the tank and is passed through a well-lit, shallow container of the algae. Another filter on the return side of the system prevents the algae from entering the main tank.

INTEGRATED TOTAL FILTRATION

Modern advances in filtration technology have produced total integrated systems, which are aimed particularly at the marine end of the fishkeeping market. They include some form of mechanical filtration followed by biological filtration, including a denitrifying filter. For marine tanks, such a set-up also has protein skimming. In an integrated system, filter parts are modular and easily serviceable, but the combined bulk of some of the systems on top of the tank often makes special hoods and lighting necessary.

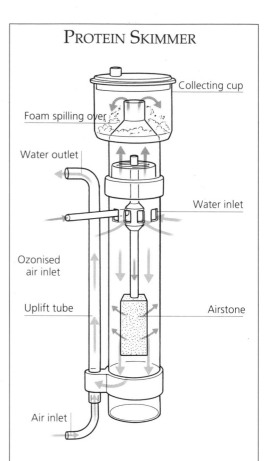

PROTEIN SKIMMER

Collecting cup
Foam spilling over
Water outlet
Water inlet
Ozonised air inlet
Uplift tube
Airstone
Air inlet

The red arrows show air introduced via an airstone. Another intake (green) pulls water down the main tube and back into the tank. The bubbles created in the main tube spill over into the collecting cup.

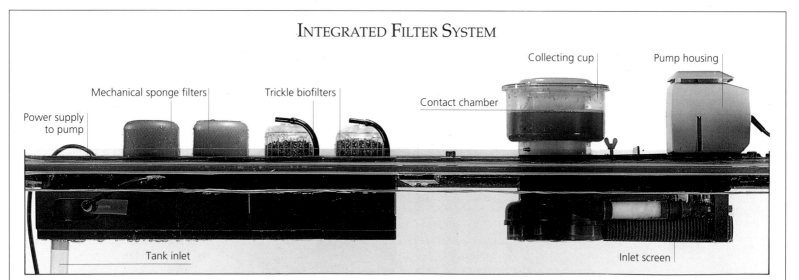

INTEGRATED FILTER SYSTEM

Mechanical sponge filters
Trickle biofilters
Collecting cup
Pump housing
Contact chamber
Power supply to pump
Tank inlet
Inlet screen

These systems are integrated and sized to the tank. They aim to filter the water mechanically, then pass a proportion on for biological filtration in a nitrifying trickle filter. The water is then passed through a denitrifying filter before being returned to the aquarium. The protein skimmer runs independently of the rest, pumping water through a contact chamber into which a venturi feeds air to generate the foam that traps soluble and fine particles of waste.

HEATING AND LIGHTING

A part from the various aspects of water chemistry and filtration (*see* pp. 154 and 159), there are two additional important areas of concern for the home aquarist in ensuring a healthy, well-balanced, and flourishing aquarium: heating and lighting.

Modern heating and lighting units can be used for many different tank habitats and sizes, provided that their outputs are sufficient to give the optimum conditions for the fishes, plants, and invertebrates you intend to keep. When consulting a stockist before purchasing heating and lighting equipment, always make sure that you know your tank dimensions, the volume of water it will hold and, if you are just starting out as an aquarist, the type of tank environment that you are intending to create.

HEATING

The heater/thermostat is a critically important piece of the aquarist's equipment. It might be days or even possibly weeks before a failure of the filtration equipment significantly affects certain species of fish or invertebrate; a heater failure, however, could become life threatening to the inhabitants of your aquarium within hours.

Technology has come a long way since the days when "state of the art" meant paraffin lamps strategically placed under a slate-based tank. Today, the internal heater/thermostat combination unit is the norm. Ideally you should position this unit in the tank where you have easy access should any fine-tuning of settings or maintenance become necessary. Also, the unit should have an easily visible display that indicates the temperature for which it has been set. Unless you are using a cable heater, you should always follow the manufacturer's instructions and set up the heater at an angle, so that rising hot water does not prematurely switch off the built-in thermostat.

CABLE HEATERS

With this type of heating system, you bury the heat-generating cable in the gravel at the bottom of the tank, and its output is controlled by a probe in the water connected to a thermostat. Despite the unnatural arrangement of heat coming from underneath the plants, in the region of their roots, the majority of aquarium plants do not seem to be adversely affected by this system.

Average temperature requirements

Few species of fish live in a natural environment where water temperature is always constant. In fact, many aquarists report better breeding success with a wide range of species by taking this fact into account and simulating the effects of natural, seasonal temperature variations, and adjusting the heater/thermostat accordingly for "winter" or "summer". The degree of adjustment is dependent on the temperature variation experienced by particular species of fish in their natural environments and, therefore, cannot be generalized.

As an average, year-round temperature (unspecific to breeding), however, you can work on the basis of keeping tropical freshwater and tropical marine tanks at 24°C (75°F); specialist discus tanks at 28°C (82°F) or even higher; and reef tanks at 26°C (79°F). Other tanks may well have other temperature requirements; the appropriate temperatures have been given for each of the aquaria featured in this book.

ASSESSING HEATING NEEDS

The heater that you choose for your aquarium must be powerful enough to heat it properly, and you should always follow manufacturers' recommendations regarding the requirements for a particular type and size of aquarium. Overequipping any tank is not a good idea, since this causes too many "on/off" cycles of the heater, which may reduce the life of the unit.

For the averagely heated home in a temperate region of the world, you should calculate your tank-heating requirements as follows: 10 watts/4.5 litres (1 gallon) for aquaria smaller than 60 cm (2 ft) long; 6 watts/4.5 litres for aquaria smaller than 120 cm (4 ft) long; and 4 watts/4.5 litres for aquaria larger than 120 cm (4 ft) long.

SUITABLE AQUARIUM LIGHTING

TYPE OF LIGHT	COMMENTS
Tungsten bulbs	No longer recommended. They have nothing to offer to the aquarist.
Fluorescent Enhanced red/blue	Output contains the correct spectrum for plant requirements and is thus good for plant growth. Light output is low, however, so this type of light is usually used in conjunction with a full-spectrum bulb.
Full spectrum	This simulates daylight and is extremely useful where space permits only one bulb.
Actinic Blue 03	Produces long-wave ultraviolet radiation, which penetrates the water well and encourages algal growth.
High-pressure mercury vapour (HPMV)	High-power lighting for tanks more than 45 cm (18 in) deep. It is less costly than metal halide, it has a fairly broad spectrum, but is lacking in blue/green wavelengths and needs blue supplementary lighting.
Metal halide	More pleasing to the human eye than HPMV because it has improved red/yellow output. Produces an intense light suitable for marine tanks, especially deep ones. This is the most expensive form of lighting and it usually requires a large housing.

SUITABLE AQUARIUM LIGHTING *Installing the correct type and intensity of lighting for your tank is essential for all its inhabitants. Both fishes and plants, as well as any invertebrates, have specific preferences when it comes to illumination. Although many are tolerant of less-than-ideal conditions, they will not necessarily flourish.*

LIGHTING

The correct type and amount of lighting are essential in the aquarium. Plants are quite demanding in their requirements and incorrect lighting may favour the growth of certain undesirable algae, for example, at the expense of algae and plants you do want to encourage. It is interesting to note that plants growing under a clear sky at sea level receive only 20 per cent less light than those growing at the same latitude at a height of 4,000 metres (2.5 miles). Yet this same degree of light loss occurs within just the first 2 metres (6 ft) of sparkling clear sea water, or the first 20 cm (8 in) of cloudy water!

Types of light In general the human eye responds to aquaria lit with a yellow/green light because it appears warmer and more appealing. Plants, however, prefer the red/blue ends of the spectrum. Although some light is absorbed in water, the average aquarium is not deep enough, or normally cloudy enough, for this to make an appreciable difference.

Manufacturers of lights have responded to the different needs of aquarists by producing an extensive range of bulb types and qualities.

Measuring light Assessing the quantity of light without the aid of a light meter is very subjective. If you already have a special camera light meter, then you can use it in this situation, but it really is not essential.

Light from a particular source is measured in lumens, but for the aquarist it is more important to know the amount of lumens per square metre (or "lux") of water surface area than simply the light's total output.

Light requirements The actual requirements of many aquatic plants vary tremendously: some have evolved to grow in dim light, while others are habituated to the full glare of an equatorial sun. Although many plants are adaptable, nearly all have preferences for specific light levels. Providing lighting levels outside of these tolerance ranges for extended periods may adversely affect growth. For comparison with the chart shown above right, young trees

LIGHTING SUITABILITY

APPEARANCE	INTENSITY	SUITABLE FOR
Subdued	<500 lux	Cryptocoryne, Vesicularia
Moderate	500 – 1,000 lux	Anubias, Echinodorus, Nomophila, Sagittaria
Quite bright	1,000 – 1,500 lux	Bacopa, Ceratopteris, Egeria, Ludwigia
Bright	>1,500 lux	Cabomba, Hygrophila, Microsorium, Myriophyllum, Synnema, Vallisneria
Very bright	6 – 8,000 lux	Anemones
Dazzling	12 – 16,000 lux	Macroalgae (e.g. Caulerpa)
Very dazzling	15 – 20,000 lux	Most corals (except for most red corals and sponges, which prefer shade)

HEATING AND LIGHTING FACTSHEET

TANK SIZE (L × D × W)	SURFACE AREA	VOLUME OF WATER	HEAT	LIGHT
61 x 46 x 38 cm/ 24 x 18 x 15 in	2,322 sq cm/ 360 sq in	106 litres/ 23 gallons	200 watt	45 watt
91 x 38 x 30 cm/ 36 x 15 x 12 in	2,787 sq cm/ 432 sq in	106 litres/ 23 gallons	200 watt	50 watt
91 x 46 x 38 cm/ 36 x 18 x 15 in	3,484 sq cm/ 540 sq in	159 litres/ 35 gallons	200 watt	80 watt
122 x 46 x 38 cm/ 48 x 18 x 15 in	4,645 sq cm/ 720 sq in	212 litres/ 47 gallons	300 watt	120 watt
122 x 61 x 38 cm/ 48 x 24 x 15 in	4,645 sq cm/ 720 sq in	283 litres/ 62 gallons	400 watt	160 watt

LIGHTING SUITABILITY *In the first chart (see* top*) you can see the recommended lighting intensity, as well as an approximate description of its appearance, for use in various tanks, depending on how they are stocked.*

HEATING AND LIGHTING FACTSHEET *In the second chart (see* above*) you will find a useful round-up of standard heating and lighting requirements for different-sized tanks. Bear in mind that this data is very general and does not take into account special requirements.*

require approximately an average of 15,000 lux, and rapidly growing cereal crops as much as 60,000 lux.

Lighting balance As you can see from the chart above, marine organisms tend to prefer intense levels of light. Freshwater plants, however, usually prefer light levels lower than those of algae – the maximum rates of photosynthesis occur at 10 to 20,000 lux for many common species of vascular plant, and yet algae continue increasing until 35,000 lux (values that actually inhibit plant growth). This means that excess illumination, either from the aquarium lights or from sunlight, may favour algal growth over plant growth. It is also important that you replicate the natural diurnal period expected by both

fishes and plants, so light the aquarium for only about 10 to 16 hours per day. To avoid stressing the fishes, never switch the lamps on and off suddenly; switch off the aquarium lights a few minutes before turning off the room light, and switch the room light on before the tank lights. Some marine aquarists leave a low-wattage red light on the tank all night. This is because in nature, marine fishes rarely experience total darkness.

The standard level of fluorescent light required is in the region of 0.016 to 0.022 watts per sq cm (0.10 to 0.14 watts per sq in). For marine tanks the fluorescent tube should be accompanied by an Actinic Blue 03 tube. For a coral reef tank (see p. 138), metal halide lamps are better than fluorescents. Use as recommended by the manufacturer.

AQUARIUM PLANTS

Hundreds of fascinating and attractive plants are available to the aquarist who is willing to make the effort to find the best specimens. Even the most common aquatic plants can be very beautiful in the right setting, and this book uses mainly the more easily available specimens. Plants are an important part of most freshwater environments, therefore it is worth taking considerable care when choosing and handling them.

Apart from their obvious appeal as attractive elements in a tank, aquatic plants support the fish inhabitants in several ways. They provide shade for those fishes that like it, as well as shelter for shy species. Some fishes rely on plants for their breeding sites, and they can provide part of the diet of vegetarian species. However, in certain tanks, such as those containing larger cichlids that eat vegetable matter, real plants are doomed from the start, and you should choose plastic plants.

THE NEEDS OF AQUATIC PLANTS

"Water gardening" has many similarities with conventional gardening, with the plants requiring good conditions and a certain amount of care for healthy survival. Plants create their own food in special green cells by absorbing carbon dioxide and giving off oxygen in a process called photosynthesis. To do this, they also need light.

Food for plants Like their land-bound counterparts, aquatic plants need certain nutrients – nitrogen, phosphorus, and potassium. They mostly take these from the water, although some plants feed through their roots.

Trace elements (*see* p. 180) are more important to some species than to others, but it is usually a good idea to add them in supplements for healthy growth. It is important to use those specially prepared for aquaria. Iron is needed for plants to make chlorophyll, the green pigment involved in photosynthesis. Other elements, like copper and zinc, are involved in various important metabolic processes.

Carbon dioxide Carbon dioxide, the fuel for photosynthesis, promotes optimum growth in plants. The purpose of carbon dioxide dosing systems is to keep the carbon dioxide level in the region of 5 to 12 mg/litre. (Higher levels may affect fishes' kidneys.) The dosing systems used in aquaria are based on those in horticultural greenhouses. They range in sophistication from straightforward, manually controlled models to those that are fully integrated with pH meters. They can also be linked with the lighting circuit, so as to shut off at the same time as the lights.

Light The levels of light needed for strong plants are quite high (*see* p. 164), and may need increasing as a tank matures. Three to five watts to every 4.55 litres (1 gallon) should produce heavy growth. Long light cycles of 12 to 16 hours may promote growth, but this can be too much for many tropical plants that live close to the equator. Although used to 12 hours of daylight, the sunlight is only strong enough to affect the plants materially during ten of these hours. Some plants thrive in lower light-levels – the anubias, particularly, prefer shade and appreciate being planted close to or beneath other specimens.

Plants and filtration Filtration systems obviously benefit plants in the aquarium by keeping the water clean, thus promoting photosynthesis. Undergravel filtration appears in some of the tanks described in this book, but not where particularly strong plant growth is wanted. This is because the constant movement of water around their roots does seem to upset plants, and prevents them from growing properly. Power filters, on the other hand, can be beneficial to plant growth, as the movement of water due to the outflow keeps plants on the move. This stops certain sections of plants being continually in shadow; it also prevents suspended material from clogging some of the finer leaves.

CHOOSING AND HANDLING PLANTS

It is well worth buying strong-looking, first-class specimens of plant. Retail plant displays are usually in flowing water under good illumination, which keeps most in prime condition. As much detailed research as possible on the needs of particular species will pay dividends. When choosing a selection for a particular tank, remember that different plants like different types of water. As long as you are careful to bear

COMBINING PLANTS *Plants add considerably to the overall look of an aquarium. Here the dark-coloured Java fern* (Microsorium pteropus) *is combined with the lighter, broad-leaved* Cryptocoryne.

this in mind, aquatic plants from differing habitats all over the world generally mix perfectly happily.

Before planting, check the specimens for signs of damage around the stems or leaves, and trim away any dead or dying (perhaps yellowing) leaves or roots. Integrating the planting with the placing of rockwork and wood can give a natural, informal look to the tank.

For most tanks, the substrate needs to be reasonably chemically inert. Fine gravels provide a better purchase for roots than the larger gravels. Baked clay granules can be mixed with the gravel to vary its texture; these often include benefical trace elements.

To give new plants an extra boost, special aquatic soil can be laid under the gravel. Standard potting mixtures are not suitable; they often contain components that float or fertilizers that may be dangerous. Special soil supplements, or planting pots sold with fertilizer tablets, are also available.

— ACHIEVING GROWTH QUICKLY —
Many plants that have a bushy, rapid growth habit are sold as bunches of top-cuttings (this is the way they are propagated, *see* right). This type of plant is ideal for creating a dense background or for screening unsightly components such as heaters. It can also provide welcome shelter and security for nervous or very small fishes.

Cuttings like this have yet to develop proper roots and may need weighting in the tank to hold them in position while they do so. Thin strips of aquarium lead can be placed around the

stem, but it is very important not to crush it or it may simply rot and the plant will float free or die.

— PROPAGATING AQUARIUM PLANTS —
Although permanently submerged, some groups of aquatic plants have varying methods of reproducing asexually – that is, without flowers and seeds.

Runners Some plants, like vallis, put out runners above the substrate, while others produce runners that grow through the substrate – cryptocorynes and swordplants, for example. At the end of each runner grows a new plant, or "slip". Some swordplants put out thicker, shorter growths called "offsets", where the new plants grow.

Top-cuttings The majority of aquarium plants are simply propagated by top-cuttings – that is, by rooting the growing part of the stem. This involves cleanly cutting off a section up to 30 cm (12 in) long. Many of the plants will form roots easily if the cutting is left floating in the water, or weighted down on the substrate. The roots usually grow from nodes along the stem, although some can produce roots from any part of the stem. Typical plants sold in bunches of top-cuttings include *Bacopa caroliniana*, green cabomba (*Cabomba caroliniana*), waterweed (*Egeria densa*), water star (*Hygrophila polysperma*), ambulia (*Limnophila aquatica*), *Ludwigia mullertii*, *Myriophyllum hippuroides*, and water wisteria (*Synnema triflorum*).

Rhizomes and tubers Many aquatic plants have a special kind of root called a rhizome that acts as a storage organ. Rhizomes consist of underground stems that have roots sprouting off them; they are recognizable by small scales and buds on the surface. They can be cut into thick slices, each of which will root

PLANT MAINTENANCE
Top cuttings can be taken from many plants, including this giant hygrophila (Nomophila stricta). *This will, in any case, be necessary as a pruning exercise.*

and produce a new plant. A tuber is another kind of storage organ, but it cannot be split into several pieces as it only has one growing point. Several aponogetons produce tubers.

Adventitious shoots Some of the more popular species produce adventitious shoots – small plantlets that grow from various parts of the mother plant. Echinodorus, for example, produce new plants from nodes on the stem, while Indian fern (*Ceratopteris thalictroides*) grows daughter plantlets on the edges of its leaves. Eventually these detach and float to the surface, but if pinched off, they can be planted. The Java fern (*Microsorium pteropus*) produces enormous clumps in this way, with small plantlets falling from the mother plant and attaching themselves to any nearby surface.

— GENERAL PLANT MAINTENANCE —
Most of the techniques involved in water gardening are a matter of common sense – removing plant debris regularly to keep the tank clean, as well as pruning, thinning, dividing, and replanting as necessary. Special tools are not really needed, although there is a useful device available for tucking plants in among dense growth, and scraping algae off the tank glass.

AILING PLANTS

Plants often start out well in the aquarium but then fade. The major reason for this is that in the wild, most aquatic plants experience an annual period of low water-levels when they are at least partially out of the water. This is when they reproduce, bearing flowers with seeds that are pollinated by insects. (The majority of aquatic plants started as land plants that later colonized rivers and streams.) Most of the plants will not flower when submerged in the tank; after about a year they weaken and fade, although some may last up to three years. Some plants need a seasonal resting phase, but this, too, is impossible in a tank. The only solution is to replace the plants with new, strong and healthy specimens.

TROUBLESHOOTING

THE TANK

Maintaining the balance of the habitat is crucial. Initially you should check pH, ammonia, and nitrite daily. Once the tank has settled, after three to four weeks, weekly checks are sufficient (fortnightly for nitrite) for the next few months. After this, monthly checks are adequate. More tolerant species render such frequent checks unnecessary.

Rinse mechanical filters weekly or fortnightly, depending on stocking level, and empty protein skimmers as necessary. Remember, heavy stocking levels put a serious burden on filtration, and it therefore needs regular maintenance.

Position the tank where it cannot be bumped accidentally, and stop people from tapping on the glass – this shocks and stresses the fishes. Similarly, avoid loud noises near the tank, like slamming doors or the sound of a television set.

VIGILANCE *Feeding offers a chance to check the health of your aquarium inhabitants.*

Switch the aquarium lights off and on gradually, to avoid stressing the fishes. At nightime, switch off the aquarium lighting before the room light, and on dark mornings, turn on the room light before the aquarium lighting.
Always remove uneaten food before it decays and pollutes the water. As a general rule, it is better to underfeed than overfeed: leave fishes looking for more so that no food escapes uneaten.

Check corners and crevices for accumulations of waste and remove them promptly. Regular accumulations in one part may suggest inadequate water distribution and require minor changes in tank layout to alleviate the problem.

If waste food accumulates in the aquarium, check that all fishes are feeding and reduce feed rates if necessary.

With marine tanks in particular, add trace elements on a regular basis, since protein skimming tends to remove them.

In the marine aquarium, you need to monitor and correct salinity frequently – check levels at least weekly.

THE INHABITANTS

Always aim to reduce stress. Take time to equalize temperatures between the transport bag and the tank water before releasing a fish into a dimly lit quarantine aquarium, which should have plenty of hiding places. Always quarantine fishes before introducing them into a long-standing, stable system – particularly reef tanks, which can be difficult to medicate effectively.

With marine tanks in particular, do not hurry the process of introducing the fishes. Bear in mind that it may take you a year or more to establish a healthy, thriving coral reef habitat.

Keep a careful eye on fishes and check that they look well and are feeding. With reef tanks you will often have to remove a sick fish to a hospital tank for treatment. This may not always be easy, or indeed possible, but it is the best course of action. Disinfect nets used to transfer sick fishes with a good pro-

TRUE COLOURS *Any loss of colour in this anemone (Anthopterra elegantissima) would demand investigation.*

prietary aquarium disinfectant. In other, less-delicately balanced tank environments, you can often treat fishes in situ.

Watch out for aggression. Some fishes can become very troublesome as adults. Also watch out for species that eat too much plant material or destroy invertebrates in marine tanks.

Do not allow excess algal growth, and thin it out as necessary. Otherwise it tends to choke everything it grows on. Excess growth is a warning that the balance of the water is slipping and that nitrate levels may be increasing or that light levels are too high.

In marine tanks, check the size, colour, and behaviour of invertebrates regularly to ensure that they are healthy. Fading colour in anemones may indicate that the lighting is too low or that they are receiving insufficient food.

Trim dead leaves from plants and prune excess growth to stop other plants from smothering.

Freeze-dried shrimp

FEEDING, BREEDING, AND HEALTHCARE

Fishes have become highly specialized during the course of their evolution, and it seems logical to assume that their feeding preferences would be equally specialized. Fortunately for the aquarist, this is not really so. In this chapter you will see that such factors as the shape of the mouth dictate whether you need to offer food that either sinks or floats, and that you need to account for the carnivorous or herbivorous preferences of your tank inhabitants. This chapter also looks closely at

Angelfish
Pterophllum Scalare

Dwarf gourami
Colisa lalia

breeding and healthcare – two areas closely linked
with correct diet. Fishes will breed only if the
conditions are right in terms of water chemistry and environment, an important part of
which is diet. When it comes to fish diseases,
the speed with which you respond is paramount,
and this chapter includes identification photographs
of the commonest fish health problems, as well as
detailed information on corrective action.

Hermit crab
Paguridae

Sea cucumber
Holothurioidea

FEEDING

Fishes, like all animals, require a balanced diet including protein, carbohydrate, fat, vitamins, and minerals. In aquaria the majority of fishes are fed on a diet of manufactured foods – usually in the form of flakes or crumbs – although natural live food should also be provided as appropriate for the types of fish that you have in your aquarium.

In the same way that an unbalanced diet can lead to health problems in the tank, so a carefully managed intake of food can play an active role in helping fishes resist disease and infection.

When estimating how much food to offer, the general rule of thumb is to feed little and often. This is usually the amount of food that can be consumed in two or three minutes, two or three times a day. Every few weeks you should also impose a fast day on the fishes. It is always best to leave fishes a little hungry, since a percentage of food

taken in by a fish fed to satiation will pass through its system undigested, and thus contribute to pollution of the water in the aquarium.

— GENERAL DIETARY REQUIREMENTS —
The major constituent of most natural foods is water, but the dry portion can be broken down into the components of the balanced diet noted earlier. Because of this, fish food manufacturers make dried foods, which, in terms of their dry-matter components, are similar to the natural foods of fishes. Food manufacturers also rely on the fact that fishes eat to a particular calorie intake. This means that most are on a self-imposed diet. In practice, most fishes have fairly similar requirements, and so an average can be used quite satisfactorily in most instances.

Protein All animal tissue contains a fairly high proportion of protein, and a constant amount is needed in the diet to maintain normal growth. As you might expect, younger fishes have a greater

SELECTIVE FEEDING *An angelfish (*Pterophyllum scalare*) spits out a small pebble that it has collected during its constant foraging for food in the tank.*

need for protein than older individuals – often 40 per cent of total dry matter as opposed to 35 per cent.

Carbohydrate If too much carbohydrate is given, excess stores may develop in the liver, interfering with its normal function. As a general rule, carbohydrate should not make up more than about 15 per cent of a fish's food intake. Levels in excess of 25 per cent may be harmful, although herbivores usually cope with carbohydrate better than do most carnivores.

Fat The bodies of fishes contain a higher level of polyunsaturated fats than that found in mammals. The omega 3 (ω3) series of fats, which research indicates is important in the prevention of heart disease in humans, appears to be important to fishes as well; it is certainly found in them at relatively high levels. Most of the fats obtained by fishes derive from plankton, and the fats from this source are generally polyunsaturated. The fat level in fish food is usually about 10 per cent. There can be problems if the balance of fatty acids in fish food is any higher than this.

MIDWATER FEEDING *Gouramis (*Trichopterus *spp.) and tiger barbs (*Barbus tetrazona*) turn their bodies to feed at the surface after being offered a meal of flaked food.*

SURFACE FEEDING *Killifish* (Aphyosemion australe) *with an upward-turned mouth feeding as they would in their home swamp.*

Vitamins Vitamins are usually added to manufactured foods at higher levels than they are actually needed. This at least partially allows for the leaching out that occurs when the food enters the water. Food is the only source of vitamins for fishes – there is no evidence that specifically adding them to the water is beneficial. Indeed, their presence in the water may encourage unwanted bacterial growth. Particularly beneficial vitamins for fishes are A and E, which stimulate the immune system, and vitamin C, which is very important in times of stress.

Minerals Minerals are added to many fish foods and they can also be absorbed to some extent directly from the water, although in soft-water tanks they are present only in small concentrations. One of the hidden benefits of carrying out regular water changes (*see* p. 45) is that they successfully replenish these mineral levels. Also, in more natural marine tanks (*see* p. 138), containing a considerable amount of living rock, adding minerals can be of great importance for maintaining the general health of the entire aquarium.

PIGMENTS

As well as being present in some natural foods, pigments, or colour enhancers, are sometimes also added to manufactured foods. They are a non-nutritional part of the diet, but they are important in permitting the development of natural skin colour. Pigments are also laid down in fishes' eggs, where they appear to influence hatchability.

DIFFERENT TYPES OF FEEDER

Fishes can be divided into three types, according to their anatomy and feeding habits (*see* p. 32). Surface-feeding fishes, such as most killifish, have upturned mouths designed for snapping up insects and other prey floating on the surface of the water. Midwater-feeding fishes, such as angelfish, take their food as it falls through the water, consuming algae and other food carried by water currents. Those species of fish, such as catfish, that normally forage for their food at the bottom of the aquarium, have specially adapted, characteristically downturned mouths.

Fishes can also be broadly classified according to their diet: carnivores, herbivores, omnivores, and scavengers. This categorization does not, however, take into account variations in feeding habits within fish families. For example, there are more than 170 species of cichlid in Lake Victoria, which have a range of feeding habits encompassing grazing algae from rocks, to eating snails and other fishes. There are also such fishes as the Bermudan angelfish (*Holocanthus bermudensis*) that are basically herbivorous in the winter and spring months, but become carnivorous when live food is readily available in the summer and autumn.

EASY GOING *Large cichlids, such as this* Cichlasoma spp., *may accept fresh peas as food.*

"Scavenger" is an often misused term. Bottom-feeders tend to be lumped into this category when, in fact, the majority of fishes, habitually feeding at any level, will at least pick at a dead fish on the bottom. There is no justification for regarding these fishes as aquatic "vacuum cleaners", yet this is precisely what happens. The consequence is that bottom- feeders are often left to take waste products sinking down from higher levels, which, in a well-managed tank, may be insufficient for their needs. Bottom-feeders are, like most people, simply omnivores – not really fussy about what they eat.

BREAKING THE RULES *Many bottom-feeders will come to the surface for food. Shy species, however, need heavier food that sinks.*

PRACTICAL ASPECTS OF FEEDING

The size of food offered should be appropriate to the fishes concerned. Livebearers, for example, produce fry that are able to take algae or flake food, but egg-layers are smaller and their offspring will only be able to manage tiny morsels. Food for the tiny fry of such egg-layers as gouramis, tetras, and barbs includes cultures of infusoria (a protozoal and algal culture known as "green water") as well as newly hatched brine shrimp (*Artemia salina*). If your tank includes specialist collections of freshwater discus, or Lake Malawi and Lake Tanganyika cichlids, then you may have to devote some time and effort to the preparation of suitable food, such as beef hearts (*see* opposite).

Marine fishes will take an array of foods. Many fishes when first imported are reluctant to feed on flaked food, but once fed in captivity, they soon learn to accept, and indeed thrive, on it. Beef heart can also be given to marine fishes, using a cheese grater to shave off suitable pieces from frozen larger chunks of the prepared meat mixture. Carnivores also enjoy such delicacies as fresh cockles, whelks, and prawns. Some species, however, have feeding habits that make them unsuitable for the home aquarium. For example, certain butterfly fish eat live coral polyps and you should therefore not purchase them.

MANUFACTURED FOODS

Processed foods are available in crumb, pellet, tablet, and flake form. These are formulated to act differently from each other in water, to cater for fishes feeding at all levels. Flake food is suitable for all types of feeder, since it floats on the surface before becoming saturated and slowly sinking to the bottom.

COMPATIBILITY

Aquarists need to take care to match fishes with their habitat. Most cichlids, for example, in their quest for food will treat a planted aquarium as a salad bar, or simply dig up shallow-rooted plants while rummaging around or nest-building. Equally, some fishes will eat coral polyps, as will fire worms (*Hermodice carunculata*). It is well worth doing some research before putting a tank together to ensure that all the occupants will be compatible. Make sure that you check on dietary preferences, to ensure that one occupant is not on the menu of another.

NATURAL FOODS

There are now a wide range of natural foods to choose from. These foods include plants, protozoa, and annelids (earthworms), as well as arthropods (flies, brine shrimps, and so on).

Fishes enjoy hunting live foods that you intoduce into their aquarium. You can obtain many forms of live foods from nature, but bear in mind that you must always vet all such foods extremely carefully, since they can quite easily transmit disease to the tank. Check collected food to ensure that you never introduce predators that can be dangerous to fishes, such as dragonfly larvae, water boatmen, and leeches, into your tank. After feeding live foods, remove all uneaten matter immediately – when dead, these animals will decay and pollute the tank.

On the opposite page, you will find advice on the suitability of the most common natural foods.

PELLETS *These are suitable for larger fishes and do not tend to pollute the tank.*

TABLETS *These are valuable for giving bottom-feeders sufficient, balanced nourishment.*

FLAKE *Developed for smaller aquarium fishes, flake can be ground up for tiny fry.*

You can readily culture them at home by soaking scalded vegetable matter in ordinary tapwater. You generally feed protozoa only to the very smallest of fry. If, however, the culture goes black and smelly, it indicates that bacteria have taken over and you should discard it and start again.

Rotifers These minute aquatic invertebrates are generally available from fish dealers as starter cultures in commercial kit form. They breed rapidly, and are an excellent food for small marine fry, or for feeding to brine shrimp, which, in turn, you can use as food for the fishes in your aquarium.

Nematodes These tiny microworms, found in most types of habitat, are very good as the next size up from brine shrimp when feeding small fry in the aquarium. Microworms are an ideal nonaquatic live food for adult fishes,

BOTTOM-FEEDERS *Catfish pellets are important for many bottom-feeders. These Asian catfish (*Pangasius sutchii*) are feeding greedily.*

Plants Many fishes require vegetable matter, such as algae and duckweed (*Lemna minor*), in their diet. As a supplement, however, you can also offer pieces of lettuce, weighted down so that they sink to the bottom, and peas. This will reduce the damage the fishes are likely to inflict on aquarium plants such as *Vallisneria* and *Aponogeton*.

Protozoa Collectively referred to as infusoria, these organisms include various amoebae, *Paramecium*, and *Euglena*.

TUBIFEX *Live foods of aquatic origin need to be selected carefully. They can be a disease risk.*

FRESH FOOD *Lettuce is a useful food supplement, as it reduces the wear and tear on aquatic plants such as this* Hypostomus.

CORDON-BLEU COOKERY

Homemade foods consisting of about 80 per cent beef hearts can be very successful for species such as discus and cichlids. Buy fresh hearts, remove all the fat, cube the meat, and blend it with wheatgerm, vegetables (such as peas), and flake food. The degree of blending depends on the age of the fishes – fry, for example, need a finer blend than older specimens. Add a general vitamin supplement, e.g. one with vitamins from the A, C, E, and the B group. Put the mixture in freezer bags and deeply indent them with the back of a knife. This will allow you to break pieces off once the mixture has set.

BRINE SHRIMP *Artemia salina eggs can be hatched to provide a disease-free food.*

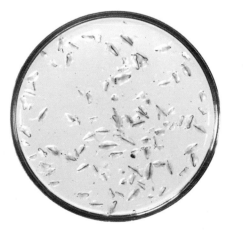

DAPHNIA *A common live food said to stimulate breeding, but it may carry disease.*

and they are free of the potential problem of disease associated with most other types of aquatic live food.

Annelids Many species of fish respond well to these types of worm in their diet, and they are also reputed to stimulate breeding (*see* p. 175). Earthworms are an ideal food for larger carnivorous fishes, such as catfish and oscars, while whiteworms are suitable for smaller fishes. Redworms, known as tubificids, are most commonly found in the organically rich mud around sewage plants. All varieties of worms will be eaten voraciously by fishes, but they may carry disease. Tubifex worms are also available in freeze-dried cubes.

Arthropods This type of live food is a useful addition to the aquarium diet. An important benefit of using them may be that the fishes get to chase their dinner. Water fleas (daphnia) are a popular food, and they are also available in frozen form. You can culture these at home in tanks left in the sun. Brine shrimp, however, must be grown only from purchased eggs.

Vertebrate prey Keeping the larger carnivorous species of fish does sometimes entail feeding them on other fishes. If this is the case, as with belonesox (*Belonesox belizanus*), which rarely accept other foods, you can either contact local breeders of guppies or establish your own breeding tank as a food source. Be careful to avoid sickly fishes that are being sold off cheaply, since they are likely to be carrying diseases. As an alternative, you can offer rainbow trout fry, since most trout hatcheries are free from disease.

FEEDING INVERTEBRATES

Invertebrates can be divided up into four categories according to their diet: plankton-eating invertebrates, carnivores, herbivores, and scavengers.

Planktonivorous invertebrates Included in this category are such species as stone and horny coral, tubeworms, bivalves, certain sea cucumbers, and crustaceans, all of which filter plankton from the water. You can feed them on manufactured plankton feeds or commercially prepared frozen foods, as well as on newly hatched brine shrimp. Plankton-feeders need to be provided with small and frequent, approximately daily, amounts of food.

DESTRUCTIVE BEAUTIES *Herbivorous sea slugs may look beautiful but they can wreak havoc on aquatic plants unless given fresh green food.*

Carnivorous invertebrates These include crabs, starfish, sea anemones, shrimps, lobsters, and octopi, and they will usually take pea-sized chunks of prawn, crab, or fish, plus flake food. Anemones are the most commonly found carnivorous invertebrate in aquaria, and you need to feed them twice a week. When in "blooming" condition, drop the food on to the tentacles, not directly into the mouth. Do not offer food if the tentacles are retracted.

DEADLY EMBRACE *Carnivorous anenomes should be fed when blooming so that the tentacles can manipulate the food into their mouths.*

Herbivorous invertebrates Most sea urchins, molluscs, and some sea slugs are herbivores, and to try to limit the damage that they can do to ornamental plants in the aquarium you should feed them on a diet of lettuce and kelp. You can quite easily blend this material, just like the beef hearts for carnivorous fishes (*see* p.173). Freeze in freezer bags as described for beef hearts, and store in the refrigerator until ready for use. Alternatively, combine the mixture with gelatin and freeze it in ice-cube trays.

Scavenger invertebrates These are mobile invertebrates that search for food at the bottom of the tank. Sea cucumbers are a useful addition to the mature aquarium, since they feed on organic material extracted from coral sand (in a similar fashion to earthworms) and thus help to keep the medium clean. These scavengers will devour any left-over food and they do best when stocked in a mature aquarium where there is plenty of detritus to clean up. If you keep these scavenger invertebrates you should ensure that you do not clean the bottom of the tank too thoroughly.

BREEDING

In general, the aquaria featured in this book are not laid out as specific breeding tanks, although many fishes will breed whenever the conditions are suitable. However, because fishes will eat each other's spawn or fry, the usual practice is to arrange for extra privacy for the parents, and protection for their offspring.

There are many different reasons for aquarists wanting to breed from their fishes. Sometimes it is to stabilize new varieties of colour or body shape; for other people, it is simply for the pleasure it gives them when they see their fishes behave in a totally natural fashion; while some people view it as a way of generating funds towards the sometimes considerable cost of their hobby. Another important reason has to do with conservation – many fish species are threatened with extinction in their native habitats.

If you are seriously interested in breeding fishes in your aquarium, then you will find an extensive resource of literature to be tapped, as well as a rich body of knowledge available through the shared experiences of members of specialist, or even local, societies.

Bear in mind that accurate records of breeding are very important in investigating the environmental or behavioural requirements of various species, and in

EGG DUMMIES *Many male African mouthbrooders have egg spots on the anal fin. As the female gathers her eggs, she also collects sperm from the male to ensure fertilization.*

EGG MASS *The eyes of these larval bullheads (Cottus gobio) can be seen within the eggs, while a newly hatched yolk-sac fry sits on top.*

this regard, home hobbyists can make a real contribution by their membership of fishkeeping societies.

—THE ENVIRONMENT AND SPAWNING—
There are many influences on fishes as they come into breeding condition. Consistently successful breeding may depend on you being able to replicate these special circumstances in the controlled environment of the tank. Almost certainly the circumstances that trigger breeding are multifactorial, consisting perhaps of a combination of factors, such as water temperature, food availablity, length of daylight, and changes in water chemistry.

Seasonal change Fishes in their natural environment are subject to seasonal change, and in general they have adapted their behaviour to ensure that their fry are born at a time of year when food is most plentiful.

Water condition In many fish species originating in the rivers of the rain forests along the equator, an important trigger to breeding is the sudden cooling of their environment, often by a few degrees, after heavy rain. The rains flood new areas, and bring a surge of nutrients from the land into the food chain. Other fluctuations in water chemistry can also occur, such as a temporary reduction in hardness, pH, and perhaps an increase in humic acids. These factors may all combine to act as a trigger to breeding. Many of these species breed several times a year and have short incubation periods.

Amount of daylight With fishes from more temperate regions, photoperiod (the hours of daylight per day) and temperature are the main triggers to breeding. Photoperiod is less important in the tropics because light levels are more constant there throughout the year. Some coldwater fishes spawn in winter, the eggs developing slowly until the water warms and daylight increases again in spring.

Nutrition Nutrition has a big part to play, and the availability of live foods seems to stimulate breeding. This may be due to the fresh food providing essential vitamins, the general stimulation that is brought about by the chase,

egg to divide, but not to contribute any genetic material to the offspring, all of which are therefore female. Consequently, all offspring of *P. formosa* are clones of the mother.

EGG-LAYERS AND LIVEBEARERS

The division of fishes into egg-layers or livebearers is fundamental. Within these basic groupings, though, different species have their own ways of ensuring

the survival of at least a proportion of their offspring. With the livebearers, techniques include various methods of nutritional support within the body of the female. In contrast to livebearers, which produce young that are capable of free-swimming when they are born and that can fend for themselves, the fry of egg-layers are small and helpless when they hatch. Some marine species may produce vast numbers of eggs, most of which end up being eaten. However, the sheer number of eggs released increases the likelihood of at least a few surviving to carry on the line. By contrast, other egg-layers deposit just a few

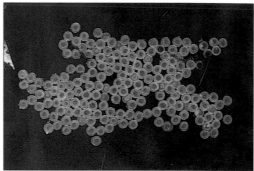

DESERTED *Corydoras barbarus eggs stuck to the front glass of the aquarium. These fishes usually select a smooth site for egg-laying.*

EGG-EATERS *Egg-scatterers, such as these glowlight tetra, commonly eat their own eggs.*

or a connection with the natural conditions that might provide such foods for the fishes in the wild.

THE BASICS

The golden rule of fish breeding is that fishes break all the rules. This means that you must accept generalizations as being at least partially error prone.

Fishes are no respecters of convention when it comes to breeding. They show all manner of sexual variations, including the traditional male/female, species that are both sexes at the same time or at different times during their life cycle, and some species that are even self-fertilizing.

One particularly interesting species, the Amazon molly (*Poecilia formosa*) – the result of natural hybridization of the sailfin molly (*P. latipinna*) and *P. mexicana* – requires a male of either of these latter two species to stimulate the

ON GUARD *The male and female of many species of catfish, such as this loricariid, take turns to guard the eggs that are laid by the female.*

NURSERY DUTY *This jewel cichlid (Hemichromis bimaculatus) is showing the typical cichlid behaviour of standing guard and fanning fresh water over the eggs.*

TENDER PARENTAL CARE *Here, the jewel cichlid is herding her brood around her territory; while breeding, she will defend this territory against all other fishes.*

eggs in sheltered or protected places and even guard them from predators. Egg-layers can be further grouped by what they do with their eggs. They may simply scatter them at random, they may deposit them and then leave them undefended, or they may deposit them and guard them. Some species from among this last category actually incubate their eggs in the mouth, providing a very secure environment.

Egg-scatterers It is not common for this group to breed successfully in the main tank, due largely to the fact that they, and the other fish species, will eat nearly all the unguarded eggs. To breed from these fishes, you should separate the sexes as soon as possible and condition them separately for breeding before introducing them as pairs to a specially prepared tank.

Such familiar characins as the cardinal tetra (*Paracheirodon axelrodi*) and its relatives, and the barbs, like the tiger barb (*Barbus tetrazona*), are egg-scatterers. These fishes will generally tolerate quite a range of water conditions in the aquarium, but they prefer some change to water chemistry for breeding purposes so that conditions conform more closely to their home waters. For breeding, both species like water acid and soft, the cardinal preferring a pH of 5.5 to 6 and a hardness of 18 to 36 mg/litre $CaCO_3$, and the barb a pH of 6.5 and a hardness of 90 to 140 mg/litre $CaCO_3$. Barbs like the water a couple of degrees warmer than the neons' 24°C (75°F).

Both species benefit from the use of a blackwater extract and feathery plants in which they can scatter their eggs. Some aquarists cover the bottom of the breeding tank with glass marbles or similar-sized stones, so that the eggs can fall to safety, between them.

The zebra danio (*Brachydanio rerio*) and its relatives require a similar tank with plants and marbles, and a temperature of 28 to 29°C (82 to 84°F). They are, however, not particularly fussy about water chemistry, preferring close to neutral water, at pH7 and with a hardness below 200 mg/litre $CaCO_3$.

These are, of course, ideal conditions for these fishes all year round, but particularly so for breeding purposes. The majority of egg-scatterers are also egg-eaters, and so you will need to remove the parents when they have finished spawning. The fry from egg-scatterers are tiny, and will have to be fed on infusoria or artificial fry food until they are large enough to move on to powdered fry food or crushed flakes.

MATERNAL CARE *A female angelfish (*Pterophyllum scalare*) guards her eggs. Using her fins to fan them, she ensures a constant flow of water, and thus oxygen, across their surface.*

cichlids are frequently aggressive as adults, choosy about their mate, and can be difficult to sex as juveniles, it is usually best to keep a number of juveniles together, as in the tanks featured in this book, and to allow natural pairing to take place.

When pairing has occurred, remove any surplus (non-paired-off) fishes to other tanks, leaving the original habitat tank as the breeding tank. As an alternative to this method, you can move fishes to new tanks as they pair up, but do not attempt to do this when they are actually breeding; it will almost certainly disrupt them and prevent them from spawning.

Angelfish (*Pterophyllum scalare*) provide excellent examples of some of the problems associated with breeding cichlids. They are reputed to breed without too much trouble, but often have eggs that are prone to attack by fungus. This is most often due to the "pair" being comprised of two female fishes – they

MOTHER'S "MILK" *Discus fish* (Symphysodon discus) *take maternal care to the extent of producing a body mucus on which the fry feed.*

both produce eggs (as do chickens), but of course they are not fertilized. Conversely, you may provide seemingly ideal conditions, yet the fishes still will not breed. In these circumstances, intervention is called for and some compulsory partner swapping is necessary.

Cichlid fry are large enough in many cases to take fine flake, powdered fry foods, or algae growing in the tank. You can also offer brine shrimp. Discus actually produce a body mucus on which the fry feed for the first week or so. During this period the parents need to be provided with plenty of good-quality food to sustain them.

Egg-depositors and buriers Some rasboras, such as the harlequin (*Rasbora heteromorpha*), are often fairly difficult to breed. They require the same type of water and attention as the tetras, but they take more care about where they place their eggs – on the undersides of leaves in the case of the harlequin. But just to emphasize how difficult it is to generalize about the behaviour of fishes, other rasboras, such as the scissortail (*Rasbora trilineata*), are like tetras and barbs in displaying little concern for the placement of their eggs.

Corydoras catfish take considerable care in choosing a site to deposit their eggs, without being considered fussy, and they prefer water to be soft and slightly acidic. Preparatory to breeding the parents select a spawning site, and clean it to suit their requirements by sucking up any debris and moving it to another part of the tank. Then they lay

their eggs as they would in a river in their natural habitat, after a sudden flush of rain cools them, bringing (in the wild) new areas of vegetation underwater as the river bursts its banks.

You can simulate these conditions by raising the tank temperature for a couple of months to 30 to 32°C (86 to 90°F) and then suddenly dropping it by as much as 5°C (9°F) for a day or two.

Killifish are prime examples of egg-buriers, laying their eggs and often mating within the soft peat at the bottom of the tank. In the aquarium, some species will adapt their spawning methods and lay their eggs in dense plant growth.

Nest-builders and mouth-brooders Prime among this group are the cichlids, the majority of which lay their eggs in a nest of some description – usually this consists of a hollow or other depression on the tank bottom. Because

LIVEBEARERS

The bearing of live young is seen in 14 families of fish, comprising less than three per cent of the bony fishes but more than half of the cartilagenous fishes. There are two types of livebearer: in viviparous species, the young develop within the uterus of the mother and are nourished by the female's bloodstream before birth, while in oviparous types, nourishment is provided by the yolk-sacs. The majority of livebearers produce small numbers of fry compared with egg-producers. This allows the fry to grow to a large size and an advanced stage of development before birth, thus increasing their chances of survival. Some marine species, however, including the red fish (*Sebastes marinus*), show a basic form of viviparity yet still produce large numbers of very small fry. Offering the parents the correct food is also a factor – stimulus provided by live food (*see* p. 172) seems to act as a trigger to breeding.

Four groups of livebearing fishes are commonly kept in domestic aquaria: Poeciliidae, Goodeidae, and Anablepidae from the fresh and brackish waters of Central and South America and the Caribbean, and Hemirhamphidae from Southeast Asia and Malaya.

Sexing livebearers Sexing livebearers is usually quite straightforward. In order to fertilize the female, the anal fin of male livebearers has developed into a structure that, in most aquarium species, is known as a gonopodium (*see* p. 38). This is used to insert the packets of sperm (spermozeugmata) into the female fish.

Once fertilized, a female livebearer can produce several broods from one mating, since she is able to store the male's sperm in her body for several months. You should be able to tell when a female is about to give birth: a dark mark, known as the gravid spot, appears close to the urino-genital vent.

ARTIFICIAL SECURITY *You can dress up cichlid breeding tanks by using artificial plants, which will withstand the attentions of the fishes and provide some cover and security.*

TAILOR-MADE NURSERY *Catfish like to have a dimly lit, soft-water aquarium with plants and flat stones. They will carefully prepare the area intended as their breeding site.*

Breeding tanks Breeding is not a problem with most livebearers, although you will usually need a special breeding tank, since they do unfortunately have a habit of eating their own newborn young. In a breeding tank, serious fish breeders will keep species of the same genus apart to prevent hybridization – and some of these hybrids will even be fertile. Your breeding tank should have some means of providing shelter for the fry, perhaps heavy planting or some other barrier, to prevent larger fishes from gaining access and eating them.

The filtration equipment for your breeding tank should always be chosen with care, as if the flow is too strong, the tiny fry can be sucked into it (*see* p. 159). On no account use an undergravel filter with the smaller egg-scatterers, as small fry can be pulled into the gravel.

NEST-BUILDERS *Red devils* (Cichlasoma citrinellum) *clean up an area and create a nest among the rocks, where the female can lay her eggs.*

HEALTHCARE

I t is true to say that the health of any animal is closely related to the "health" of its environment. This is even more the case with fishes, where the environment plays a direct part in the levels of stress felt and their susceptibility to disease.

In the aquarium, whenever there is a health problem you will need to look at three factors: the fishes themselves, the environment in general, and specific disease organisms. You should maintain a regular routine for observing fishes – for example, at feeding time. This will enable you to immediately establish when any of them are ill, and to act to prevent a disease from spreading to other fishes in your aquarium.

In practical terms, an outbreak of white spot or a bacterial skin disease can often be traced to the introduction of a newly acquired fish to the aquarium. It could have been that only one week earlier that same fish was swimming around in a rearing tank in, say, Singapore. It would have been fasted for a few days, packed with 50 or more others in a small plastic bag, inside a polystyrene box, and finally flown halfway around the world.

Conditions during transportation are often far from ideal: the water will certainly cool down a little and waste products from the highly stressed fish will accumulate. The fish would then have been unpacked and introduced to the wholesaler's tank, where it may have been properly quarantined. On the other hand, it may have been given a general treatment, such as chloramine T, sold on within the day to a local stockist, and then, hours later, to the home aquarist.

COMMON DISEASES

By following all the points on the disease-prevention checklist you will go a long way in minimizing problems within the tank. However, almost inevitably you will at some stage need to deal with a sick fish, and the earlier you catch the problem, the greater the chance of its complete recovery, and the less the chance of other fishes succumbing.

TRACE-ELEMENT DEFICIENCY

Trace elements are minerals present in the water in minute concentrations. Although generally not detectable by the home aquarist, they are important for the all-round health of fishes. Deficiencies of specific trace elements can result in the problems noted below. You can buy trace-element supplements from good fish stockists and you should follow the instructions regarding dosage levels to suit your aquarium.

Element	Result of deficiency
Calcium	Poor growth
Phosphorus	Poor growth, anaemia, deformities
Magnesium	Poor growth, kidney disease
Manganese	Deformities, cataracts
Zinc	Cataracts, wasting
Iron	Anaemia
Copper	Anaemia, poor growth
Selenium	Muscle damage
Iodine	Poor growth, goitre

DISEASE-PREVENTION LIST

Purchase new fishes from a reputable dealer, and make sure that they are compatible with other species in the tank.
Follow the correct procedure for handling or transporting fishes to minimize stress (*see* p. 44).
Where the main tank is difficult to medicate, such as a reef tank or those with invertebrates, always quarantine new fishes for a few weeks in a separate tank before transferring them to the main aquarium.
Similarly, isolate a sick fish in a hospital tank (*see* below) when treating a serious disease.
Be careful to disinfect nets and tanks after using them for a sick fish.
Regularly monitor and correct all aspects of water chemistry demanded by the fish species in the aquarium (*see* p. 154).
Do not overfeed fishes.
Periodically remove any detritus build-up from the bottom of the tank.
Maintain the tank's filtration system on a regular basis.

SETTING UP A HOSPITAL TANK

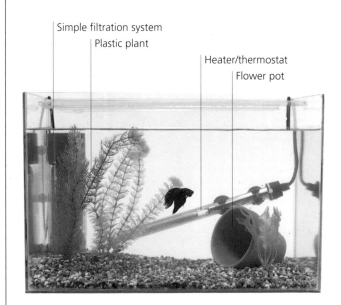

Simple filtration system
Plastic plant
Heater/thermostat
Flower pot

A hospital tank often doubles as a quarantine tank for new fishes before they are introduced into an established tank that is difficult to treat, or that contains valuable fishes. For quarantine or hospital use, requirements are similar, with security being of prime importance. You can provide for the fishes' wellbeing by the use of shelters, such as rocks or flower pots, and by "planting" the tank with plastic plants that you can disinfect between uses.

HEADSTANDING *Nitrite poisoning can simply kill fishes, but tiger barbs* (Barbus tetrazona) *show this strange headstanding and swimming-on-the-spot behaviour, with their fins outstretched in the early stages.*

FISH WARTS *Lymphocystis affects a wide range of fish species, but this viral disease is particularly a problem for marine fishes, such as this blue-masked angelfish* (Euxiphipops xanthometapon).

VIRAL INFECTIONS

Relatively little is known about the various viral infections that attack ornamental fishes. However, viruses are known to have caused serious losses in dwarf cichlids (*Apistogramma ramirezi*), although this is something that is unlikely to be seen by the home aquarist. Viruses are also suspected as being the cause of a disease known as S.A.D. (Singapore angel disease).

The virus most familiar to tropical fishkeepers is lymphocystis, and marine fishes are particularly at risk. It causes warty growths to appear on the fins or body. The strains of this virus appear to be, to some extent at least, family or even species specific. There is no actual treatment for this virus, although, strange as it sounds, taking a fish that is affected by the virus out of the tank and scraping one of the growths seems sometimes to alert the fish's immune system to the problem and causes it to react.

In general, vaccines are the best solution to viral infections, but so far research into vaccines has been restricted to commercial food-fish farming. Some of this research would undoubtedly be

FIN ROT *The cause of fin rot is often initial damage by aggressive fin nippers. This will be worse if tank conditions are not clean.*

TUBERCULOSIS *This can affect any fishes; wasting is the most common symptom, but some fishes also develop ulcerated nodules.*

applicable to ornamental species, but up until now vaccines have not been available to the aquarium hobbyist.

BACTERIAL DISEASES

Pathogenic bacteria, such as *Aeromonas* and *Pseudomonas*, are found in aquarium water and these will cause disease if the fishes are at all susceptible. Bacterial diseases are very common and range from fin and tail, and body ulceration to septicaemia (indicated by a reddening of the skin). Research has shown that up to 70 per cent of fishes arriving at wholesalers have these bac-

teria in their blood, but if kept properly they should be expected to recover. If, however, aspects of water chemistry (*see* p. 154) and heating and lighting (*see* pp. 163 and 164) are not ideal then serious losses may result.

Bacterial skin and gill diseases, the most common being columnaris, or cotton wool disease, are also caused by another group of pathogenic bacteria known as *Myxobacteria*. The bacteria seem particularly to affect black mollies (*Poecilia* hybrid) in freshwater aquaria; these are a brackish-water fish species that become more susceptible to disease when kept in acid water. You can help to treat the disease by placing the infected black mollies in a saltwater solution at a concentration of 5 to 9 g per litre (about 1 oz per gallon). Bacterial skin and gill diseases are very virulent and you must treat them quickly to prevent them from spreading to other fishes in the aquarium.

You can add various antibacterial compounds, such as benzalkonium chloride or chloramine T, to the water, but if the infection has actually penetrated into the tissues, then veterinary antibiotics are needed. You should administer antibiotics by adding them to food. If they are deposited directly in the water they may adversely affect filtration. Different groups of bacteria have different susceptibilities, so you should seek veterinary advice.

Fish tuberculosis is another fairly common illness caused by bacteria. Signs include a progressive wasting of the body and in some cases ulcerated swellings under the skin. Tuberculosis spreads easily once in the tank, mainly by cannibalism, so always remove sick, dying, or dead fishes quickly. On rare occasions these bacteria can infect humans, so make sure that you wash your hands thoroughly every time you come in contact with aquarium water. You should always seek veterinary advice about treating these types of bacterial infection.

FUNGAL INFECTIONS

The most common type of fungus is known as *Saprolegia*, which causes cotton-wool-like growths to appear on the fins, mouths, eyes, and gills. Fungal infection seems mainly to attack a fish that is already injured or weakened in some way. In the majority of cases, this will be a secondary infection following on from white spot or bacterial disease. Treatments for fungal problems are

"ICH" *White spot is the commonest fish disease. When stressed, a fish's defences are suppressed and it is then that signs may appear.*

usually based on malachite green, which you can paint directly on to the affected areas or add to the water.

PARASITIC DISEASES

Several very common health problems and diseases, mostly affecting the skin and gills, are caused by parasites.

Velvet and coral fish disease *Oodinium*, or *Amyloodinium* in marine fishes, belong to a group of parasites known as dinoflagellates, which are related to algae and contain chlorophyll within them. Stages of these parasites are free-swimming, and attach themselves

MARINE "ICH" Cryptocaryon *causes the marine equivalent of white spot and is just as common. It can be more troublesome to treat.*

firmly to the skin and gills of the host fish. *Oodinium* causes velvet disease in freshwater species, and coral fish disease in marine species. All fishes can be affected by these diseases, which particularly cause damage to the gills. Copper-based treatments are the best remedies, but they are toxic to invertebrates and should not be administered to marine tanks that contain them.

White spot, "Ich" This organism (*Ichthyophthirius multifiliis*) is visible to the naked eye as tiny white spots on the skin or gills. When the parasite reaches its full size it bursts out leaving a hole behind. A large number of parasites doing this can cause loss of body fluids, not unlike the effect of a severe burn. The Ich then divides into "tomites", the infective stage, which are free to infect more fishes. In the tropical aquarium this process may take only 12 to 18 hours. The majority of fishes live at peace with this parasite, but when they

CORAL FISH DISEASE *This disease is seen as a fine, golden "dust" on the body. Fishes invariably show signs of respiratory distress, with rapid movements of the gill covers. The usual copper-based treatments can be a problem in tanks containing invertebrates.*

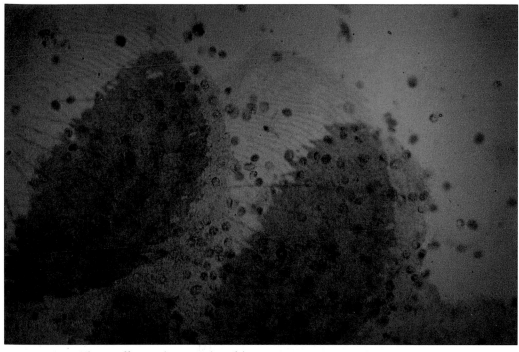

SLIME DISEASE *The small parasites causing this disease are always present in huge numbers, as shown by these many* Trichodina spp. *seen in a skin scraping with two fish scales.*

Flukes There are two types of these parasites: monogenetic flukes (single host) and digenetic flukes (several hosts). Although recognised as a common affliction among coldwater fishes, monogenetic flukes do not often bother freshwater tropicals. Skin flukes are not unusual on tropical marine fishes, often appearing as dandruff-like flakes or minute black threads. The effects of proprietary treatments are variable because of resistance on the part of the organisms. Formalin baths are sometimes used, but proprietary or veterinary organophosphorus treatments are more commonly employed.

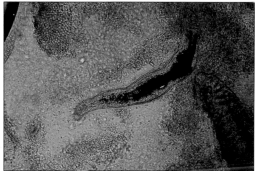

FLUKES *Gill flukes such as* Dactylogyrus spp. *can do considerable damage to a fish's gill before its existence is suspected. Treatments are not always successful because many are egg-layers and leave a resistant stage behind.*

are stressed their immunity wanes and the parasite multiplies. Ich usually responds well to proprietary remedies, and there is also a vaccine that may become available to stimulate immunity. The marine equivalent of this disease is *Cryptocaryon irritans*.

Grey-slime disease Slime diseases have similar signs but they are caused by several parasite families that can be distinguished only under a microscope. The principal families are: *Chilodonella* (in fresh water), *Trichodina* and *Costia* (*Ichthyobodo*) (in all types of water), and *Brooklynella* (in sea water). Fishes react to these parasites by producing large amounts of mucus, which dulls their colours, and hence gives this disease its common name.

Grey slime is less easy to treat than white spot, because the parasites are often resistant to treatment. Some may respond only to a high-concentration formalin bath, which is itself stressful to small fishes. Do not follow this course of action without expert advice.

Hole-in-the-head disease This disease, attributed to the parasite *Hexamita*, causes holes to appear in the head, along

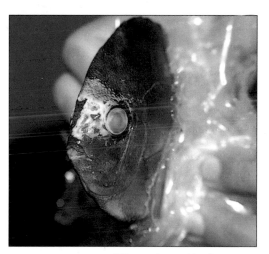

HOLE IN THE HEAD *Discus in particular are susceptible to this protozoan disease. Fishes may be infected when young and carry the organism for years before it causes a problem.*

the lateral line, and at the base of the dorsal fin. The parasite is very commonly found in the intestines of young cichlids and gouramis, and this commonly leads to outbreaks of the problem when the fishes are stressed. Veterinary treatment is usually with metronidazole or dimetridazole via the water for acutely infected young fishes, and mixed in the food for larger fishes. There is evidence to suggest that some of the fishes need vitamins A, C, and E supplements for healing. A similar disease seen in marine fishes is generally ascribed to vitamin-A deficiency.

GENERAL ADVICE

As a general rule, if there is no positive response to proprietary treatments, or if bacterial diseases are suspected, consult a veterinary surgeon or other expert.
Check the water chemistry and filtration, making sure that these are correct for the species of fish (*see* pp. 154 and 159).
If any water parameters are doubtful, carry out a water change or tank clean-up (*see* p. 156).
Do not mix treatments. Carry out water changes between treatments.
Avoid using antibiotics in the water, or methylene blue in tanks with biological filtration.
Learn by experience and keep detailed records to help you if a similar problem recurs.

APPENDIX

UNDERSTANDING WATER CHEMISTRY

Creating and then maintaining the correct water chemistry for the types of fish – as well as invertebrates, corals, and plants – you want to keep are factors that are fundamental to maintaining a healthy aquarium habitat.

In order to do this in the most effective manner possible, you may find it useful to understand something of the more technical aspects of such terms as acidity, alkalinity, hardness, pH, and so on, all of which relate to water chemistry. In nearly all cases, however, testing for these aspects of water chemistry is either by simple-to-use meters or colour-comparison charts, already dealt with on pp. 154–157, and should represent no problem even for the most inexperienced aquarist.

Water (H_2O)

"Pure water" is in fact a molecule with the very familiar chemical description of H_2O, meaning that it is composed of two hydrogen atoms bonded with one oxygen atom. Overall, the electrical charge of the water molecule is neutral – in other words it is neither positively nor negatively charged.

From a fishkeeping viewpoint, however, it is interesting to note that the atoms that comprise water can become positively or negatively charged as a result of either losing or gaining electrons. When this occurs the atom affected is known as an "ion": a positively charged ion is a "cation"; a negatively charged ion an "anion". The common ions of water are a single hydrogen atom (H^+) and hydroxyl (OH^-). This is significant because it is the ionization of water that affects its ability to dissolve minerals and chemicals present in your aquarium water. High levels of dissolved minerals are often not wanted by aquarists and indeed may be harmful to fishes.

Tapwater and rainwater

Tapwater contains a range of different substances, including calcium, magnesium, and sodium, as well as trace elements of such metals as copper or iron. It may also contain additives such as chlorine and chloramine, which are used for killing harmful bacteria, as well as fluoride and water-softening chemicals.

Rainwater, meanwhile, dissolves minerals and chemicals from many sources, including roofs, pipes, and pollutants in the form of dust. In addition, due to acid rain – the result of largely avoidable waste-gas emissions from chimneys, factories, and cars forming acids in the atmosphere – calcium, magnesium, and potassium may be dissolved from soil by the water. As if this were not enough, such toxic metals as mercury, aluminium, zinc, and manganese may also be released, sometimes in sufficiently large quantities to kill fishes in rivers, lakes, and reservoirs.

Water acidity

Acidity is described in terms of "pH", a convention used to express conveniently the number of hydrogen ions in a solution. A pH of 7 is chemically neutral, while solutions below pH7 are said to be acidic, and those above pH7 alkaline. Any substance that increases the concentration of hydrogen ions in water is an acid; any substance that reduces it is an alkali. The great majority of fish species are happy in water within a range of 6 to 7.5, but others need water maintained to an even more exact specification.

When you take a pH reading you need to pay close attention to the results, since the pH scale is logarithmic. In other words, a decrease in pH from 6 to 5 indicates a 10-fold increase in hydrogen-ion concentration – a very significant variation indeed.

General conditions within the tank, and particularly the level of carbon dioxide (see right), have an effect on the water's pH levels. This makes it even more important that you monitor the water carefully, since a sudden shift in pH, even a small one, may represent a danger to aquarium life. This is especially true in soft, acid-water tanks where there are more hydrogen ions present than in hard water. Abrupt increases or decreases in pH, known as "pH pulses" (see below), can lead to an inability in fishes to control salt levels in their own bodies. This inability to control salt levels can result in serious stress, lack of co-ordination, or, in extreme cases, general organ failure and death.

In a well-planted tank, where there is a substantial uptake of carbon dioxide and nitrate by the plants, hydrogen ions will be steadily used up, and so there will be an increase in pH, unless you take steps to replenish carbon levels. In an aquarium that contains poor, or scant plant growth, however, the trend is towards a rise in potentially harmful nitrate levels (see opposite) and a decline in the levels of both pH and alkalinity.

Carbon dioxide (CO_2)

Carbon dioxide is a waste product produced by almost all living things. Plants, however, have a positive use for it. By the process of photosynthesis they take up carbon dioxide and produce organic compounds for their own growth, as well as the oxygen that is vital for all life.

pH pulses

During the night, when you have turned off the lights in your aquarium, photosynthesis stops, but plants continue to produce amounts of carbon dioxide and consume oxygen as they continue to respire.

The surplus carbon dioxide present in the water leads to an increase in hydrogen ions, with a consequent increase in water acidity and a fall in pH. During the day, however, with the aquarium lights on again, these aspects of water chemistry reverse as plants begin to photosynthesize once more. It is this change in chemistry that is known as a "pH pulse".

The fall in the level of carbon dioxide that occurs during the day also encourages "biogenic decalcification", as the plants endeavour to obtain carbon dioxide directly from calcium carbonate, a mineral common in hard water. This causes calcium deposits to form on the leaves, which may ultimately kill the plants. To overcome this problem, use a trickle filter (see p. 157).

Water hardness and alkalinity

The levels of dissolved minerals in water can be described as the water's "hardness". Different minerals, however, are responsible for different types of hardness: carbonate (CO_3^{2-}), bicarbonate (HCO_3^-), and hydroxyl (OH^-) are associated with "carbonate hardness" (°KH or "alkalinity"); metals with sulphate (SO_4^{2-}), chloride (Cl^-), and nitrate (NO_3^{2-}) are responsible for noncarbonate hardness (°NKH). "Total hardness" (°GH) is the term used to describe the sum of carbonate and noncarbonate hardness.

It is important to note that in this context "alkalinity" is a term reserved for describing levels of carbonate hardness; it is not an indication of alkaline pH.

Of the above minerals, bicarbonates are by far the most important. Because of their ability to accept or release hydrogen ions they help to stabilize the pH levels of a body of water. Water's ability to resist changes in pH is known as its "buffering" capacity (see p. 157).

Temporary and permanent hardness

Water hardness caused by calcium and magnesium carbonates and bicarbonates is often referred to as "temporary hardness". This is because bringing the water to the boil changes the solubility of these compounds, causing them to precipitate out as solids. It is this type of deposit that is left behind on the electrical element of a kettle. So when preparing water for the aquarium, you can remove temporary hardness from the water simply by boiling it first.

This procedure does not affect "permanent hardness", however, which is caused by other minerals, particularly calcium sulphate. To remove these minerals as well you need to deionize the water using exchange resins, or run the water through a reverse-osmosis unit (see p. 154).

Levels of hardness

For simplicity, levels of hardness of any type are expressed as milligrams per litre of calcium carbonate ($CaCO_3$). In the United Kingdom, water hardness has been described in °Clark (1°Clark = 14.3 mg/litre $CaCO_3$), although it is now more common to express it directly in mg/litre $CaCO_3$. In the United States it is sometimes described in °Hardness (1°Hardness = 1 mg/litre $CaCO_3$). An even more recent measure is to express hardness and alkalinity in milliequivalents (meq), where 1 meq/litre = 50 mg/litre $CaCO_3$. The measure German hardness (°dH) actually refers to calcium oxide not calcium carbonate, but it is convertible to 1°dH = 17.9 mg/litre $CaCO_3$.

The following table gives a general indication of levels of mg/litre $CaCO_3$ to be found in various hardnesses of water:

Very soft < 10 mg/litre $CaCO_3$
Soft 10-100 mg/litre $CaCO_3$
Hard 100-200 mg/litre $CaCO_3$
Very hard > 200 mg/litre $CaCO_3$

Just as some species of fish cannot tolerate changes in pH, others suffer in soft water, or water of low alkalinity. In such unfamiliar water, fishes may suffer scale damage, fin erosion, and slow growth, as well as in generally poor condition.

Trace elements

Trace elements are minerals present in water at very low, or trace, levels. Of general interest to the aquarist are those needed physiologically by fishes or plants (see p.180). Common trace elements include cobalt, iodine, iron, copper, and selenium. Most often, the tank water will contain naturally occurring trace elements, and they are also added as supplements to many manufactured fish foods (see p. 180).

It is simply not practicable to test for the presence of trace elements in water without sophisticated equipment. In fact, many aquarists never add trace elements to their tanks and never report any problems. If, however, you have a soft, acid-water tank or you are using demineralized water, or if you observe your fishes behaving anything less than optimally, you should consider adding trace elements. These can be bought from fish stockists.

UNDERSTANDING BIOLOGICAL FILTRATION

In nature, water undergoes a complex series of processes as part of the system of biological filtration. These same processes have now become fundamental to successful fishkeeping. The four fundamental processes are mineralization, deamination, nitrification, and denitrification.

All of the processes of biological filtration occur naturally and unseen in rivers, streams, and ponds, as well as in your aquarium, and all are dependent on bacteria – primarily "heterotrophic" bacteria, which obtain nourishment from organic substances.

In nature, most bodies of water are subjected to constant renewal, from rivers, rain, or run-off from the land. In a closed system, such as that found in a tank, however, these biological processes can lead to a lowering of pH values. This is an aspect of water chemistry you need to monitor carefully and correct promptly (see p. 154) to avoid subjecting fishes to stress.

The four processes

The first process, mineralization, is carried out principally by *Micrococcus*, *Flavobacterium*, and *Achromobacter*. These bacteria feed on the waste nitrogenous products in the water, using part of them as food. These waste products include protein and their breakdown products – amino acids, found in uneaten or undigested food, urea, and uric acid – bacterial breakdown of plant materials, and compounds such as phenols from algae.

In deamination, the second process, the amino acids that are left behind by mineralization are further broken down to produce ammonia, which can be toxic in an aquarium.

This ammonia is then converted by nitrification, the third process, into nitrite and then nitrate. This conversion is carried out by "autotrophic" bacteria, those that obtain nourishment from inorganic substances. But for these bacteria to do their work efficiently they need a plentiful supply of oxygen.

The first part of the change, from ammonia to nitrite, is carried out by the *Nitrosomonas* group of bacteria, and the second step, the conversion from nitrite to nitrate,

is performed by *Nitrobacter*. Effective nitrification is pH dependent; bacteria have their own preferences for pH, as do fishes and other aquatic creatures. The process of nitrification is most efficient at a high pH – around 9 – and virtually ceases at around 5.5. Consequently, in water with a pH as low as this, there is a danger that ammonia levels will build up. Fortunately for fishes that are suited to soft water, the effects of this inefficiency are made less drastic by the fact that in acidic conditions ammonia is less toxic, since it is transformed into ammonium (see below).

In addition to the bacteria responsible for nitrification, there are bacteria that break down nitrates themselves and, in so doing, produce both free nitrogen and oxygen. This process – the fourth and final link in the "nitrogen cycle" – is known as denitrification, and it can be recreated in the aquarium where nitrates may build up to unacceptable levels.

The nitrogen cycle

Nitrogen is found in water in five forms: organic nitrogen, ammonia-nitrogen (NH_3-N), nitrite-nitrogen (NO_2-N), nitrate-nitrogen (NO_3-N), and dissolved nitrogen. These all form part of the nitrogen cycle. Unless all parts of the cycle are in good working order, the water will not be able to support plant and fish life properly.

Organic nitrogen

Organic nitrogen is derived from proteins and amino acids that are contained in waste food and dead fishes, and by the bacteria that feed on them and break them down into ammonia.

Ammonia-nitrogen

Ammonia is the main nitrogenous excretory product of most fishes. Once excreted into the water it ionizes, to a degree dependent on pH and water temperature. In other words, in cool, acidic water, one ammonia molecule should pick up a spare hydrogen ion, with the result that it becomes ammonium (NH_4^+). The more acidic and cool the water, the greater the degree of ionization.

Ammonia that has not been ionized is very toxic to fishes, although the susceptibility of different species varies. Generally, exposure to levels of ammonia-

nitrogen higher than 0.1 mg/litre for extended periods can cause chronic thickening of the gills, while higher levels still may result in death. The ionized form, ammonium, on the other hand, is not toxic to fishes.

Nitrite-nitrogen

The oxidation of ammonia into nitrite is carried out by aerobic (oxygen-consuming) bacteria. Levels of nitrite-nitrogen higher than 0.1 to 0.2 mg/litre retard the growth of fishes and are considered harmful to many species. If nitrite-nitrogen levels are allowed to rise to higher than 0.5mg/litre it is likely that fishes will die. Marine fishes are protected from the effects of nitrite by the minerals present in the water, although you should still keep levels below 0.1 mg/litre in marine aquaria.

Nitrate-nitrogen

The transformation of nitrites into nitrates is also by oxidation. Nitrates are thought to be nontoxic in fresh water, but in sea water they do cause serious problems. Tapwater may have as much as 50 mg/litre nitrate, and many inexperienced aquarists fail to remove this when setting up a marine tank (see Denitrifying filters, p. 161).

Marine invertebrates are also usually particularly sensitive to high levels of nitrate. Delicate corals, such as Goniopora, can simply wither away if they are exposed to levels of nitrate higher than 20 mg/litre for any length of time. Certain species of fish, such as the Moorish idol, are also badly affected.

Dissolved nitrogen

Some nitrates may, by the process of denitrification, be converted into free nitrogen in the water. Much of this is removed from the water by bubbles.

GLOSSARY

A

Acidity/alkalinity The measure of the number of hydrogen ions in water, expressed in terms of *pH*. A pH of 7 is considered neutral (neither acid nor alkaline). Solutions below pH7 are acidic and those above pH7 alkaline. A secondary meaning of alkalinity describes the levels of carbonate hardness of water.

Algae Primitive aquatic plants ranging in complexity from single-celled, microscopic types to large seaweeds.

Ammonia (NH_3) A highly soluble gas and the main nitrogenous excretory product of most fishes. Highly toxic to many species of fish.

Ammonium (NH_4^+) A molecule of *ammonia* plus an additional hydrogen ion and charge. This ionized form of ammonia is fairly nontoxic to fishes.

Arthropod An *invertebrate* animal which has a distinctively segmented body, jointed limbs, and a shell.

B

Barbel Whisker-like growths from the corners of the mouths of some bottom-feeding fishes. Used to detect food.

Brachiopod A marine *invertebrate* animal of the phylum *Brachiopoda*, with a pulsating, hair-like-covered (ciliated) feeding organ, and a shell with *dorsal* and *ventral* valves.

Brackish water A combination of fresh water and sea water, occuring in and around estuaries where these mix.

Buffering The process that allows water to resist changes in its *pH*. The higher the *calcium carbonate* content of the water the greater the buffering capacity.

C

Calcium carbonate ($CaCO_3$) A white, crystalline mineral found typically in high concentrations in hard water.

Carbon dioxide (CO_2) A waste product produced by nearly all living things, and used by aquarium plants in the process of *photosynthesis*.

Chloramine Additive used in drinking water to kill harmful bacteria. Can be toxic to fishes.

Chlorine (Cl_2) Additive used in drinking water to kill harmful bacteria. Can be toxic to fishes.

Community tank A tank containing different *species* of compatible fishes.

Compare with *Species tank*.

Conductivity The measure of water's ability to conduct an electrical current. The higher the concentrations of *minerals* the greater the water's conductivity.

Coral sand Pulverized coral with a particle size similar to that of sand.

D

Demineralized water Water that has been treated to remove all *minerals*.

Denitrification The process by which nitrogen and nitrogenous compounds are removed from water.

Dorsal The top surface of a fish. Compare with *Ventral*.

E

Egg-layer Any species of fish whose eggs are fertilized and hatched outside the body. Compare with *Livebearer*.

F

Filter Any device that is used to keep aquarium water clean.

Fry The newly hatched young of fishes.

Full-spectrum lighting An artificial, fluorescent light source emitting illumination with the same type and proportion of wavelengths as natural light from the sun.

Fungus Cotton-wool-like, parasitic growth most commonly seen attached to the fins, mouths, eyes, and *gills* of fishes.

G

Gastropod Any mollusc of the class *Gastropoda*, which includes slugs, snails, whelks, and limpets.

Genus The name for a group of closely related *species*. In the nomenclature of plants and fishes, the genus designation is the first part of the scientific name. Plural: genera.

Gills The fish's equivalent to our lungs, which extract oxygen from water.

Gonopodium The modified, rod-like anal fin of male *livebearers* used to deliver packets of sperm inside the female.

H

Habitat The physical environment of a particular species.

Hardness, water Describes the concentration of certain dissolved *minerals* contained in fresh water (see *Salinity* for sea water). Hard water has high

concentrations of dissolved minerals; soft water, low concentrations. Different species of fish have different preferences for water hardness.

Humic acid An acid that is derived from humus, a dark brown or black conglomeration of partially decomposed organic material.

Hydrometer Device for measuring the *specific gravity*, and hence the *salinity*, of salt water.

Hybrid A fish resulting from a mating between significantly dissimilar parents, generally when the individuals are from different *species*. Interspecies hybrids are usually infertile.

I

Ichthyology The study of fishes.

Invertebrate An animal without a spinal (vertebral) column.

Ion-exchange resin Material used to remove *minerals* from, and hence soften, water. See also *Hardness, water*.

L

Lateral line A sense organ consisting of a tube within the skin, running longitudinally on each side of a fish, through which vibrations in the water are transmitted to the nervous system.

Length The number of fishes that can be supported by a given volume of water is often described as a total "length" of fishes. When calculating the length of a fish, you should always measure from the tip of the snout to the beginning of the caudal fin (tail).

Livebearer Any fish whose eggs are fertilized and hatched inside the body.

Lux A measure of the intensity of illumination at a particular point.

M

Mineral Naturally occurring inorganic substance found in water. High levels of dissolved minerals in aquarium water may be harmful to some species of fish, and some minerals at trace levels are important for the health of fishes and plants. See also *Trace element*.

Mineralization The breakdown by bacteria of nitrogenous waste products.

Mulm An accumulation of decayed organic matter, for example fishes' waste products, undigested food, or plant leaves.

N

Naturalized Fishes that have adapted to living in a different natural environment from that in which they evolved.

Natural pairing The process by which fishes mate, without any exterior encouragement or intervention.

Nitrate The final compound produced by the process of *nitrification*. Nitrates in freshwater aquaria are thought to be harmless. In sea water, however, marine invertebrates are usually adversely affected by high levels of nitrate.

Nitrification Chemical process carried out by bacteria in which toxic *ammonia* is converted into *nitrite* and then *nitrate*.

Nitrite The compound between *ammonia* and *nitrate* produced by the process of *nitrification*. High concentrations in freshwater aquaria can be fatal for fishes. The high levels of *chloride* in marine aquaria tend to protect fishes from nitrite.

O

Organic Relating to carbon-based plant or animal constituents or products.

Osmosis The movement of water through a membrane from a weaker to a more concentrated solution.

P

pH A logarithmic scale used to describe water's *acidity/alkalinity*.

Photosynthesis The process by which plants absorb *carbon dioxide* to produce

compounds for their growth, and emit oxygen as a byproduct of this process.

Polyps An aquatic animal, usually cylindrical in shape with a ring of tentacles around the mouth. Once dead, polyp skeletons form the building material of coral reefs.

Power filter A filter with an integral electric motor.

Protein skimmer A filter device for marine aquaria that creates and collects an electrically charged, active foam which attracts waste products from the water. Also known as an electrostatic filter.

R

Redox potential An abbreviation for a body of water's potential for "**red**uction" or "**ox**idation". Water with a high redox potential is clear, of high quality, and contains much surplus oxygen. A low redox potential indicates water that is of poor quality, and deficient in oxygen.

Reverse-flow filtration An arrangement that pumps water through the gravel covering the base of the tank, thereby dislodging any solid waste material, and making it available for collection by the *power filter* doing the pumping.

S

Salinity Describes the relative concentration of *minerals (salts)* that are present in sea water.

Salt A term in common usage for sodium

chloride, which is very important in marine aquaria (see *Salinity*). Also used more widely for various minerals.

Soft water See *Hardness, water*.

Species A subdivision of a *genus* containing closely related plants or animals capable of interbreeding. In the nomenclature of plants and fishes, the species designation is the second part of the scientific name.

Species tank A tank containing only a single *species* of fish. Compare with *Community tank*.

Specific gravity The ratio of the density of a substance to that of pure water. See also *Hydrometer*.

T

Thermostat A device that can be preset to regulate the output of a heating unit. Commonly found as part of an integrated heating unit for tanks.

Trace element A *mineral* present in water at extremely low, or trace, levels. Of interest to the aquarist are those trace elements needed physiologically by fishes or plants. These include cobalt, iodine, iron, copper, and selenium.

Trilobite An extinct marine *arthropod* characterized by a segmented exoskeleton divided into three parts.

V

Ventral The lower surface of a fish. Compare with *Dorsal*.

BIBLIOGRAPHY

Allen, G.R. and Cross, N.J., Rainbowfishes of Australia and Papua New Guinea, TFH, 1982.

Andrews, C., Exell, A. and Carrington, N., The Manual of Fish Health, Salamander, 1988.

Carrington, N., A Fishkeeper's Guide to Maintaining a Healthy Aquarium, Salamander, 1985.

Colin, P.L., Marine Invertebrates and Plants of the Living Reef, TFH, 1978.

Fryer, G. and Iles, T.D., The Cichlid Fishes of the Great Lakes of Africa, Oliver and Boyd, 1972.

Haywood M. and Wells, S., Manual of Marine Invertebrates, Salamander, 1989.

Holliday, L., Coral Reefs, Salamander, 1989.

James, B., A Fishkeeper's Guide to Aquarium Plants, Salamander, 1986.

Lagler, K.F., Bardach, J.E. and Miller, R.R., Ichthyology: The Study of Fishes, J. Wiley and Sons, 1962.

Leggett, R. and Mernck, J.R., Australian Native Fishes for the Aquarium, J.R. Merrick Publications, 1987.

Loiselle, P.V., The Cichlid Aquarium, Tetra, 1985.

Lowe-McConnell, R.H., Ecological Studies in Tropical Fish Communities, Cambridge University Press, 1987.

Masters, C.O., Encyclopedia of Live Foods, TFH, 1975.

Mills, D., The Practical Encyclopedia of the Marine Aquarium, Salamander, 1987.

Post, G.W., Text Book of Fish Health, TFH, 1987.

Ramshorst, J.D., The Complete Aquarium Encyclopedia of Tropical Freshwater Fish,

Elsevier, 1978.

Rataj, K. and Horeman, T.J., Aquarium Plants, TFH, 1977.

Richter, H.J., Gouramies and Other Anabantoids, TFH, 1988.

Sands, D., A Fishkeeper's Guide to South American Catfishes, Salamander, 1988.

Sands, D., An Interpet Guide to African and Asian Catfishes, 1986.

Sands, D., Catfishes of the World, Vols. 1 to 6, Dunure, 1985.

Sterba, G., The Aquarist's Encyclopedia, Blandford, 1983.

Vierke, J., Dwarf Cichlids, TFH, 1988.

Wood E., Exploitation of Coral Reef Fishes for the Aquarium Trade, Marine Conservation Society, 1985.

Wood, E.M., Corals of the World, TFH, 1983.

INDEX

ACKNOWLEDGMENTS

Author's Acknowledgments
I would like to thank all of the team at Dorling Kindersley who made this project actually happen, in particular Alan Buckingham for taking my original concept and developing it into a final book, which would not have seen the light of day without Krystyna Mayer bringing the bits together. Jane Burton and Kim Taylor deserve very special thanks for their endless patience in taking the photographs which are so important to the book, as does Ursula Dawson for her input on the tank layouts and design of the book. Thanks to Waterworld, Enfield, who supplied most of the fishes and equipment for the aquaria, and to Brian and Paul, who helped in setting up the tanks. Also Sea Life Centre, Weymouth, and Brighton Aquarium, whose staff donned waders to collect the fishes used in the temperate marine aquarium. Other people whose brains have been unashamedly picked include Dr. Chris Andrews, David Sands of Aquadventure, Dr. David Ford of Aquarian, and Miss Horder, Chief Librarian at the Royal College of Veterinary Surgeons.

Picture credits
Key: t = top; b = bottom; l = left; r = right; m = middle; f = far

All photography by Jane Burton and Kim Taylor except for:
Ardea: L. and T. Banford 38b; P. Morris 119t; Ian Beames 119r
R. Benson 181tr
Bridgeman Art Library: 6tl, 6ml, 7tr, 9tl
Bruce Coleman: K. Balcomb 110t; R. Boardman 51l; M. N. Boulton 16b; A. Campost 17t, 37b; B. Coales 17bl, 84t; P. Davey 16t; G. Dore 146; M.P.L. Fogden 19br, 90t; J. Foott 39tr, 129br, 155, 167r, 169; M. Freeman 13t, 13b, 14t, 14b, 15m, 15b, 54t; Frith Photo 19 bl, 21t; G Gibitt 78t; F. Lanting 35bl; J.R. MacKinnan 22t; L.C. Mango 15t, 60t; C. Ott 17br; A. Paver 34m; D. and M. Plage 19t; G.D. Plage 27l; M. Plage 122 t; H. Reinhard 18l, 30t, b, 31bl, 32bl, tr, 33bl, 34t, 35br, 37ml, 51m, br, 57bl, 63r, 75 far l, r, 81t,

(**Bruce Coleman**, continued) ml, 87m, 168; C. Roessler 31br, 34b; Dr. F. Savier 20br; W. Townsend 81b; F. Vollmar 72t; P. Ward 102t; B. Wood 20bl, 21b, 33t, 33br, 143r, 174
Camera Press: 45l
J. Allen Cash: 8–9 bm
Mary Evans: pp. 6–7m, 7tl, br, 8t, bl, 9r, b
NHPA: K. Omtals 22b; G.E. Schmeide 87l
Planet Earth: 6b, 125c; S. Aven 96t; D. Clarke 134 bl; A. Kerstritch 142r; D. Maitland 149; P. Oliveira 57br, 63l, 63mr, 75 fr, 113r; C. Petron 142l; K. Scholey 116; P. Scoones 27r, 81mr, 134tl; N. Septon 43bl; J. D. Watt 138
Mike Sandford 176l
David Sands: 43tr, br, tl, 51tr, 57tl, tr, 63ml, 69l, m, r, 87r, 99l, m, r, 105, 113tl, bl, c, 125 tl, tr, 128bl, 134tr, br, 135, 143l, c, 167l, 171, 172, 173, 176r, b, 178, 179, 182
Peter W. Scott 181bl, br, 183
Survival Anglia: A. Root 36

Dorling Kindersley would like to thank the following for their help in the preparation of the book: David Sands and Dr. Chris Andrews for advice on the text; Patrizio Semproni and Hazel Edington for design assistance; Kuo Kang Chen for the illustrations; Hazel Taylor for hand modelling; Jemima Dunne for initial work on the project; Caroline Wilson for editorial assistance; Peter Moloney for the index; and Hilary Stephens for production. Also Paul and Brian of Waterworld for supplying material for the aquaria, as well as Brighton Aquarium, Kew Gardens, and Weymouth Sea Life Centre.